THE HEART OF
BURROUGHS'S JOURNALS

John Burroughs

THE HEART OF
BURROUGHS'S JOURNALS

EDITED BY
CLARA BARRUS

BOSTON AND NEW YORK
HOUGHTON MIFFLIN COMPANY
The Riverside Press Cambridge
1928

The Riverside Press
CAMBRIDGE · MASSACHUSETTS
PRINTED IN THE U.S.A.

PREFACE

THE Journals of John Burroughs cover the period from the year 1876, when he was thirty-nine years of age, to within a few weeks of his death in 1921, when he was eighty-four. But long before beginning his Journals, in 1854 — from the age of seventeen onward — he tucked away in sundry notebooks his groping, half-formed thoughts, reflections on what he was reading, immature philosophizing, and arresting words, phrases, and quotations. Thus the Notebooks and Journals, as a whole, supply a practically continuous record of more than sixty-seven years, a record, so far as I know, unparalleled, in continuity and duration, by that of any other well-known American author.

Since the Journals of Burroughs have not been published in their entirety, as have those of Emerson and Thoreau, the editing of a single volume from the entire record (which covers some two thousand typewritten pages of transcriptions from the originals), presents somewhat different problems than must have occupied the editors of the other volumes in this series. Still some parts of Burroughs's Journals have already appeared in print. The present editor made a few excerpts from them when writing 'Our Friend John Burroughs,' and copious excerpts when preparing 'The Life and Letters.' And Burroughs himself occasionally drew from them in writing his essays. Now and then the reader of this book will come upon a passage almost identical with one long familiar to him in the books of Burroughs, as well as upon others which he will recognize as germs of passages elaborated in the essays.

It would have been far easier to arrange the Heart of Burroughs's Journals were there a complete edition of the records to which the reader might turn. As it is, the editor has all along had the uncomfortable feeling of robbing the reader in bringing away so little of the treasure to which she herself has had access. She finds small comfort in the assurance concerning the fate of him that's robbed ——

> ' Let him not know it,
> And he is not robbed at all.'

However, in the rather harrowing task of separating the wheat from more and more wheat in the overflowing bins, the valued help of Mr. Francis H. Allen, who has read the entire transcription of the originals, has greatly lightened the work, and to him grateful acknowledgment is here made.

When Mr. Burroughs gave me his early Notebooks, he declared: 'They are of no value, but I can't bear to throw them away. Here is where I practiced when I was learning my trade.' One dissents from the slighting estimate the author himself put upon these records when, by their means, he is enabled to follow that country-bred youth through his groping years, to see the handicaps he overcame, and to watch him evolve into the author holding the assured place which Burroughs holds in literature. One sees the aspiring, self-taught youth ploughing his way through the great authors, and struggling to express

the thoughts thus generated, and others which came from
listening to his own soul. Leading thoughts which emerge
in his youth recur again and again, some of which, as
later entries show, became the fixed stars by which he
steered his course through life. The earlier entries show
how essentially spiritual-minded Burroughs always was.
He began as a thinker and an incipient philosopher, long
before he became the keen observer and interpreter of
Nature; but all through life, while retaining his objective
interest in Nature, he sought her chiefly for what lies back
of her.

He often said that Emerson was his spiritual father.
In 1837, when Burroughs was not yet a year old, Emerson
was delivering his lectures on Human Culture; sending
forth upon the air those germinal ideas which, like ferti-
lizing pollen, were to be disseminated and fructify the
soul of many a child just born. Eagerly did Burroughs
take to heart two of Emerson's rules for attaining true
culture: Sit alone, and Keep a Journal.

'Men who write Journals,' said Burroughs himself in
the last volume to come from his pen, 'are usually men
of certain marked traits — they are idealists; they love
solitude rather than society; they are self-conscious, and
they love to write... their Journals largely take the
place of social converse. Amiel, Emerson, and Thoreau,
for example, were lonely souls, lacking in social gifts, and
seeking relief in the society of their own thoughts. Such
men go to their Journals as other men go to their clubs.
They love to be alone with themselves, and dread to be
benumbed or drained of their mental force by uncongenial
persons. To such a man his Journal becomes his duplicate

self, and he says to it what he could not say to his nearest friend. It becomes both an altar and a confessional.'

True, but one thinks of other than 'lonely souls' that have kept Journals, or, more often, Diaries, with the vivid pictures of their days, their times, their associates, and themselves. Boswell quotes some one as saying that, as ladies like to see themselves in a glass, so a man likes to see himself in his Journal. The inimitable Pepys is not the only one who delineates himself at every turn, while chiefly intent on holding the mirror up to the ladies and gentlemen of his day. The introspective journalist also, while confiding to his silent companion, achieves a like self-delineation, even though, ostrich-like, with head buried in self-communing, he thinks himself hidden. The diarist who looks himself squarely in the face is bound to reveal himself at every stroke of the pen, not only in his self-assessment, but also in the account of his downsittings and uprisings, and in his comments on others. While the aim, in making this selection from the large mass of the Journals, has been to include the more strictly journalistic entries, and to omit much of autobiographic interest already used in the 'Life and Letters of John Burroughs,' still enough has been included, it is hoped, for the faithful self-portrait we always crave from the Diarist.

The wistful backward glance toward youth and home which dominated Burroughs before he reached middle life, a heritage from his Celtic forebears, was aptly described by him as a 'homesickness which home cannot cure.' Apropos of this trait, when, in the early years of my acquaintance with him, he sent me some of his Journals, he wrote:

'I do not expect you to read them all — only here and there where you get some real glimpse of me. I looked into some of them last night. They seem too sad. I seem to have put all my sunshine into the books, and all my gloom into the Diaries. Remember they were written for my eyes alone — a sort of cemetery where I could turn and mourn over my vanished days and vanished thoughts.'

If, like Carlyle, Burroughs had journalized only when in low spirits, a more general tone of sadness might be found than is the case in the section on which he comments here; but sunshine falls athwart many a page; he accepted the universe with such abiding joy — the dear, common flowers; the birds; the light of day; the soil underfoot, the stars in the sky; it was all good, all as it should be, the best of all possible worlds; and he yielded himself joyously to the perfect Whole.

It is true he did have an abiding anxiety about the weather, and cussed and discussed it, in season and out of season. The Journals as a whole are 'packed as full of weather as they can stick,' and then some will be found bulging beyond the edges. Perhaps he did not actually count one hundred and thirty-six kinds of weather in twenty-four hours at Riverby, as did Mark Twain in New England, but to his natural concern about it, as an observer of nature, was added that of the practical husbandman, so, when untoward conditions threatened, he suffered all the tortures of the imaginative man; and when he witnessed the devastations wrought in his vineyard by the debauches of the weather-gods, his rage, though impotent, was by no means inarticulate. But even his

weather bulletins are good reading, whether as vigorous
railings, or glowing descriptions, or merely choice bits of
cadenced prose. The reader invariably shares his mood,
frowns with him when Nature frowns, and rejoices with
him when she is kind. And Burroughs is ever more ready
to praise than to blame, so when the good days come, he
says, in effect, with Mark Twain: 'There, there! I forgive
you now. Go, and sin no more. . . . You're the most
enchanting weather in the world.'

He knew how to snub his Journal. There are sometimes gaps of weeks, again long periods when only comments on the weather occur, or brief jottings of natural
history. He elaborates little concerning significant events
in his own life. Sometimes when living the most intensely,
he gives little indication of it; again he condenses much
into a few terse sentences; but, on occasion, lays bare his
heart in long frank entries.

His life was rich in friendships. The types welcomed
show his catholicity; so long as the person was genuine,
rank, talents, station, mattered little. There was a great
deal of the milk of human kindness in Burroughs. He
shows his strong warm interest in the humble lives that
touched his own — his kin, his neighbors, his hired men
— no less than in such comrades as Walt Whitman, Myron B. Benton, and Theodore Roosevelt. We see his abiding love for country folk and country ways, and witness
his hospitality at Slabsides and Woodchuck Lodge. And
always we come upon his curious interest and his tender
but unsentimental love for the flowers, the birds, and all
wild creatures, and for his dog friends.

The deepest attachments of his life are poignantly

dwelt upon, especially his vague, yearning homesickness
when away from the Old Home, and his strong love of
kindred. These yearnings find full expression both before
and after his kindred are gone from the earth; and after,
he calls them back with peculiar vividness in his many
pilgrimages to their graves, in keeping the anniversaries of
their passing, and in the persistent mingling of memories
of them with the scenes of which they are for him forever
a part.

It must be confessed that momentous current events
often receive but scanty mention in the Journals, and
that subjects sometimes appear suddenly, and as suddenly disappear. Clearly he made no systematic attempt
to keep an accurate record, either of personal experiences
or of public events, but wrote as he listed. And yet one
does get here his outspoken comments on men and measures; his reactions to the wars of his time, the Civil War,
the Spanish-American War, the Boer War, the Russo-
Japanese War, and, decidedly, the World War. In brief
paragraphs he shows the wide grasp he had on public
questions, and how sanely his patriotism was broadened
and fused into internationalism.

His candor in giving his impressions of the great ones of
the past, and of his contemporaries in literature, is re-
freshing; likewise of public men, whether he stands in
close friendly relations with them, or merely knows them
from scrutinizing their careers. His honest-mindedness is
seen, again and again, in his frequent examination of the
conventional religious attitude of his times; the unflinch-
ingness with which he faces scientific facts, and their import; and his tender regard, almost envy, for the religion

of his fathers, from which he was debarred by the Time-Spirit of his day. One rejoices in his independence of thought as he examines into any question, literary, scientific, religious, or philosophic. Clearly his life was, as he naïvely says in one of his youthful notebooks, 'an apprenticeship to the truth.' Not even Darwin, whose truth-loving mind he so revered, was a more ardent, patient searcher after the truth. His love of truth is shown in his checking himself up, from year to year, after insufficient observation and hasty deduction; it is shown in his appraisal of himself, of his kin, of his friends, of public men — never does his love for any of these betray him into mere eulogy, nor blind him, even when he is sorrowing acutely over their loss; in a few, terse, clear-sighted sentences he sets down their outstanding traits as he knew them — warts and all.

We often find him fumbling with his pen. Much in the Journal is experimental. It was actually his workshop. Here are his undressed thoughts. For his artistry, as a rule, one must turn to his books. And yet, now and again, we come upon passages as beautiful as any in his published work. In the books, however, one finds only so much of the man as he permitted the world to see; in the Journal one comes close to him; sees him as he looked to himself; as he was. It is in the unstudied character of the records, then, that so much of value lies; in that, and the fact that he always regarded his Journal as his 'house of refuge.'

In offering this single volume culled from the originals, the aim has been to show Burroughs in his beginnings; show his mental growth, his absorbing interests, his com-

radeships, his forthrightness as revealed in his question-
ing and sifting of creeds and conventions, his ready
acceptance and application of scientific discoveries, his
penetrating criticism of books and authors; in short, by
means of this glimpse into the heart of the Journals of
Burroughs, to afford the reader a glimpse into the mind
and heart of Burroughs himself.

After 1876, the place where the entries were made, unless otherwise specified, or shown in the entries themselves, may be understood to be at West Park on the
Hudson — at Riverby, usually, but sometimes at Slabsides. When an entry is dated from Roxbury, it is usually
written at Woodchuck Lodge.

Whatever else of interest the Journals hold, of self-
communings, of opinions on persons, on literature, on
life, they prove how completely Nature was Burroughs's
guide and liberator, from beginning to end. News about
the May warblers opens the Journals, proper, in 1876,
and, by a fitting coincidence, the last sentence which
closes the long record in 1921 is a brief observation on
Nature.

CLARA BARRUS

ROXBURY IN THE CATSKILLS
April, 1928

CHRONOLOGICAL TABLE

1837. John Burroughs born at Roxbury, New York, April 3.

1837–44. Life on dairy farm in Catskills.

1844–54. Attended rural schools. Began keeping early notebooks.

1854–63. Taught school, with a few months' attendance at Hedding Literary Institute, Ashland, New York, and at Cooperstown Seminary.

1856. First appearance in print ('Vagaries *viz.* Spiritualism,' by 'Philomath').

1857. Married Ursula North. Came under influence of Emerson.

1859. Wrote philosophical articles for New York 'Saturday Press' — 'Fragments from the Table of an Intellectual Epicure' by 'All Souls.'

1860. Wrote for New York 'Leader.' 'Expression' published in 'Atlantic Monthly.'

1861. Wrote 'From the Back Country' series for New York 'Leader,' and thus found his own field of work.

1862. Read medicine for a few months. Wrote the poem 'Waiting.'

1863. Began to study the birds. Wrote 'With the Birds' and 'The Adirondacks.' Resigned as a teacher. Went to Washington, D.C. Met Walt Whitman.

1864. Appointed clerk in Currency Bureau of Treasury Department.

1867. 'Notes on Walt Whitman as Poet and Person' published.

1871. First European visit ('An October Abroad'). 'Wake-Robin' published.

1872. Resigned position in Treasury Department.

1873. Appointed receiver of a broken bank, and Special Bank Examiner. Bought land on Hudson and began building.

1874. Established home (Riverby) at West Park on Hudson.

1875. 'Winter Sunshine' published. Began fruit-farming.

1876. Began keeping a regular journal.

1877. 'Birds and Poets' published.

1878. Birth of son, Julian.

1879. 'Locusts and Wild Honey' published.

1881. Built chestnut-bark Study at Riverby. 'Pepacton' published.

1882. Second European visit.

1884. 'Fresh Fields' published.

1885. Bank-examining ended.

1886. 'Signs and Seasons' published.

1888. Extended acreage of vineyards and fruit-farming.

1889. 'Indoor Studies' published.

1894. 'Riverby' published.

1895. Began the building of Slabsides.

1896. 'Whitman: A Study' published.

1899. Joined Harriman Alaskan Expedition.

1900. 'The Light of Day' published.

1901. Edited 'Songs of Nature.' 'Squirrels and Other Fur-Bearers' published.

1902. 'Literary Values' published. 'Life of Audubon' published. Traveled in Jamaica. Built cottage for son at Riverby.

1903. Traveled in Florida. 'Real and Sham Natural

History' (March 'Atlantic'). Trip to Yellowstone
Park with President Roosevelt.

1904. 'Far and Near' published.

1905. 'Ways of Nature' published. Wintered in Bermuda.

1906. 'Bird and Bough' (poems) published.

1907. 'Camping and Tramping with Roosevelt' published.

1908. 'Leaf and Tendril' published. Established summer home (Woodchuck Lodge) at Roxbury, New York. Wintered in the South.

1909. Traveled with John Muir in Far West and visited Hawaiian Islands.

1910. Received the degree of Litt.D. from Yale University.

1911. Second trip to California. Received the degree of Doctor of Humane Letters from Colgate University.

1912. 'Time and Change' published. Wintered in the South.

1913. 'The Summit of the Years' published.

1915. 'The Breath of Life' published. Received the degree of. Doctor of Letters from the University of Georgia.

1916. 'Under the Apple-Trees' published.

1917. Death of his wife, Ursula North Burroughs.

1918. Wintered in North Carolina. (During World War wrote many letters to New York dailies.)

1919. 'Field and Study' published. Third winter in California. Worked on 'Under the Maples' (published posthumously, 1921).

1920. 'Accepting the Universe' published. Fourth winter in California. Worked on 'The Last Harvest' (published posthumously, 1922).

1921. Died March 29.

'Keep a Journal. Pay so much honor to the visits of truth to your mind as to record them.'

EMERSON

THE HEART OF
BURROUGHS'S JOURNALS

1854–1858

[THE early Notebooks of John Burroughs form a motley group, covering the period from 1854 to 1876. They give touching evidences of his earnestness and honest-mindedness, and his persistent efforts at self-culture. The first little book contains penciled entries, often so blurred as to be illegible. The spelling, punctuation, and grammar reflect his meager elementary training. A quaint touch is given by occasional flourishes, and the use of long *s*'s. Jottings of small amounts due him, algebraic problems, a sample of a promissory note, and other entries, are records of that West Settlement schoolboy at Roxbury in the Catskills in 1853. These are followed by a record of days taught in his first school, at Olive, New York (April 13 to September 23, 1854). One glimpses the young teacher's social activities during his first months away from home. An expense account shows that if he danced, he paid the fiddler, and fiddler's bills, the charges for horse and sulky to attend the country dances, the cost of additions to his wardrobe, necessitated by his entrance into the society at Olive, and other incidentals, are carefully set down.

From November, 1854, to February, 1855, he attended school at the Hedding Literary Institute, at Ashland,

New York. A copy of the curriculum shows him studying Algebra, Geometry, French, Chemistry, Physiology, Milton, and Logic. (He said that he chose the study of logic because he had not then the least idea what it was.) Quotations from Thomas Dick, a Scots philosopher whose works the youthful Burroughs had bought on his first visit to New York City, are transcribed in the little book. Biblical references are in amusing juxtaposition to his laundry lists, and to statements of historical facts. A careful record is kept of his standing in the various branches during the winter term at the Ashland Seminary, the chief interest here being in the fact that his lowest marks were in Chemistry, the highest in Composition. I recall that once in commenting on the contents of this and other early notebooks, Mr. Burroughs said, 'Oh, those days of the callow youth, when he is taken with words, words, words! He has no ideas of his own, so the more grandiloquent a thing is, the more it takes his fancy.' Concerning a long defense of phrenology he said: 'Poor, high-flown stuff! I had no ideas and was just playing with words. I suppose that is the way many begin to write.'

The next Notebook is dated 1854–59, and quaintly named, 'A Book of Solitude, Sentiment, and Study.' In this, one can trace the thought-life of Burroughs through his formative years; see what he was reading; and how deeply he was delving into his own mind and heart, and into the life of the universe.

Much of the time between 1854 and late 1863, Burroughs was teaching in various rural schools in New York and New Jersey, with one winter term at Buffalo Grove, near Polo, Illinois. His teaching during these

years, was, however, interrupted for a period of three
months at the seminary at Ashland, New York, and another of six months at Cooperstown Seminary. He married Ursula North in September, 1857.]

The disposition to swear and make use of oaths, so
natural in men of ardent temperaments, I take to come
from the poverty and weakness of our language. When
the soul is excited and aroused we naturally seek for the
most expressive terms and figures in which to embody our
thoughts and feelings, and to the vulgar there are no terms
so terrible and expressive as 'devil,' 'hell,' 'damnation,'
etc. Hence these and the like come immediately to the
tongue as the most fit symbols with which to unburden
their feelings. The cultivated seldom swear or make use of
oaths because the extent of their vocabulary and the
refinement of their feelings enable them to use terms
which to them are more appropriate and expressive. An
uncultivated man seldom swears until he is excited and
then, without he is a cold, phlegmatic temperament, he is
pretty sure to make use of language not allowable in the
Sunday-schools. The feelings of the most refined, however, will sometimes get to so high a pitch that they are
obliged to call in some of those excommunicated terms
to their aid. I doubt if there is that man living but that
has uttered an oath of some kind. Even the good Washington did once. Everybody occasionally uses a byword.
In fact, a byword seems to serve the same purpose in
talking that a cane does in walking. Young men are
more apt to use a byword than old men, but then the old
ones use the cane in walking.

It is a good thing to let your MS. matter stand a while before publishing; much sediment and personal conceit that was stirred up and held in solution during the freshet which it caused in your soul will settle from it and precipitate itself to the bottom.

A man is only worth the appellation so long as he preserves his own personal identity, acts and thinks from what is born within him. . . . The idea of genius is most clearly expressed by him who is most thoroughly his own master, who owns himself, keeps himself, and governs himself. Democracy is its twin brother . . . that democracy which guarantees Equal Rights to all men — which inspires a true independence in thought and a liberality in sentiment, which is a protest against sectarianism, . . . which is synonymous with the idea of Christian equality and which asserts the true dignity of human nature. . . . I have a right to be just what I can be honorably and justly. If I am born with talents to be great and useful, no man shall stand between me and the attainment of my destination. . . . Launched upon the ocean of life like an innumerable fleet, we have a right to spread whatever sail God has given us, whether we be ship, brig, schooner, or man of war, and no admiral or commodore shall dictate the amount of canvas we may carry, or the course we may pursue.

Poetry is spiritual facts represented by natural symbols; hence the most poetic writer, as well as the most pleasing and instructive, is he who conveys his ideas in illustrations drawn from natural objects, who makes the world of matter mirror forth the world of mind, who translates

things into thought. Nature when rightly seen is but a
representation of spirit; its face is radiant with celestial
smiles, and to him who is pure and true to the law of his
being 'it speaks a various language.' To the pure in
heart Nature is a volume full of the sublimest truths.
The soul active, all things are representative; the sky
mirrors its purity and serenity, the ocean symbolizes its
depth and grandeur, the mountains are its thoughts, the
vale with its brooks and [an indecipherable word] pictures
the beauty and richness of its spiritual harmony, and the
myriad melodies around us that are the daily offering of
earth to heaven are like the incense of love and prayer
that go up from its pure devotion. An original writer is
told by his language. Is it pure? that is, is it the natural
uttering of a soul in communion with the great fountain
of truth and Nature? Is it fresh and teeming with the life
that streams around and through us to-day?

How one's life at certain times will blaze up out of
the coals! Then the flame goes back again, the coals
slumber or emit nothing but smoke, and ashes accumulate over them. But presently excitement or some
startling circumstance sweeps away the ashes and we
blaze up again.

Buffalo Grove, Illinois, March 26, 1857

On Wednesday evening, March 25, I first learned what
was meant by a 'wild-goose chase.' He who has not
realized its signification, can do so by roaming over the
prairies in Ogle County, Illinois, in search of geese when
the ground sinks under his feet about six inches every step.

May 15, *Sunday*

The following truths occurred to me while walking to church: Art is something more than a mere daguerreotype of outward Nature. It is a blending of the natural and the divine. It must be radiant with that Eternal spirit of Beauty and Unity of which Nature is but the shadow.

Do not imitate. The imitator dooms himself to perpetual mediocrity. He can never rise above his model. He leaves the infinitude of his own soul to take a minor share in another's. Cato's imitators were called *left-handed Catos*. It is so in every case; the tendency of great minds is to subdue and captivate weaker natures, and hence every original writer or actor is followed by a host of imitators, but they are all left-handed. We have left-handed Shakespeares, and left-handed Byrons, and left-handed Platos. But it is much easier for a man to be right-handed — to be himself. Originality is Nature expressed, imitation is Nature suppressed. What comes under the law of my being to me is original because it is natural, and if I go beyond this, I am an imitator, a pretender, a liar. Imitate nothing but the sun. Like him be a center dispensing life and light and beauty on every hand. Continue thy course bright and cheerful, and like him grow larger at thy setting.

Little things explain big things. A grain of sand is the Alps on a small scale. A drop of water illustrates the laws of the ocean. The fall of an apple revealed to the mind of Newton the laws of the spheres. A man's life explains all history. What is true of me is true of a nation. Plutarch

throws more light on the character of his heroes by casual
events, impromptu repartees, or the [avowal?] of opinions
and incidents in their private lives than by all their outward or public acts. A man's outward life is artificial, but
his private or indoor life, natural. We are like the moon,
we always keep one side to the world and the other side to
the stars.

Thinking is like catching pigeons with a net. You may
pull your rope never so quick sometimes and catch nothing but a feather.

It is a fact that extremes meet everywhere. Good and
bad, order and disorder, light and darkness, growth and
decay, beauty and deformity, affirmative and negative,
substance and show, spirit and fact, are but different sides
of the same great law. What Nature neglects in one thing,
she makes up in another. How clearly this is illustrated
in the condition of different nations! Look over the world
and you will see that where Nature has lavished her
bounties on the soil and the physical conformation of a
country, she neglects the moral and intellectual growth
of the people. But where the country is rough and rugged,
its productions not spontaneous, but the fruit of labor and
earnest exertion, there you see the Titans; there you see
civilization and progress. It seems that it requires friction to develop the electricity in men as well as in other
things. When man makes the soil beautiful and productive, he makes his mind beautiful and productive. He
absorbs whatever he creates. His growth is commen-
surate with the work of his hands. His mission is to sub-

due the earth and not let it subdue him. Rome, by wars
and conquests, flourished in beautiful and productive
Italy for a millennium, but the rich spontaneous earth
soon intoxicated her with pleasure and enervated her
with idleness, and so at last completely absorbed her.
Stout old England possessed no natural advantages, but
she has made a garden of her island and produced a race
of Titans.

Oct. 6, 1857

Every good book has a spirit, a living, moving spirit
underlying and animating all its thought. Here is where
its power is. This gives it an influence in the world greater
than that of Cæsar or Alexander. This makes a book live.
This brings Plato and Shakespeare down from age to age
and makes them always new and inspiring. A poor book
has not this spirit; it may have facts and truths, but if
they are not embedded in and animated by this spirit, it is
but a mechanical contrivance and must soon sink to the
bottom like all mud and sediment. But a live book, that
is, one whose truths and principles float in spirit as a ship
on the ocean, can never die. Some books have a great
influence in the world that contain no very important
facts. Such are spirit books, and they belong to what De
Quincey terms the literature of power. Such are the
writings of Milton, of Scott, of Shakespeare, and, in fact,
all imaginative works. We read them, not to find facts of
history, or science, or art, etc., but for the delicious spiritual power that flows into us from their pages. This
beauty, or this real worth, cannot be shown by any craft
of criticism; it eludes the most skillful analysis; it can be

discerned only by tuning the soul to the same harmony. The same is true of a work of art, or a landscape.

Jan. 30, 1858

If one is struggling in his library to utter or give tangible form to a truth which he clearly feels but cannot fully grasp, let him step to the door or window and look out upon the hills and mountains, or the moon, or the setting sun, and he shall readily speak what in his closet was too big for him to utter. His soul seems to expand and to 'partake of the largeness of his vision,' and he breaks over his prison walls and comprehends that which once comprehended him.

Why is it that a train of thought is better sustained by connecting our senses with some physical object? If you have a statue, a painting, or any clear distinct object in your library upon which you can fix your eyes, you can think more vigorously and continuously. It seems to concentrate your thoughts and place your subject at a right focal distance. When immersed in thought, how unconsciously one rises from his seat, walks the floor, or busies his hands with something! One of the English poets said his thoughts and images never came so palpably to the surface of his mind as when gazing upon a waterfall. And Scott relates of one of his school-fellows who could never recite a lesson without fumbling over the buttons on his coat. I suppose it is a good sign, the mind being so 'het up' that the electricity must needs flow off and escape through these channels. It is like throwing water on the fire to release the heat and let it out.

Proposed essays, April, 1858: Revolutions, Mystery, Silence, Universality, A Man and his Times, The Affirmative Man, Analogy, The Boy and his Education, Character and Faculty, Emerson, Carlyle, The Philosophy of the Porch, Genius, Individuality, Nicknames, Mohammedanism, Expression, Opposites, Reason, The Indian, The African, Quakerism, Grammar, St. Pierre, Memory, Shakespeare.

I saw the moon run over a poor little star to-night. I suspect it will never open its eye again.

I suppose if we could grasp the handle of the Big Dipper, we could dip up the heavens and all their shining pebbles.

Those are not the best books which settle and compose us, which flatter our knowledge and make us contented with our condition and attainments; but, on the contrary, those are the best books which unsettle and disquiet us, which undermine our opinions and complacent knowledge, which take down the narrow walls in which we have so long rested secure, and place us on the confines of the unconfinable, and make us pray and fear and tremble and struggle for a firmer footing and a surer purpose.

There is a good deal of music in a boy if one knows how to play upon him.

The novelist but reports himself magnified; he gives latitude and expansion to his inward tendencies; his secret hope he realizes, and latent plans that would never have risen to the surface of his life, he executes; he can write nothing he might not have experienced.

The ocean is clear and calm in its distant depths, but grows foul and turbid just where it touches the shore; so the lives of many great men are as pure and beautiful as the sunlight in their higher developments and manifestations, but mean and sordid when they touch the affairs of common life. Bacon's for instance.

Literature is the union of the abstract and the concrete, the Ideal holding in solution the Real. Energy is the male principle of life, but it must be cast into a purpose before it can become the father of events.

Under every one of our individual necessities Nature conceals a prospective end. The outlook to my garden and onion bed is also an outlook to the stars and the mysteries of the heavens. Like the planets, we each obey a private end, and work out our own plans and purposes as complacently as if nobody else was concerned; but all the while, night and day, asleep and awake, a great law bears us on, and we unintentionally go to help make up the sublime harmony of the spheres. . . . We advance the interests of all by making sure a laudable purpose of our own. Generalities are reached only through particulars; and the only way we can do good to others is by doing it to ourselves. We may talk eloquently about the general good and universal emancipation, and prescribe remedies with learned accuracy for the ills of humanity, but we must give the pill to a personated fact, not to impersonal generalities; to a man, and not to Humanity. . . . When a man works honestly for his own bread, he is earning wages for all mankind. . . . The great benefactors of the race were as selfish as any of us, yielded obedience to an inward necessity, to a voice unheard by other souls, and the grandeur of the result arches itself over the proposed end, as the sky over the meanest molehill. It was as necessary for Paul to preach as for me to teach; he sought to justify himself in his own eyes, and in the eyes of his Maker, by giving expression to the faith within him. I seek to earn my bread, and to gratify a childish love for communicating instruction; but I suppose other results than these are realized, results that neither Paul nor I planned or proposed, or had the least adequate conception of.

My author must suggest and define, convey by accurate analysis and definition, and by casual hints and imperfect revelations; some truths must be evolved in a clear white light, their boundaries and relations unmistakably pointed out; others only partially revealed, like the moon in gibbous; some again merely adumbrated, and so back to the [indecipherable] glimpse of light. Some paths he must go with me the whole way, but leave the byroads and intersecting trails for me to follow through at my leisure. He must [not] tell me all, but leave something for me to find out myself. He must not hem or bind the fabric of his loom, but leave the ends and shreds for me to knit on my own bordering. When he is showing me any particular constellation, tracing its boundaries, and remarking its significance, I love to be permitted to look through to

remote stars, or nebulous fields of light, beyond. There is
nothing like suggestiveness in an author, and throwing out
hints and provocations to the reader that shall keep up an
undercurrent of thought of his own beneath the main current of the book; nothing like conducting him to a grand
prospect through a grove with innumerable openings and
outlooks, through which we may glance at sunny fields
and quiet villages which are not seen from the main summit. With my author it must be perpetual spring and
perpetual autumn, perpetual seed-time and perpetual
harvest. He must be a Bahama Isle with ripened fruit,
full-expanded blossoms, half-opened buds, and mere
germinal twigs. The whole process, the whole metemp-
sychosis [metamorphosis?] of growth and development
must go on before me.

1859–1860

[THE next book, dated 1859, bears on the fly-leaf this legend:

'A Notebook containing a few smooth pebbles which the waves of Thought leave, from time to time, upon my Shores,

J. Burroughs, Newark, New Jersey.'

At this time Burroughs was teaching at East Orange, and living in Newark, New Jersey. Here the young philosopher is more articulate, speaks in a more assured tone, and ranges all over creation in thought. Ideas crowd his mind, and he labors unceasingly to utilize them. His 'pebbles' are by no means always 'smooth,' but are more so than in the preceding 'Book of Solitude.' Everywhere he seeks analogies between facts in nature and moral and intellectual truths.

Perhaps some of these entries went into the philosophical fragments which he wrote for the New York 'Saturday Press,' and the New York 'Leader' between 1859–60, those in the 'Press' appearing under the title 'Fragments from the Table of an Intellectual Epicure.' In these long entries one traces much which is all of a piece with his first essay in the 'Atlantic Monthly' — 'Expression.'

Some 'pearly shells' were added in the next book to the 'smooth pebbles' that the 'Waves of Thought' left upon the shores in the preceding one. This is dated December 3, 1859, to March, 1860. Two significant things are placed

on the fly-leaf: the statement, 'My life is an apprenticeship to Truth,' and a carefully drawn eye — the eye pos-
sibly placed there as a symbol. The contents certainly
show that the observant eye is an appropriate illustration
for the book.]

April 9, 1859

My friend Herder is like some springs: you can get
very clear, pretty talk out of him with a small cup
and by not dipping near the surface, but sink down in
him the bucket of a sound philosophical question and
he is so roiled that you will not be able to get a clear
draught from him again in a day or two.

Writing is the spoils of living; it is reporting what we
saw after the vision has left us; or, more familiarly, it is
catching the fish which the tide has left far up on our
shores in the low and depressed places. We can only say
a thing after it has become detached from us and passes
from an unconscious active power of the soul, to a conscious tangible formula of the intellect. Our thoughts are
our feelings gone to seed.

Life is the rounded circle, speech only a segment. The
highest states of feeling, either of joy or grief, utterly beg-
gar our meager craft of expression, and, indeed, generally
never seek to embody themselves in outward articulation.
Who has not had the tide, the real divine afflatus of
ecstasy, in some serene beatitude, flow in upon his shores
till all the old landmarks — the docks and wharves of
speech from which he had usually launched his frail cargo

of knowledge, or landed the result of his piratical excursions in Science — were entirely obliterated, and he could embark at any point upon the sea of bliss? In such moments, speech is clumsy and impertinent, and only as a bucket to the ocean.

Living is genial feeling, exuberant growth, expansion of soul, full, uncontained and uncontainable energy, overflowing in gladness of heart, in liquid sunshine, in aptness, willingness, joyful unconsciousness, filling everything with its own exhaustless life and meaning. It is genius equalized and pervading the whole being with transparent life; not genius condensed into intellectual diamonds, hard and lifeless. Lambs playing upon the green, Puss chasing her tail, birds singing from the fullness of their joy; the cattle capering and lowing upon the hillsides; and the movement, buoyancy, and pulsing energy of all animate and inanimate Nature on a bright spring morning, is the lower phase of its development. Youth realizes it in all its innocence, purity, and spontaneity; and the boy who looks toward the horizon and longs for the future with its golden harvest of manhood, and who expects to take down the Big Dipper and quaff the nectar of the heavens from its starry bowl, is its poetic embodiment. Youth never theorizes and conjectures, never hesitates and doubts, never shuffles or prevaricates, has no logic or creed, but, borne on by the flood-tide of life, dissolves and assimilates everything; leaps and bounds through rain and shine, foaming and sparkling as it dashes upon the old shores and limitations of conservatism; takes hold with both hands and with gloves off when the thing is to be done; is impatient of argument, or precedent, or explanation, but must face the matter at once, and taste the joy of doing.

The great difference between Beecher and other preachers and writers consists in his intense motion, and the completeness with which he evolves an idea. Most writers never more than half uncover their thoughts; their leverage is not sufficient to raise them clear from the ground. Beecher not only detaches his, but tosses them in the air, throws them up from the solid earth of the understanding, against the clear blue of his imagination, and so not only liberates them full before your eyes, and sets them off by a beautiful background, but gives them the additional charm of motion. The thoughts of ordinary preachers are half-live coals, half buried in the ashes. Beecher's are the same coals hurled through the air, blazing, sparkling, coruscating, and rebounding in so many fresh forms and angles, and darting off in so many unexpected curves as to feast the eye with perpetual novelty.

Lies at all times are dangerous things. Much of the difficulties and jars in society and in families are caused by old lies being uncovered. A lie is like a sliver in your hand; sooner or later it will fester and cause trouble.

July 4

That which distinguishes this day from all others is that then both orators and artillerymen shoot blank cartridges.

A man trying to analyze his own thoughts is like Puss
trying to catch her own tail — the greater the effort, the
less chance of success. It is only by surprise, by a sudden
instantaneous movement of the mind, that we can get
an objective view of our own thoughts, as Puss, if she
succeeds at all, does by a sudden twist and outreaching
before her whole body is fully in motion. The mind can
at best get but a mere glance at its own workings. Our
thoughts, like woodcock, are always rising to take flight
when we see them. Attempt to consider your own
personal identity, to get out of yourself, to take an external objective view of you as you, and, if you succeed, it
will not be by a laborious logical effort, but by a kind of
felicity — quick, instantaneous as a lightning-flash, and
entirely inexplicable.

There is a tradition of an old German who won his way
to the source of the Danube; placing himself in the little
stream, and damming the water with his huge boots, he
exultantly cried out, 'How the nations will wonder why
the Danube does not come!' So those supertextualists
who take any particular passage or isolated declaration
from the Bible and build thereupon a sect of religion, and
claim Scriptural teachings as the rock upon which they
build, are just as much in error as was the old Dutchman
in supposing that the mighty waters of the Danube were
controlled solely by one remote mountain rill.

It is the tendency of the Book that we should look to;
the net result, after all the facts are digested. The bee
makes one honey from a diversity of elements; so there

is one tendency, one undercurrent, steady and unvarying, beneath the surface facts and cross-currents of every book; that is, in every book whose growth is organic and not mechanic; which obeys an inward law, and not an outward necessity. There is a Spirit in the Bible that floats all its facts as a river floats its ice and driftwood; there is a great catholic sense, a mighty ocean current, that is as unchanging as the revolutions of the earth; and the church or religion that reaches down to this is borne on by the forces of nature, and in the very teeth of the surface winds and currents.

Nov. 2

Light is only seen when reflected back by opaque bodies; it is in itself invisible and no man hath seen it. So it is with the spirit of Life: itself cannot be seen, but only its manifestations.

That man is my Pilot who has traversed the seas before me; that man is my Master in whom I can see my own green, crude feelings and grub instincts ripened and hanging upon him like apples, absorbing the rich, golden autumn sunlight. Hence men become leaders only by greater power of expression; by affording a free passage to that which is choked and obstructed in others. They shape into notes and cadences the music that, unexpressed, is ravishing other souls. That man is our Hero who is more ourselves than we are; who beats us at our own game; who surpasses us in our own directions.

When I am introduced to a man, the first thing I want

to know, after his name, is what his thought is, what
helm he obeys, and what compass he steers by. After
this he is no longer a stranger to me. I can then account
for everything he says or does, knowing that according to
his general idea will all the particular facts arrange themselves. For it is true that every man has some one central
principle, some one predominant idea upon which he is
built, as a ship upon its keel, and which determines the
course and character of all his lesser timbers. A declaration of a man's principles is a letter of introduction, and
gives us a key to his attainments and possibilities; for if
they are a growth, and are not borrowed, they are characteristic, and carry somewhat of a man's personality
along with them. What an endless amount of gabble and
gossip and misunderstanding and false moving it would
save if every man would hang his sign out, and tie his
principles or professions to his coat button!

Nov. 17

In all history I find no man so thoroughly intellectual as Emerson; in all history I find no man so thoroughly sane as Franklin.

Every man has an inlet into the great deep if he will
only keep it open and free from sticks and rubbish. In
youth the passage is free, but the cares and business of
the world soon clog and choke it up, so that we become
a little muddy bay, cut off from the great ocean. A man's
soul can only be kept pure and healthy by a constant
reception of truth; or at least a free communion with
truth.

Nov. 27

I love to get a back view of a man's character, to see the private, everyday side of him, as I love to get a glance in the rear of imposing residences; the back yard, and not the front yard with its gravelled walks and smooth greensward, is the place where the character and tendencies leak out. For my part I like the spirit of the old farmer who insisted on having as much cornice and architectural beauty on the back part of his house, and as nice grass and trees in his rear yard, as on and in front.

Dec. 2

The scholar's life is an alternation of two moods, the conceptive and the receptive; the miracle of gestation and birth with him is perpetually renewed. At one time he is full and overflowing with thoughts and fancies, and, like a brimming cup, cannot be disturbed by speech without letting drop jewels; everything he looks upon is flooded with exhaustless meaning and beauty, and to his eyes the landscape seems waiting and ready to float away into the upper heavens. Facts and clods become transparent; the walls of his own being become clear as glass, and he seems to see through the very pores of his skin. The laws of Nature that shoot and radiate like great nerves throughout the universe, making every part vital and related to the whole, come out beneath his penetrating vision. His senses are sharpened and refined, and he hears musical sounds in the air, sees signs and signals in the earth, 'sermons in stones, and running brooks,' and meaning everywhere. The trees seem to nod to him, and rustle their leaves in his presence; the hills seem to purr, and great broad smiles to beam from their rugged visages when he looks upon them. He finds himself talking to the flowers, singing with the birds, and making love to the stars. But soon the mood changes. The soul cannot always keep summer; such fruit and sunshine impoverish and leave us bleak and desolate. Nothing satisfies us; we suck a thing empty the moment we look upon it. We feel restless and lank, like a woman that has borne a child. We long for books, and society, and travel, and excitement to fill us up again. We are like pigs at the teats of Destiny, and must spend much time in kneading and rooting for one full draught.

We are just as much in the heavens now as we ever can be. If a man was in the Pleiades he would be no more in the heavens than is Paddy in the ditch.

Subjects for essays: Growth by activity and by incubation when the universe broods over us; Action and Reaction, or the Law of Antagonism; The Law of Silence; Local Physical Laws soon show themselves in spirit; Climate and Character; England and Englishmen; Mountains, Islands, and Men; The Law of Rainbows; Man an Epitome of the World; Root and Branch; The Law of Births and Deaths.

Dec. 29

It is justly maintained by Ruskin that the painter who cannot paint great deformity, great blackness and horror, cannot paint their opposites in any degree of sublimity; he who cannot make the sky frown, cannot make it smile;

and he who cannot paint a fiend, cannot paint an angel. So it is in life; he who cannot, or dare not, confront an evil, cannot support a good; he who does not kick Satan, dare not kiss his Lord; he who cannot be intensely melancholy, cannot be intensely gay; he who cannot feel indignation, cannot experience generosity; he who cannot hate, cannot love; and the savagest natures have been known to exhibit the greatest degree of tenderness. These things go together as day and night, and are opposite sides of the same law. This corresponds to Plato's doctrine that the capacity for the greatest good can become the capacity for the greatest evil; that the best saint makes the best devil; that it requires as much genius to perpetrate enormous crimes as it does to achieve great good. Small minds are capable of no vast reach in either direction, their latitude and longitude is only 8 by 10. The greatest shore indicates the deepest sea.

Jan., 1860

It is a strange idea which people have of use — as if a man must go jingling his money in his pocket, or reciting passages from books, to establish his claim to wealth or to wisdom. You know a man cannot jump much without calves to his legs; and if I put a bottomless abyss between you and me, must I show my calves to convince you that I really jumped it, when there was no other possible way for me to get over? If you will bring me gold, I will not ask for the pick and spade which you used in digging it.

Jan. 5

In the finest strain of music, or the most masterly

strain of art or eloquence, there is something that un-
satisfies; that promises more than is performed; that
hints somewhat that is not realized. Immense possibilities
beckon to us. The dome is uncapped and the great heavens are beyond. The highest problem of literature and
art is to lift us up in sight of these huge possibilities; not
to realize, but to break down our limitations, and let us
flow out into the Infinite. Art must not be a wall against
which our thoughts rebound, so that one idea can be projected a thousand times, but an open space, a sky-mall,
an outlook into perennial day, giving one room to think,
as the sun has room to shine; so that there is a constant,
unimpeded outflow of ideas; no echo, no reaction, no
corners to turn, but on, on.

A man is but a little piece of earth, with a little piece of
sky over him; and all the laws of this outward earth and
sky are repeated in him on a higher scale.

The biggest eyes by no means see the sharpest; in
fact, they never see quite so sharp as your calm, middle-
sized, deep-set eyes. Their focal distance, somehow or
other, is not well defined; they seem to diffuse the light
instead of condensing it or drawing it to a point. So I
think a man can have so much feeling as not to feel
sharply and intensely; the curve is not sufficient to bring
it to a point.

The best thinking is extemporaneous. 'Tis with
thoughts as with apples; the ripest fall the easiest. When
a man's ideas are fully matured, a slight effort, a gentle

jogging of his branches, brings the golden pippins down. But to get them fully matured, there's the rub. Knots and knurls grow on every branch, but full-orbed, umber-seeded fruits is a *desideratum*. When the corn has germinated, it appears at the surface; so, I think, when our thoughts are fully matured, they will blossom in speech. It is the action of the mind which matures them; this gets up the heat, the magnetism, that makes the seed fructify.

I like old Ben Jonson with all his faults. There is a good deal of light in him, with all his opacity. He is like the old-fashioned tin lantern which gives a shower and not a flood of light. Bright patches and stray beams dance on every page of his works.

What an immense seacoast Carlyle has! Most men have no seacoast; no outlook to the great ocean of truth; no port or harbor therein; but are mostly inland — their relation to truth relative and second-hand; and consequently have no treasures upon the great deep.

Aristotle observes that all great men are melancholy; it is certain that the greatest men are melancholy; the highest mountain is oftenest clouded.

Ruskin says that in art a mass of subdued color may be balanced by a point of a powerful one, and a long and latent line overpowered by a short and conspicuous one. The same is true in life. A single shot will go farther, and do more execution, than a handful of lead filings.

Humor is the wit of the heart.

The fancy is a kind of under-wing of the imagination —
like, but finer and inferior to it. It does not lift a man
off his feet, or set him spinning like the planets, but grace-
fully relieves and lightens his burdens, gives pliability
and ease to his movement, and assists the imagination in
its empyrean flights.

A man of great conceit can never be a great thinker;
cannot think long and continuously and go on a Columbus
voyage of discovery. He cannot forget himself long
enough; he must come home to roost. The centripetal
overcomes the centrifugal force, and his thought is constantly returning to himself. It is like a bird held by a
string; it can only flutter and gyrate about his head, and
then fall back upon the hand that holds it. The greatest
thoughts are the most impersonal, just as the greatest
circles possess the least curve. A great egotist is always
narrow; he may be intense, but not comprehensive; and
you can see the sweep of his circle at a glance. He is
excursive, abrupt, sallies out like a cowardly, saucy dog,
snaps here and there, and hastens back to his own kennel
to defy all other dogs from his master's doorsill; while the
good hound will pursue the game days and nights without the least thought of self.

The more personal a thought is, the narrower is its
range. The condition of deep, far-reaching thinking, of
pure creation, is that we forget self; that we go beyond our
conscious personality and view the universe in its own
light, and measure it by its own standard. A man must

not form a part of that which he sees, if he would see cor-
rectly. Or, we may say, the condition of right seeing is
that we do not form a part of that we would see, or
bear any personal relation to it. If we would see the
landscape aright, we must not be in it, but stand on the
adjacent hill. When Shakespeare created Hamlet, he did
not take a cast of himself and interject his own accidental features and peculiarities in him; but forgot himself,
and dealt with the eternal elements of our common humanity, keeping his work between himself and the sun, so
that his own shadow left no trace therein.

I have observed that the boy in the school learning to
write at first imitates his copy for a few lines, and then
turns naturally to imitating himself; and so, in obedience
to the law of imitation, which always keeps the man below his model, writes poorer and poorer all the way to the
bottom of the page. The same is in a measure true of us
all: the high resolve, the pure purpose, the convictions
and determinations, of our calm, serene moments, are
soon lost sight of, and the writing of our lives yesterday
is made the copy for to-day.

Jan. 27

This is one of the cleanest, purest days heaven ever
let down upon earth. It is an intellectual day; — it has no
vapors, fogs, or clouds, but is clear, deep, bright, and cold.
It is such a day as always rests upon the highest mountain tops; vegetation and growth lie far beneath in the
latitude of [indecipherable], fogs, and change. The virgin
snow rests like a heavenly fleece upon all the earth, hid-

ing the dirt and filth; only on the paths and public highways of men is it soiled and mixed with dirt; as is generally the case with heavenly influences that fall upon the courses of our lives. They are soon stained, ground into the earth, robbed of their starry lustre, and made to subserve the meanest ends. Still, how pure is everything that comes out of the heavens! Behold the rain, the dew, the snow, the air, the sunlight; only when it reaches earth is it tainted and diluted and trafficked in.

Feb. 1

There is originally, and in the abstract, but one tree; or, perhaps we might say, but one root, for the first vegetable kind that grew contained within itself the possibility — and demonstrated it — of every other type or modification that has ever grown. So in the animal world: all classes and tribes and genera can be traced back through all their ramifications, as a river to its source, to the first sole type and beginning. We may say, in short, that all phases of life, both animal and vegetable, in all their multiple, complex, widespread relations, are reducible to a single, simple beginning, as all colors and combinations of colors spring from a colorless ray; or as all motion (which is the first and primary condition of life) springs, or sprang, from a simple impulse. I believe the whole universe, in fact, grew from a single atom. Have given one atom, and a little push, and the whole creation is demonstrable.

March

March is certainly a step from winter towards summer,

yet its sour, blustery, fickle weather, if one looked no
further, and did not consider the law, would induce the
belief that the earth had taken the wrong road, and that
summer did not lie in this direction.

In the progress of the mind there are periods when we
seem to be farther from truth and a right knowledge of
things than when we set out. Thought and study change
our standpoint, and before we have worked through to
another, so that we see things from the ground of intellect,
and not of experience, we are apt to be unbelievers, scof-
fers, and skeptics, having no faith in anything permanent
and solid; we lose all sense of sacredness and veneration;
and our instinct is to deny and trample down. In this
case, the course for an individual or a nation to pursue is
not to deny its unbelief, [nor] to turn back and say the
tendency of culture is evil, but to persistently follow it
out, push it to its legitimate results, and the curve of the
circle will bring all right again; and science and culture
shall be found, not to end in skepticism and doubt, but
in hope, love, and a sublime faith in the essential veracity
and justness of things.

Botanists say that thorns are imperfectly developed
buds which have become indurated, and which a more
favorable situation and cultivation would have converted
into luxurious branches. It is certainly a very significant
fact. How many thorns of human nature — hard, sharp,
lifeless protuberances that tear and wound us, narrow
prejudices, bristling conceits that repel and disgust us —
are arrested developments, calcified tendencies, buds of

promise that should have lifted a branch up into the sunny
day, with fruit and flowers to delight the heart of men,
but now all grown hard, petrified, for want of culture
and a congenial soil and climate! the tender germ which
folded into itself such rich and beautiful possibilities,
grown a knot of offence, a thorn to poison and wound!
Surely a significant fact.

Twilight — blank leaves in the volume of the day —
a broad margin for reverie and annotation.

Man seems at best a kind of tide-mill. Poor devil!
he has no dam or perennial stream within himself; but,
placed as he is on the shores of the sea of Infinite Being,
with its ceaseless ebb and flow, he manages to get a little
impetus and grind his grist more or less indifferently at
last.

Well, March has gone out, as she usually does, angry
and sniffy, and slammed the door behind her.

1861–1876

[THE many and varied entries in the remaining Note-books are chiefly on nature and literature.

After Burroughs's 'Expression,' which had appeared, unsigned, in the 'Atlantic Monthly' in November, 1860, had been attributed by the critics to Emerson, the young writer, being too fervent a disciple of Emerson to wish to imitate him, decided he must get on ground of his own, and that to do it he must write of things at first hand, not merely from what he had acquired from the push of reading. Accordingly, he began in 1861 to write a series of sketches about farm life and farm experiences, entitled 'From the Back Country,' and immediately found his own field of work. These appeared in the New York 'Leader.'

Burroughs read medicine a few months in 1862 with a country doctor at Olive, New York, while teaching in that locality. At that time he wrote the poem 'Waiting.' Medicine was soon dropped, but essay-writing and school-teaching continued. It was in 1863, while he was teaching at Buttermilk Falls on the Hudson, near West Point, that Burroughs began the systematic study of the wild flowers and the birds, a friendship with a botanist there, in the one case, and Audubon's spirited portraits of the birds, in the other, determining the course of his studies. He had come upon Audubon's work in the library of the Military Academy. A camping trip in the Adirondacks followed, and out of that, and the ardor begotten by his new studies, he wrote his first essays on the birds — 'With the Birds' and 'The Adirondacks.' It was that year, at West Point, that he first met Emerson.

In the autumn of 1863 he abandoned school-teaching and sought employment in Washington, D.C., first obtaining work in the Quartermaster's Department, and later as Treasury Clerk in the Currency Bureau. The most momentous event of the Washington period was the meeting and quickly formed comradeship with Walt Whitman. The poet was forty-four and Burroughs twenty-six at the time. In these various Notebooks, especially those filled between 1863 and 1868, are voluminous notes about the 'Good Gray Poet,' as William O'Connor named Whitman. One can fairly watch the young man's mind seething with the thoughts and emotions that the encounter induced. He records his first impressions of Whitman, recalls his first reactions to 'Leaves of Grass,' which he had read a year or two before going to Washington, and describes at length his subsequent reactions as he reads both book and man together. He gives us glimpses of their comradeship, occasional reports of their conversations, and graphic accounts of Whitman's ministry to the soldiers, both during and after the War. Here we see some of the earliest tilts of Burroughs with a critical lance in defense of his hero.

Some of the matter which went into Burroughs's first printed article on Whitman ('Walt Whitman and his Drum Taps,' 'Galaxy,' December, 1866), and much that went into his first book, 'Notes on Walt Whitman as Poet and Person' (1867), with much else never published, is found in these significant little books. Much found here was later incorporated in the essays 'Before Beauty' and 'Before Genius' ('Birds and Poets'); and Burroughs evidently even turned back and levied on these early records, many years later, when writing his second book on the poet, 'Whitman: A Study' (1896).

Quite different entries than those concerning Whitman are now beginning to creep into the little Notebooks. Certain ones, long familiar to the reader of 'Wake-Robin' (published in 1871), fairly jump at one from these early penciled pages; tentative beginnings to favorite essays, such as 'In the Hemlocks' and 'The Adirondacks,' are found here.

In the autumn of 1871 Burroughs first went to Europe, but the only reference to this experience found in the Notebooks is in some jottings about the notes of European birds. The trip was especially memorable to him for the meeting with Carlyle. He also met Edward Dowden, the Rossettis, and Moncure D. Conway; he heard James Martineau and Spurgeon in London, and, what meant far more to him, heard the skylarks on the South Downs. Although impressions of his journeyings are wanting in the Notebooks, they are given in 'An October Abroad' in 'Winter Sunshine'; while others are incorporated with accounts of his second European trip (1882) in 'Fresh Fields.'

At the close of 1872 Burroughs resigned from the Treasury Department, went back to his native State, bought land along the Hudson, about eighty miles north of New York City, and there established his home — Riverby, at West Park. There he continued to dwell the rest of his life, carrying on (till ousted by Cleveland's administra-

tion) bank-examining, in connection with fruit-farming
and essay-writing. In 1875 he published 'Winter Sunshine.' In May, 1876, he discarded the Notebooks for a
Journal, which he kept till within a few weeks of the
close of his life. Henceforth there is less and less philosophizing, and more and more of the writer we know
through the nature essays.

The list of titles of essays transcribed here probably
shows a tentative arrangement of contents for an early
book of essays which, in 1861, Burroughs had contem-
plated publishing, until deterred by advice from David A.
Wasson, with whom he had some valued correspondence
in the early eighteen-sixties.]

Titles of Essays: Growth of Knowledge, Spiritual
Lungs, Moral Atmosphere, Lies, Bluebirds, Growth of
the World, Theory and Practice, Adversity, Writing,
Intellect and Character, The American, Pure Reason,
Poetry, My Authors, Past and Present, Home, Teeth and
Ideas, A Little Genius, Self-Culture.

April 1, 1862

Take courage, brave heart! Difficulties in prospective,
in the distance, appear more formidable than they are in
reality. On a nearer approach they are not so terrible
after all. In a mountainous country one can never see his
way through. Huge Alps seem to lie across his path on
every hand, but be assured there is a way out, and it will
reveal itself to the unfainting traveler. So, too, clouds in
the horizon appear more threatening than on a closer
view. Floating ice in the river seems completely to hedge

up the way miles in front of the boat, but when we approach, behold, blue lanes open here and there, and wide safe passages are disclosed, where once appeared only danger and opposition!

The grossest materialists I know are the spiritualists.

A steamboat is not rocked by its own waves, but a man often is.

It is a question worthy of the consideration of any man interested in literature, how far rhyme, and what is called versification, are valuable; their true significance and relation to the matter in hand. Are they not a sort of accompaniment, quite secondary, deriving their value from the delight we take in according sounds? or perhaps, to go deeper, from the love of correspondence, of compensation, or return, innate in us? Yet, at the most, its appeal is to the ear, and it is as much of a trick as an acrostic or an anagram. It is a trick, I repeat, and may be found in great perfection entirely distinct from the true soul of poetry. How it has come to be valued so highly, and used so largely in modern literature, is a puzzle to me. Has the love of symmetry anything to do with it? does it spring from the same feeling that prompts us to set out trees in rows and regular distances, and lay out our grounds with the rule and the square? We do not want the boughs all on one side of the tree, and I notice that they are not set exactly opposite one another; and the peaks and depressions of parallel mountain chains do not coincide, but the reverse. Rhyme is entirely verbal and [labial?], and of no intrinsic value. The weakness of modern poetry is that it is obviously poetical, is meant to be so, and has no unconscious grandeur and sublimity.

March 4, 1865

To-day, for the first, I heard the song of the Canada sparrow [1] — a soft, sweet note, almost running into a warble. Brushing the coverlid of leaves from the ground, in one of those warm slopes in the woods, we found the liverwort just pushing up its buds. The claytonia also was fairly under way. Digging into the rich mould, I disclosed the bloodroot with a sprout an inch long. What miracles are going on here under the leaves, or an inch or two under the ground! What awakenings, what shooting of first sprouts! What an important service the dead leaves render — every plant tucked up so tenderly! The arbutus also was budding. The bluebird's note came down from the air overhead, like the first tremulous voice of spring. This bird always comes to me like the signs and tokens of a new era; for days and days in the air, before it takes shape before my eyes. I look and look, but as yet it is only a wandering voice; by and by I see him timidly alight on a stake or a fence.

March 12

Visited the woods again yesterday in company with Everett. It was a superb day without a cloud, with a soft wind — one of those strong, positive days — a he-day — impregnating the earth with the generative principle of sunshine. Just as we were about to enter one of those

[1] Now commonly called the tree sparrow.

deep wooded nooks on Piney Branch, eager and expect-
ant, we saw two soldiers just ahead of us. I felt vexed
and as if they had no business there. Had I possessed the
authority, I should have ordered them back, for I could
not get over the feeling that they would drive away something I was after, some influence, some wood spirit or
kindly genie that needed to be approached as gently and
devoutly as possible. I felt as I do when some fisherman
gets to the brook ahead of me, and I am obliged to cast
into holes just ravished by his hook, though habitually I
respect and love these Bluecoats above all men. So we
were obliged to lie down on the leaves and wait till the
pollution of their presence had passed off, and the privacy
of the woods restored — the coy nymphs all back again.

Of course it is all fancy, but when I do not go for game,
but for pleasure, — for such game as I shoot with my eyes
and ears and nose, and bring down with the arrows of the
imagination, — I cannot bear to have any one get ahead
of me. I miss something. The virginity of the woods is
gone, and I must sit down till the equilibrium is restored;
till the scent of [the intruder's] footsteps has exhaled; till
the woods have sloughed his presence; till his tracks are
snowed full, so to speak.

Presently the soldiers commenced firing for practice,
and I despaired of meeting my invisible friends in that
nook. I could almost hear the rustle of frightened wings
go by. So we lay basking in the warm sunshine, talking
of Spiritualism, and discussing philosophy. I say law is
but another name for the intelligence of things, and is
self-executive, bearing no analogy to human or civil law,
or to any mechanism that depends upon a motive power.

It is not effect or cause out of, and independent of, itself; it is cause and effect in one. There is no compulsion, etc., etc. And here we split.

By and by we moved on, and on a gentle slope in the woods, where one year ago to-day I was blessed in precisely the same way, I found a solitary liverwort in bloom. Everywhere they were just pushing up through the mould, but only this one in all the woods had opened its blue eye to the sun. I think I must be a favorite of the wood nymphs, for I am always led to the one flower when others search and search in vain. In January, walking in these woods with a friend, I found one houstonia in bloom, and the little lump of mould upon which it was enthroned was frozen hard as a stone. Of course there was not another in the whole woods. [See 'Spring at the Capital' for this incident.]

May 8

This morning early the veery, to my unbounded delight and surprise, came and sang in the pear tree in the garden. Of course it was for my benefit. I thought first it was one of those independent, irresponsible tricks of the imagination, as it was very early and raining, and as he did not sing fully and confidently. It was like a dream of my boyhood. There was also a burst of bobolink melody from somewhere in the air — a troop going North, I expect.

May 26

I confess my excursions to the woods are often spoiled, or at least vitiated, by taking my gun and making it a specialty to obtain a bird. I am too much preoccupied and miss everything but the bird. I am not devout and receptive, but eager and inquisitive, and, if I miss the bird, come home dissatisfied.

The full fruition of enjoyment and delight comes when I go out without any purpose except to get nearer the earth and sky, and accept the whole; ready to entertain bird and beast and tree alike — full of faith and self-forgetfulness, and pledged to no special end — all to gain and nothing to lose.

As I saunter through the woods and by the brook, the kindly and hospitable influences of the air and earth come nearer to me; nothing escapes my eye, ear, or nose. A more intimate and harmonious relation is established between me and Nature. I do not outrage the woods; I do not hunt down a bird.

As necessary as it seems to be in life, much is lost by being wedded to a particular end; and the loafer or saunterer who has nothing at stake, but looks on and contemplates, has the fullest enjoyment. Poet Piatt says in his boyhood he used to hunt wild turkeys, and would set out with his gun loaded for that purpose; but often would see no turkeys, but lots of other game, which he forbore to shoot because he was loaded for turkeys, and so came home dissatisfied. I often find I go out loaded for game which I do not see for that very reason, and miss much else I might otherwise obtain.

May 27

The voices of all birds to me express some human feeling or sentiment: the bobolink, hilarity; the bluebird, homesickness; the catbird, pride; the song sparrow, faith;

the robin, triumph; the hermit thrush, religious devotion; the white-eyed flycatcher,[1] self-consciousness; the swallow, love; the red-eyed flycatcher,[2] contentment. Indeed, I do not seem to know a bird till I have heard its voice. As soon as it speaks, I seem to recognize it, and place it. The gray-cheeked thrush is enveloped in mystery to me, because I have only seen him and never heard his voice.

Aug. 26

What a wonderful man Walt is; what a great, yearning love he has; what a hospitable soul; what soft, gentle ways; what a deep, sympathetic voice! How he appreciates, how he listens! The most cosmical and synthetical mind I ever knew, he yet has a wonderful power of analysis — keen, searching, discriminating, and subtle.

So commanding is one vital truth, he says, so much else becomes knowable when one thing is thoroughly known, that he can see how the theology of the day would fall before the standards of him who had got even the insects. 'If these things are true, if these facts are so, then these other ones are not so.' I was trying to express to him how, by some wonderful indirection, I was helped by my knowledge of the birds, the animals — cows, and common objects. He could see, he said. The ancients had an axiom that he who knows one truth knows all truths. There are so many ways by which Nature may be come at; so many sides to her, whether by bird, or insect, or flower, by hunting, or science — when one thing is really known, you can no longer be deceived; you possess a key, a standard; you effect an entrance, and everything else

[1] White-eyed vireo.   [2] Red-eyed vireo.

links on and follows. He thought natural history, to be true to life, must be inspired as well as poetry. There ought to be intuitive perception of truth; important conclusions ought to be jumped to — laws, facts, results, arrived at by a kind of insight, or inspirational foreknowledge, that never could be obtained by mere observation or actual verification. In science, in astronomy, some of the most important discoveries seem inspirations, or a kind of winged, ecstatic reasoning, quite above and beyond the real facts. It was always so with the great poet, with Shakespeare. He knew all things without collecting the facts. Why not something like this in natural history? So far as he had observed, the authorities on these subjects have been mere explorers, and have gone no farther than they could see; have caught no hints or clues by which large and important inferences can be drawn. And much more grand, glorious talk, entirely beyond my power to hint.

One delicate test by which he knew he had eaten too much of my wife's good victuals, was that he did not spring (with a peculiar motion of the hand) and respond buoyantly to such a scene as was before us — as we came down back of the Capitol.

Notwithstanding the beauty and expressiveness of his eyes, I occasionally see something in them, as he bends them upon me, that almost makes me draw back. I cannot explain it — whether it is more or less than human. It is as if the Earth looked at me — dumb, yearning, relentless, immodest, inhuman [unhuman?]. If the impersonal elements and forces were concentrated in an eye, that would be it. It is not piercing, but absorbing and devouring — the pupil expanded, the lid slightly drooping, and the eye set and fixed.

There is something indescribable in his look, in his eye — as in that of the mother of many children.

Sauntering with him one day along by the Capitol, we met a soldier, — dirty, travel-stained, and ragged, with a very friendless, careworn expression, — not a loiterer, but one evidently bent on some long journey, whom Walt kindly accosted. I shall never forget how the soldier altered the tone in which he was about answering him, as he looked Walt in the face. He had evidently been spoken to often, but not in this fashion, and the sympathy and deep, yearning love that spoke in this man's voice, and beamed in his face, completely disarmed him; and in a blushing, bashful way he answered Walt's questions. I stood a little apart and thought I had never seen anything so human and good. The soldier looked down at his boots and began to be ashamed of his appearance, since here was some one who took an interest in him. He was a Western boy, and there was some curious history connected with his story and appearance.

Walt in his tender, curious way, asked him if he should not help him a little — not enough to hurt him, but enough to get him a bit of food; for he looked hungry. The soldier did not know how to meet this charge, and came near breaking down outright; and as Walt placed some small notes [1] in his hand, and turned away, he found his

[1] Fractional currency.

tongue to say, in that awkward, constrained way, that
he hoped he would have good health and keep well. I saw
how deeply he responded to this act of kindness, and how
poorly his words expressed what he felt. That youth will
not forget, as long as he lives, the great kind man that
accosted him under the walls of the Capitol, and spoke
the first words of human sympathy and tenderness, perhaps, he had heard since his mother bade him farewell.

Walt said he had probably been guilty of some mis-
demeanor, perhaps was a deserter, or a returning rebel;
but I saw this incident would do more to strengthen and
encourage him, and help restore his lost manhood, if so it
was, than all the sermons and homilies and tracts that
have ever been preached or printed.

His book,[1] read with modern eyes, would seem to justify
Emerson's characterization of him as 'half song thrush
and half alligator;' and, by some means or other, I had
got an impression that he was at least half rowdy. Imagine my surprise, therefore, when, on being introduced to
him, I beheld a well-dressed, large, benevolent-looking
man, very cleanly and neat in his appearance, with a
grizzly, shaggy appearance about the face and free open
throat.

Without rising, he reached out to me a large, warm,
soft hand, and regarded me with a look of infinite good
nature and contentment. I was struck with the strange
new beauty of him as he sat there in the gas-light — the
brightness of his eyes, the glow of his countenance, and
the curious blending of youth and age in his expression.

[1] *Leaves of Grass.*

He was in that felicitous mood, almost habitual to him I have since found, during which his flesh and skin, as it were, become transparent, and allow his great summery, motherly soul to shine through. I was struck, likewise, by his rich, mellow voice — a voice at once an index to the man, implying not only deep human sympathies and affinities, but the finest blood and breeding — a gentle, strong, cultivated soul.

After all, there is nothing the soul loves like reality. There is nothing in literature of any value but reality; that is, that spirit, directness, rectitude, and integrity in thought and expression which tallies with the forms and movements of the visible universe.

Jan. 15, 1866

Sitting on a mountain and looking across a deep valley to a corn-field on the opposite side which, when seen near at hand, completely envelops the ground, the predominating tinge is not that of the corn, but of the earth. After the deepest snow, I am astonished to see how little of the earth is hidden after all; the color is only changed.

Jan. 17

Nature is the only fact, after all. This is the ocean from which all the streams start, and to which they return. In the great city *it* seems the only fact. How fixed and enduring it all looks, the imposing fronts, the paved streets, the marble and the iron, and the clatter of hoofs and wheels! how it all struts and spreads its huge tail! Nature is entirely crowded out; the stars seem to shine by grace, and the sun and moon look like fixtures of the corporation. And the citizen in time comes to think that they are. But get out on the hills where you can take the measure of this monster, get a rear view of it, see over it, and around it, and the ground on which it stands, and the impression is quite changed; its pride and impertinence are all gone. Now it seems accidental and transient, and the earth and sky, the only permanency after all. It is as transient as a child's playhouse, and as frail. The rains might wash it away, or the mud bury it, or a little restlessness of the earth in her sleep bury it in ruins. Fugitive, and as frail as a bubble! Absolutely considered, London is no more permanent than a village of prairie-dogs, or the pyramids more enduring than ant-hills. Longer in time, but not in eternity. They shall as surely disappear from the face of the earth as shall yonder snow-bank. Given time enough, and the air will grind them to powder. You part away the immutable waves for a moment, but how surely they close again!

Nature exists for man no more than she does for monkeys, and is as regardless of his life or pleasure or success as she is of fleas. Her waves will drown him, her fire burn him, and her earth devour him, her storms and lightnings smite him, as if he were only a dog. His success and triumph is in placing himself in the way of her beneficent tendencies, and letting her work through him. She says to man, My horses are going this way and you can vault into the saddle and ride, though always at the risk of being run over if you fail. My steam will carry you and all your traps and household around the earth, if you know how to manage it; or will rend you to atoms if you miss your hold. My streams will saw your lumber and grind your grists, or will saw and grind you if you fail to keep the upper hand.

Man is at the top, in his own estimation, and thinks the sun and the moon are for him; but he is no more an end than a frog is; and is not so much atop as the birds are. He appeared in the plan, and he will disappear in the plan, and Nature values him only as manure — squanders him as recklessly as autumn leaves. The geological ages, the convulsions, and parturient throes, were to bring him forth no more than the beetles. Are not all the wealth of the seasons — these solar and sidereal influences, this depth and vitality, and internal fires, the seas, and rivers, and oceans, and atmospheric currents, as necessary to the life of the worms and the bugs as to our own? and do these [forces?] exist for us any more than for the tadpole?

Why should Nature be choice of spending and squandering when it is her own coffers that are enriched? Is it lost if it goes to the sun, or to the stars? or if it comes from them to us? There is no loss.

What is size? what is time, distance, etc., to Nature? Nothing. She knows no time, no space, no great, no small, no beginning, no end, no life, no death; that is, she works without reference to these things. She is not powerful, she is power. Did you think Niagara a great display of power? What is that which lies silent in the earth around, and of which Niagara is only the lifting of the finger? Every display of power is but gravity claiming its own, a drop blending with the ocean again, and the power is the eagerness to blend. Man places his wheel between the two separated parts and makes gravity grind his grist. The possibility of life and movement is in breaking the equilibrium. Where is the end of this thread? Is heat first, or movement, or life, or power? You cannot corner this Proteus here, for, behold, these are all one! Where is the beginning? How was the equilibrium broken to allow life and movement to begin?

Every lover of Nature understands Thoreau's aversion to a companion in a walk, except he be a true lover also. It is a rare qualification to be a good walker. We do not go to the woods for society, or to talk politics; and he that would go with me, must leave me to myself, and leave the town behind him. A young and thoughtful boy is the best company. You do not want to be diverted or hindered, but open, like a sponge, yet ready to give or take.

The passionate delight of the sportsman, the skater, the swimmer, the boatman, the rambler in the woods, the camper-out, is more rational and human than the narrow and intense pursuit of the naturalist, or the botanist, and brings you nearer to the sense and meaning of Nature. Not to the student without love, armed with every weapon of science, does Nature yield her most precious secrets. Nature will not be conquered, but gives herself freely to her true lover — to him who revels with her, bathes in her seas, sails her rivers, camps in her woods, and, with no mercenary ends, accepts all. Why is the naturalist, the entomologist, the geologist, not enriched and ameliorated by his pursuit? Because he is a partialist, and is so intent on the body that he misses the soul; follows her rule, and does not see her inspiration. The poet's pursuit of Nature is the only true one. The study of natural history, to be profitable and true, must be grafted on a deep and abiding love of Nature; not the birds or the plants for themselves, but so far as they express and stand for the spirit of Nature. Is your delight the same, if you see no bird or flower? If not, you will never interpret aright these forms.

Feb. 13

Looking out of my window into the sunshine, this cool, still morning, the old question comes up again, Whence this beauty? There stand the naked trees, there is the gray, scarred ground, and yonder soars the sky. No ornament, no system, no gaudy coloring, no attempt at beauty, but only the nude, simple world, yet beautiful to the verge of ecstasy. The brilliant equipages in the street cease to attract notice; the most elaborate architectural edifice is of no account in this transparent sunlight. In the park, in the road, on the hill, the same uncontained and measureless beauty floods and fills the earth. The horizon is the brim of a cup that swims with the divine elixir.

The book[1] is still a problem to me. I am delighted, and shocked, and stunned, and ravished, and aroused, all at the same time; and I am yet unable to decide whether the fault, if fault there is, is in me, in my habits and training, or in the poems.

I cannot rid myself of the impression that the poet is sometimes putting on airs, and is wilfully perverse and defiant. He need not have laid it on quite so thick, to

[1] *Leaves of Grass.*

begin with. The public made wry faces at his first poem, and he seems to have said, 'If you make wry faces at that, I will give you something to make wry faces for,' and so wrote the poems of procreation.

There is no greater or more significant fact in the universe than that of sex; none with larger and deeper running analogies; nothing like the love of the man for the woman, and the responding love of the woman, nothing so ravishing and fearfully uncontrollable as the sexual desire, nothing so sacred and beautiful as the consummation of love; and no instincts more certain and constant than those which throw the veil over these things. And this tragedy of love must be rendered, if at all, with perfect fidelity to Nature and the natural instincts and promptings.

April 5

Let me work all day in my garden, the next day ramble in the fields and woods, with a little reading, and the third day I can give myself to literary pursuits with a new freshness and vigor.

The first step which a man or a people takes toward culture is a love of the artificial, as such, while the last and crowning step is a love of the natural and the simple.

July 3, 1867

One of the secrets in writing, I find, is to choose a commanding position, a central stronghold, as it were, which easily commands long ranges and vast tracts of thought. An eminence, a high point. Then what progress one makes! he can't help but write well. At other times, when he gets entangled in the byways, as it were, how hard it is!

Many writers show great spirit and activity, dart out first this way, then that, but never arrive at any results. They show special merit, but never give any grand effects. Most of the criticism of the time is of this character; it is aimless; it leads nowhere. Writers cast about them vigorously, cutting right and left, but one easily sees that they are in a corner, or ravine, as it were, and do not command the ground about and beyond them.

July 5

I think we can hardly estimate the moral value even of geography. Think of our advantage in this respect over the early Eastern nations! To know really the limitations and shape of this great wonder, the world, and all that is on its surface; to know that there are no vast countries, or possible wonders, just beyond the horizon — who does not feel that it is a great point gained? There is no cure for superstition like Science.

July 10

This, then, would be my ideal of poetry: human speech that conveys to the soul the sense of the health and perfectability that pervade Nature, the Whole. As soon as one breathes the spirit of poetry, he sees how insoluble things are, and how and why they are insoluble; and how vain and foolish all the disputes and systems and theories of the logicians and philosophers. Folded in the poet's speech like an aroma, is the sense of the All. His words are not beautiful merely, but good. How they strengthen my faith! how they absorb into my soul!

April 6, 1868

It seems to me that one great defect in [W. D.] O'Connor's mind is that he lacks the perception of identity. This shows itself more particularly in his admiration of, and remarks upon, the great poets and authors. What is common to all, he sees clearly enough; but what is peculiar to each, I think, he totally fails to see. Thus Æschylus and Rabelais, Hugo and Whitman, all awaken the same emotion in his mind, and he applies the same epithets to each.

April 16

Made a trip to the woods. Nothing mentionable to report. The day was bright and warm, no wind, not even a breeze. A delicious hush pervaded the gray, sunlit woods, which was rather enhanced than otherwise by the sweet, plaintive song of a single wood sparrow, and the cawing of a passing crow. Spiders and ants were crawling about on the dry leaves. Occasionally a bumble-bee sounded his mellow bass. In some pines, heard the fine, insect-like warble of the black and white creeper.

Swallows appear in Washington from the first to the middle of April. They come twittering overhead just as they do North. The swift, or chimney swallow, comes like the rest and is [abundant?] here all summer. The purple martin appears in April, and again in July and August. One singular sound, and to a Northerner a very precious one, may be heard on some bright morning in May. You are walking forth in the delicious air, and suddenly there comes a burst of bobolink melody, half a dozen throats breaking out in one hilarious shout, and as suddenly ceasing. There is a mysterious remoteness and uncertainty about it, but a little attention reveals its source skyward. A quick eye may detect them far up against the sky, pushing northward. They seldom alight here, yet one season they not only alighted, but tarried nearly a week, owing, no doubt, to a sudden change in the weather — a cold spell at the North.

Nov. 30, 1870

It seems to me the greatest of all gifts to have in one is the rationale of the universe — to see and feel in one's inmost consciousness that the universe is good; that it could in nowise be different from what it is; that things are an arch — a span — in which every stone is a keystone, all mutually dependent, interdependent; and that it will not do to seize upon one point, or thing, and run it, as some do. I sometimes think there are men of real genius whose minds do not present this similitude of an arch or a span, and who do not feel at all the authority and binding force of Nature. Make a statement or assertion, to such a person, that has not an immediate logical sequence, but that harmonizes or accords with general Nature and experience, and he denies it at once.

Feb. 11, 1871

No book can deeply please, or long last, that has not a good, lovable man behind it. The final background of every book, or poem, or essay, is the character of the author; here we bring up at last.

Feb. 14

How quickly one can tell in the morning before he gets
up that it has been snowing! The room is filled with a
soft, white light. Then there is a strange silence without.
One hears voices — the gleeful shouts of boys, or the bell
of the milk-man, but no other sounds. The 'meteor of the
snow,' what a happy phrase! The 'snow-loving pines,'
also, from the same source. How the snow is piled up on
them! They do seem to love it.

To-day the old farmer sits by the fire, or tends his cattle. He will not go to the mountain to haul out wood to-
day, [unless] he be entirely out; nor open the stack on the
hill to replenish the mow, nor to fodder his cattle from it
on the snow. The cattle are left in the stable till nearly
noon, and then let out to drink. See them hurrying toward the spring, their backs soon white with the snow,
and then crowding around to drink. Age generally takes
precedence here, and the young, timid heifers stand
shivering around in the snow till their turn comes. Having drunk, back they go, and congregate about the stable
door till the farmer opens it and lets them in. Again in
the stanchions, and hay before them, the discomforts of
the storm are soon forgotten. The snow melts from
their backs, their bodies steam as they reach and stretch
for the hay.

The young cattle or calves by the stack in the field, with
perhaps a yearling colt and a cosset sheep among them,
have a harder time. They huddle under the lee side and
look unhappy. They have gnawed the stack till its base is
a great hard stem that their poor noses can hardly make
an impression on. Such an abundance before them, yet

such a struggle to live! Some, more knowing than the
rest, worry away at one place till a hole is made; the solid
front of spear-ends is broken, and, if not checked, the
stack will by and by totter to its fall.

Feb. 27

Emerson stands for moral and intellectual electricity;
he is not life, he is not color, or warmth, or impulse; he is
freaky, fantastic, full of surprises, and aims always to
communicate a shock — to give off a spark. He is subtle
as lightning, abrupt, zigzaggy, far-darting; develops a
spark out of the nearest object. In this respect he has no
equal and has never had.

[On March 9, 1871, is an entry which shows the pupil
trying to step in the footprints of his teacher. It is so in
the manner of Whitman that I searched through 'Leaves
of Grass' to make sure it was not there. It occurs, without quotation-marks, along with other comments on
March weather, not written, however, in verse, as here
arranged.]

O, West Wind! wind of high-sailing clouds,
Wind of blue sky and fair weather;
Dry, intermittent wind, clear-off wind, wind of the moun-
tains and the spheres!

South Wind! moist, wooing, fragrant wind,
Streaming, musical wind from the Gulf, loaded with
vapors;
Wind of the low-hurrying clouds, rolling over the moun-
tains,
Resting on their tops, drenching the land with rain!

Southwest Wind! with your long processions, your cara-
   vans of clouds filing across the sky,
Great fleets and armadas — black-hulked, white-sailed;
   water in their bellies, and lightning in their shrouds;
Swooping up the dust, silvering the leaves, making the
   flags leap, and the sails careen!

Aug. 1

Have just been talking with Walt about Joaquin
Miller, the new California poet. He has seen only some
extracts — thinks we ought to lean to the favorable side.
In the first place, Walt said, he [J. M.] had saturated himself through and through with Byron and the stormy, passionate poetry of that school, but that he had had the good
sense, or the luck, to graft, or get grafted, upon this stock,
fresh subjects — miners, hunters, etc., from Mexico and
California. He said there was dash and spirit in the book,
and freshness; but it would not bear trying by any high,
serene standards. He said that beneath the convention-
ality of the English aristocracy, there was a chord that
vibrated to the wild-horse business — roughness, danger,
courage, etc., and that Miller had had the luck to strike
it, and John Bull was tickled. His is a fashionable success, and not a scientific success; not a success in a high
artistic literary or esthetic sense.

Dec. 21

Walt said a friend of his, Mr. Marvin, met Emerson in
Boston the other day. When Walt was mentioned, 'Yes,'
said Mr. Emerson, 'Walt [1] sends me all his books. But

[1] It seems probable that Emerson, instead of saying 'Walt,' said
either 'Whitman' or 'Mr. Whitman.'

tell Walt I am not satisfied, not satisfied. I expect —
him — to make — the songs of the Nation — but he
seems — to be contented to — make the inventories.'

Walt laughed and said it tickled him much. It was
capital. But it did not disturb him at all. 'I know what
I am about better than Emerson does. Yet I love to hear
what the gods have to say.' And, continuing, he said: 'I
see how I might easily have wandered into other and
easier paths than I did — paths that would have paid
better, and gained me popularity; and I wonder how my
feet were guided as they were. Indeed, I am more than
satisfied with myself for having the courage to do what I
have.'

Dec. 23

With Walt. Taking up an ancient atlas, I remarked,
'How strange the world must have seemed to the ancients!' 'Yes,' said Walt in a musing kind of way, 'I
wonder what advantage their ignorance was to them —
in stimulating their imagination. No doubt, very much,
for all the old literature may be said to be founded upon
fable.'

I observed that the bump of wonder seems to have died
out and become extinct, like certain bodily organs that
the anatomist finds the rudiments of. 'No,' said Walt,
'but the human mind has not yet adjusted itself to the
new lights, to science — the vast fields and expansions
laid open to us in astronomy, geology, and the like. The
staple of all our literature is an emanation from, or in some
way, the result of, the long age of fable and myth. Our
poets more or less still play at the old game. My book is

the first attempt at an expression in poetry of a knowledge of the earth as one of the orbs, and to give the wonder and imagination a new and true field — the field opened by scientific discovery.'

Jan. 30, 1872

Proposed essays: Serious Humor, The Poet's Point of View.

Feb.

Subjects for essays: The Natural History of the Boy, Serious Humor, Unction, The Point of View of the Poet, Springs, The Cow, The Apple, The Scorners — M. Arnold among the chief.

March 2

Yesterday was a bright sharp day without a cloud. Ah! there are no weather-breeders like these clear days. Last night the sun went to his rest knee-deep in haze, and this morning before he was up the storm set in — a driving, blinding 'meteor of snow,' which is equally good to look at or to be out in. It is now eleven o'clock and no cessation. I look out of the window and see it stalking by, blotting out everything.

The waves and pulsations of a snowstorm are vertical. It is so remarkable and unusual that I must commemorate it. All the impulse and mood [?] of the spring, and all the rigors of the winter combined. It excites me to see it. Such briskness and animation! I love to be pelted by such a storm; it exhilarates me; every flake seems to discharge into me its electricity. And then the privacy of the storm — how good it is! How one can write or read such a day, or do any indoor work.

Washington, April 21

One of the best-tempered spring days I ever experienced. Perfect in every respect. Neither hot nor cold; no spring languor on the one hand, and no chill on the other. The air was simply delicious, and the whole body of it softened and tempered with warmth. There were no raw, cold streaks in it. The warmth and deliciousness were uniform and all-pervasive. It was not cold in the shade, nor hot in the sun, as it was last Sunday, but equally fresh and renewing everywhere. There was no wind, and only a slight film in the air. A few clouds flecked the blue sky. I sat on a knoll in the fields and reclined for an hour in the woods, and saw no difference in the temperature. The air was elastic and bracing. Some spring days, to touch the ground with one's body is fatal. It seems to absorb one's strength and energy, to suck it out of him. In a fatal moment he throws himself upon the ground on dry leaves under the shelter of the hill, to bask in the sunshine and rest his limbs, but he rises more enervated and tired than when he lay down, and can hardly drag one foot after the other. Antæus is not renewed by touching the earth on such days. But to-day nothing enervated. There was nothing seductive or betraying in repose, and nothing fatiguing in action. One seemed to get the sun's warmth by indirection. You did not feel his beams upon you, but the air held and diffused their warmth. Later, how he will scorch! and how one will seek shelter from his arrows! Even earlier, when the

air was yet cold, how his rays beat down upon our backs
as we plodded along! But to-day he rules with love, and
his reign is so perfect as not to be felt. He is a fountain of
warmth and coolness and light. Radiant, equable day,
when shall I see your like again?

Feb. 15, 1874

Contrast Lamb, for instance, with the writers of this
class among ourselves: Lamb has real juice, real mellowness, real unction; but there is not a drop of unction in any
American writer since Irving, and he had not much. We
have witty men like Holmes, bright and smart men like
Lowell, dainty humorists like Howells, or clever mockers
like Bret Harte, but no unctuous writers. The nearest we
have produced to anything so good as Lamb is to be
found in Thoreau. As dissimilar as these two authors are,
in aim and subject, they are yet close akin. They indeed
spring from the same root. Their methods are the same;
so is their quaintness and scorn of rhetoric. Thoreau
has the dryer humor, as might be expected, and is less
stomachic. One cares all for Nature, the other, nothing at
all. One is attached to the city and to artificial life, as the
other to the country and the life of animals and plants.
Yet they both reach the heart by about the same road.
[Elaborated in 'Touches of Nature' ('Birds and Poets').]

May, 1875

What can be more exquisite, I said, coming up from the
dock, than a sparrow's nest under a grassy bank? There
it is, a structure, something built, put together, and done,
it may be, in a few days, and yet it looks as if it grew

there! How it fits its place! An excavation has been made, and yet no sign of it anywhere, not a straw, or a spear of grass has been disturbed, and not a particle of earth dropped. How commonly and coarsely it begins, and how it refines as it approaches the center! How gently the ground must have been displaced to make room for it; with what care the whole work conducted! [Elaborated in 'A Bird Medley' ('Birds and Poets').]

Sept. 4

It was bliss enough for Rab to be with me, and it was a never-failing source of pleasure for me to be with Rab. Why should my grief be so acute? Only a dog! My neighbor, or my friend, dies, or my man-servant, or my maid-servant, who has served me long and faithfully, and my grief is far less poignant. My dog is a part of myself. He has no separate or independent existence; he lives wholly in and for me. But my friend, or my neighbor, revolves in an orbit of his own. He has his own schemes and purposes, and touches me only casually, or not closely at all. Your dog is interested in everything you do. Then he represents the spirit of holiday, of fun, of adventure. The world is full of wonders to him, and in a journey of a mile he has many adventures. Every journey is an excursion, a sally into the unknown land, teeming with curiosities. A dog lives only fifteen years, but think how much he crowds into that space; how much energy and vitality he lives up!

Have you ever noticed what a harvest, midsummer sound the mowing-machine, or patent reaper, is coming to have, or, in fact, had from the first? The sound of the whetstone or of the rifle upon the scythe, pleasant as it is, is even less in keeping with the time and the air than the sound of these machines. It is like the whir and rattle of an enormous cicada, or harvest-fly, or the rasping, strident sound of a mighty grasshopper. [Elaborated in 'Touches of Nature' ('Birds and Poets').]

Feb. 13, *Sunday*

A delicious day — clear, calm; snow all gone; ice all afloat. Put in some big licks on Emerson.

Feb. 19

Began my 'Touches of Nature' to-day.[1]

March 7

One of the 'charmed days' Emerson sings of. Soft, southwest wind, no clouds, but a deep haze. Oh, the blue-birds! oh, the robins! Saw the first ducks, a level line of them skimming the water northward. Oh, the fascination of out-of-doors! I stand spellbound on the brow of the hill.

[1] See *Birds and Poets.* Later he has written near this entry: 'Finished them about March 1st. Wrote the "Final Word on Emerson" second week in February.' Events proved that his 'final' word on Emerson was not written till many years later. Emerson, like Whitman, and like the birds, was a subject which ever drew him. A considerable portion of his posthumous book *The Last Harvest* is largely a discussion of Emerson and his Journals.

1876–1886

[THE Journals as journals begin abruptly May 13, 1876. Burroughs had been living at his river home at West Park on the Hudson since 1874. We find him, during this decade, much occupied with vineyard and garden and with his 'other garden,' literature, as well as with bank-examining. In the uncongenial task of going from bank to bank and scrutinizing long columns of figures he still kept a sharp lookout on the birds and wild flowers. If he painstakingly examined the banks in his assigned territory, he investigated even more assiduously Nature's accounts. Once in commenting on the drudgery of bank-examining, he said, 'Yes, I stuck it out a good many years, but "I know a bank where the wild thyme grows," and I like to examine that a good deal better.'

From now on the reader will share his saunterings, his recurring joy in the recurring seasonal events — the calls of the birds, the trill of the toads, the shrill chorus of the spring peepers, the companionship of chipmunks and red squirrels and other fur-bearers, and the scenes and sounds which came to him in and around his little bark-covered study perched on the bank of the great river. He will see him returning again and again to the Old Home in the Catskills, trying in vain to drink at the Fountain of Youth; see him boiling sap, gathering arbutus, going on wild-honey quests on Mount Hymettus, and canoeing in the sweet wild solitude of Black Pond. He will get glimpses of Whitman in his visits to Riverby and as

Burroughs saw him in Camden, and will see the comrades as they strolled on the beach at Ocean Grove, watching 'the white arms out in the breakers tirelessly tossing.'

For Burroughs this period is one of deep sorrows and abiding joys. He loses first his mother, then his father, and, one after another, several of his dog friends. Emerson's death takes a deep hold on him, and Whitman's gradual decline keeps him sadly anxious. But compensations come in happy experiences. His son is born early in the decade; he makes that memorable summer voyage on the Pepacton; he gleans much from his second European trip, in 1882; and it is during these years that several of his most delightful early books were published — 'Birds and Poets,' 'Locusts and Wild Honey,' 'Pepacton,' 'Fresh Fields,' and 'Signs and Seasons.'

The year 1883 was especially significant for him in that he then began to study Darwin and became fairly elated at the discovery of the key to so many of the secrets of the universe. What he saw, as he looked down the long road of evolution, added immeasurably to the glory of man, and, instead of feeling any false shame, he felt a pardonable pride in his humble progenitors.

The same year was memorable for the meeting with Matthew Arnold, and productive of his later critiques on Arnold.

Throughout the Journals, the reader of Burroughs's essays will come upon familiar passages, some identical with those in the books, others strikingly similar. While many of these have been located for the reader, still others have been left for him to discover. Although we shall find here much writing on scientific and theological

questions, and much on literary criticism, for the most
part we shall lose the young philosopher so much in
evidence in the Notebooks, and find the outdoor companion who saunters at ease with Nature.]

May 13, 1876

Standing in the road over in the woods, I saw a lively
little shadow, cast by some object above and behind me,
on the ground in front of me. Turning I saw the source
of it — the redstart performing its astonishing gym-
nastics in a leafless oak tree. How it darted and flashed,
its tail spread, its wings drooping, and its whole form instinct with motion! Its shootings and gyrations festooned
the tree with a black and orange cord. It is the quickest
and prettiest of the flycatchers.[1] The game it took was
certainly invisible.

Each species of warbler, it seems, has its own range and
prey. The insects this redstart took certainly could not
have been taken by any other bird. In the lower branches
and bushes the black-throated blue warbler was pursuing
its game very leisurely, picking it up at rest, and never
taking it on the wing. About the orchards and open trees
I saw the blue yellow-back [2] probing the flowers and buds
with its beak, either for honey or else a microscopical
insect. The creeping warbler [3] was scouring the trunk and
branches for its food — not forcing a way to it like the
woodpeckers, or probing deeply like a brown creeper, but
picking it up, apparently on the surface of the bark and

[1] The American redstart, one of the wood warblers, was formerly
known as a flycatcher, or flycatching warbler.
[2] The blue yellow-backed warbler, or parula warbler.
[3] The black and white warbler.

lichens. The ground warblers find their food on lone plants and shrubs. The Kentucky warbler is often on the ground picking off worms or insects from the undersides of low, overhanging leaves.

June 1

These, yesterday and to-day, are the shining days. How the river dances and sparkles, how the new leaves of all the trees shine under the sun! The air has a soft lustre; there is a haze; it is not blue, but a kind of shining, diffused nimbus — no clouds, but the sky a bluish white, very soft and delicate.

June 27

A great event — Father came to visit me for the first time! In the seventy-fourth year of his age, and after I have been a housekeeper for nearly twenty years, Father comes and sits at my table, and smokes his pipe on my porch, and sleeps in my chamber. I can hardly realize it. He is like a boy, remarkably well and hearty, has an enormous appetite, and it does me good to see him eat.

Aug. 1

If my writings have any of the freshness which my readers profess to find in them, the secret is that my apprehension of the birds, of a scene, of the open air, or what not, is not, in the first instance, a literary or scholastic one, but a real, personal one. I do not run after the birds in order to write about them, but in order to enjoy them, and to satisfy a natural thirst for them; and I never know till after the fun is all over that I am 'like,' as the women say, for an article.

Oct. 30

It was a picturesque incident to see the fish hawk, or osprey, dive for a fish the other morning, in the river, near Marlborough. He went straight down, feet foremost, and was completely submerged in the water. I think the divided water united above him. Presently the tips of his wings emerged, then he recovered himself and got up with his fish — a goldfish, I should judge. It was not large, but the hawk made hard work with it. I watched him for a quarter of an hour, flying back and forth, from one point to another, on each return getting a little higher, but taking a very easy grade. After eight or ten bouts he reached the highest land in the vicinity, but did not alight, as I thought he would, but was still on the wing. Was he waiting for the fish to die? Perhaps he could not perch and hold a kicking fish.

Nov. 2

A soft, very warm, dreamy day — a day I shall never forget, carried deep into my heart by a rare poetic and human experience. A lady that had known and liked me when she was a girl of nine on the prairies, and whom I had known but had forgotten, now a grown woman of twenty-nine, revealed herself to me by letter, and then met me by appointment and passed the afternoon with me on the hills and in the woods in sweetest, closest converse. She touched me very closely, and the day passed all too quickly. It had been twenty years since we had met, and we may never meet again, but I shall never forget her.

Nov. 8

A flock of goldfinches in their fall plumage, numbering at least a hundred, have been picnicking about my grounds for a day or two, on the ground among the rag-weed, in the bushes and trees. This afternoon they were congregated together, and all singing with a kind of sup-pressed glee, much in the same manner as they do in May or June. There are but few of our common birds that en-gage in this congregational singing. The snowbirds some-times do, half chattering, half singing; the robins do it, in a measure, in spring, but I think of no others. How well I remember this goldfinch, or 'yellow-bird,' from a boy, along the roadsides on the thistles or dandelions, or in the orchard, its peculiar flight in the air: the male cir-cling around and around, its course a series of short arches, the wings being closed as the bird rises, and opened again as it falls, and with that note always repeated as if it were automatic, *per-chick-o-pee*, *per-chick-o-pee*. Then, on alighting, that note, *paisley*, *paisley*. It builds a sump-tuous nest.

Jan. 5, 1877

What command, what godlike symmetry and strength in those Greek faces that have never reappeared in the human countenance! The strength at the junction of the nose with the brow, that straight high embankment, it fills me with envy. The modern face, as a rule, is weak there — the arches are crushed, the brow does not rest upon such a pier of strength. It is the difference between the vaulted arch and the lintel.

Feb. 7

Last night I sat a long time on the wall in the gloaming with my pail of sap, thinking of my youth, and trying to get back the boy's feeling when he wriggled home from the woods with his pail of sap, or sat down and cried when he spilled it in the snow or at the crossing of the fence. O for some of those magic silver dimes and quarters that glowed in the pocket when the boy sold his little cakes of sugar in the spring! That was real money. It seems as if I had never seen any since those boyish days. I think Father yet owes me a few dollars of that heavenly coin that I loaned him thirty years ago. But he can never pay it back in this world.

Feb. 11

One of the peculiar sounds here is the croaking of the great ice-frogs on the river — rip, rip, they go in the still nights, and again when the sun first strikes the ice in the morning. It is a singular sound. Thoreau calls it a 'whoop,' Emerson a 'cannonade,' and, again, 'the gasp and moan of the ice-imprisoned flood.' Sometimes it reminds me of a huge gong, then of a giant staff beating the air. It seems always in the air, and to proceed from something in swift motion — it *ricochets* like a cannon-shot, and glances from side to side. It starts sometimes from under your feet, and rips or explodes and vanishes in the distance. Then again it seems like a grunt, as if some great ice-god were turning over in his sleep. [Compare 'A River View,' p. 187 *et seq.*, 'Signs and Seasons.']

Feb. 17

Returned yesterday from Philadelphia, where I spent

the night of the 15th with Walt, at Mrs. Gilchrist's.
Never saw Walt look so handsome — so new and fresh.
His new, light gray clothes, his white hair and beard, and
his rosy, godlike, yet infantile face, all combined to make a
rare picture. After ten o'clock we went up to his room
and sat and talked till near one o'clock. I wanted him to
say how he liked my piece on him ['The Flight of the
Eagle'] but he did not say. We talked about it — what
had best go in, and what were best left out, but he was
provokingly silent about the merits of the piece. Speaking of his poems, he said it was a very audacious and risky
thing he had done, and the wonder was, not that they had
made their way so slowly, but that they had got any foot-
hold at all. When the conditions were all considered and
the want of anything like matured and robust æsthetic
perception in this country remembered, it was a great
success to have effected a lodgment at all.

It is a feast to me to look at Walt's face; it is in-
comparably the grandest face I ever saw — such sweetness and harmony, and such strength — strength like the
Roman arches. If that is not the face of a poet, then it is
the face of a god. None of his pictures do it half justice.

April 13

Friday morning at six o'clock I left Roxbury for the
down train. Mother got me my breakfast. The boys and
Father were in the stable milking. As I turned to take a
parting view of home out on the knoll, I saw Father and
Hiram emerging from the stable door with the pails of
milk. Charley was going up the steps; the robins sang
loud up in the sugar-bush, where a bucket, just smitten

by the sun, sent back a tinny flash. The snow, dirty and dishevelled, belted the side of the hill above the house. I went down across the lots. It was a typical April morning: the sunlight white, the trees nude, the fields bare and sere. How the sparrows sang! how the robins laughed! how the phœbe-birds called!

June 1

Edward Carpenter left me to-day — a modest, hearty, thoughtful young Englishman.

June 7

In respect to observers, the great mass of men are like the rank and file of an army — they fire vaguely in the direction of the enemy, and, if anything is hit, it is as much a matter of chance, or of general principles; but here and there is your keen observer; he is the sharpshooter; his eye discriminates, picks out; he sees what he fires at, and hits what he sees; his eye and his bullet go to the same mark. To individualize is the secret of observation. In one sense the great poet, and the great naturalist, are the same — things take definite and distinct shape to them; they are capable of vivid impressions. The naturalist walks the real world with his eyes open; he knows a man from a stump at once. The poet walks the ideal world, and his eye disintegrates in the same way.

Oct. 18

Solitude is only more and closer company than one can have elsewhere — the company of one's self. One's best companions are those that affect him like his own waking

thoughts and sympathies — himself seen at a little re-
move. The lover of solitude understands well Thoreau's
dry remark that in his hut there on Walden Pond he had
a great deal of company, especially in the morning, when
nobody called. Solitude is a severe test of a man, but it is
no doubt necessary to insure deep and fast colors of the
spirit. Those who are most alone are most like themselves. Travel and society polish one, but a rolling stone
gathers no moss, and a little moss is a good thing on a
man. It gives him a local flavor and coloring that one
likes. Solitude makes one a shining mark for the arrows
that men dread — misfortune and the loss of friends by
death — he must meet these alone, unprotected.

The lover of solitude sows himself wherever he walks —
the woods and fields and hills and lanes where he strolls
come to reflect himself. There is a deposit of him all over
the landscape where he has lived. He likes to go the same
route each time, because he meets himself at every turn.
He says to the silent trees, or gray rocks, or still pool, or
waterfall: 'We have met before. My spirit has worn you
as a garment, and you are near to me.' He is such a lover
of the earth that a new landscape looks alien to him. After
a time, maybe a long time, it becomes colored, or, more
properly, enriched, more or less, by his spirit. The
mountains where one was born remind him of his father
and mother, and he has a filial yearning for them. When
Father and Mother are gone, I know I shall have a sad
pleasure in the look of the hills where they lived and died.

Nov. 27

We talk of communing with Nature, but 'tis with our-

selves we commune. Nature has nothing to say. It all
comes from within. The air supports combustion, but
'tis the candle that burns, not the air. Nature furnishes
the conditions — the solitude — and the soul furnishes
the entertainment. The 'something more deeply interfused' is interfused then and there by the beholder. All
lovers of Nature are lovers of solitude, and hence of themselves. They muse and dream and commune with themselves. They interpret themselves, not Nature. She reflects their own thoughts and moods. You find in Nature
only what you bring to her. If you are joyful, she is joyful; if you are sad, she is sad. The religious soul finds
Nature very religious. To the scientist she means science, and to the poet she means picture and parable.
She is all things to all men. People admire my birds, but
it is not the birds they see, it is me. I put myself in them.
Shelley's lark is Shelley, Keats's nightingale is Keats.
Who has seen or heard in Nature what Wordsworth did?
She is a book printed full of his own thoughts, nothing is
hers but the paper.

Jan. 29, 1878

Saw three eagles to-day. Two were sailing round and
round, over the river, by the dock. They approached
each other and appeared to clasp claws, then swung
round and round several times, like school-girls a-hold of
hands. [His description of this incident was the source of
Whitman's 'Dalliance of the Eagles.']

Feb. 16

Homer Lynch told me this anecdote about Levi Jen-
kins, whom we saw as we came back from Margaretville:

It was many winters ago. He lived in Batavia Kill, and, being short of fodder and grain for his cattle, used to poach a little upon Harve Keator's oat-mow. Keator suspected some one was stealing his oats, so, one cold, snowy night, watched for the thief. About ten o'clock Levi came with his oxen and sled. (The barn, by the way, was remote from Keator's house.) Levi got up on the mow and began throwing down the sheaves of oats, counting them audibly, and talking to himself the while. 'There! that makes four shocks,' said he. 'I guess that is all will stay on — No — I guess I can carry a few more — one, two, three' — until seven was reached. 'There!' he said, 'four shocks and seven sheaves — that is all I can carry.'

'How many did you say, Levi?' asked Keator, who knew him by his voice.

'Four shocks and seven sheaves, by God!' said Levi.

Poor Levi! the affair cost him his yoke of oxen. He gave them to Keator to say nothing about it. Keator was a hog. How surely a good and wise man would have said to Levi, 'Go, and steal no more.' Levi did it for love of his cattle and team.

Immortality is something to be reasoned about and proven, is it? a question to be established by a subtle metaphysical argument? Then away with it, and away with all such questions! If they do not prove themselves, like the day or the night, or health, or disease, if they are not self-evident, I will have nothing to do with them. What do I care for a metaphysical hell? or a metaphysical heaven? If I *have* existed without my body, then I shall exist again without it; if I have not, then what can you prove by argument, or what assurance give? Where was the flame before the candle was lighted? Where will it be when the candle is put out? We are immortal, just as every force and atom in the universe is immortal — that is self-evident; beyond this there is nothing to be said. No force in me was created at my birth, or in my subsequent growth, but only gathered from the outlying universe and organized into the being I am; and no force will be lost at my death, but only scattered again, to shift and re-appear in other forms. We settle back into the deep, as a wave settles back, or as it breaks and is spent upon the shore. The waves run and run, the force or impulse that fills and makes them is co-equal with the universe.

Feb. 26

I take it [as] a great compliment when my friends, those who have known me longest and best, say of my writings, 'They sound just like you; I see you in every page,' as a doctor who knew me when a boy, and who knew my people, has just written me. This removes much of the Thoreau charge; if it is my flavor, then it is not his. I really see very little of Thoreau in myself. There is a whiff of him, now and then, in a few of my pieces, as in 'Exhilarations of the Road.' I know his quality is very penetrating and contagious; reading him is like eating onions — one must look out or the flavor will reach his own page. But my current is as strong in my own channel as Thoreau's in his. Thoreau preaches and teaches always. I never preach or teach. I simply see and describe. I must have a pure result. I paint the bird for its own sake, and for the pleasure it affords me, and am annoyed at any lesson or moral twist. Even the scholar in me (a very poor one he is!) must not show his head when I am writing on natural themes. I would remind of books no more than the things themselves do.

March 16

Smoke seems to be the equivalent of flame. When the fire bursts out, the smoke is gone. I think that, intellectually speaking, I have many smoky days, when a little more draught, a little excitement, a lucky hit or thought, or maybe a determined effort, would cause the flame to come forth. Something like this always occurs with me when I write: I begin by 'smoking,' and feeling discouraged; by and by, if I put the screws on, the clear leaping thoughts and the glow come. But for the past three or four days I cannot get beyond the smoke. The combustible matter in me is very soggy for some reason, mainly, I think, because spring is here.

March 26

Could I have known, twenty years ago, all the good things that were in store for me, I should have been spoiled. My writing has brought me more fame and money than I ever dared to hope. For the past fifteen years I have had a good income — the last five years as high as $3500 *per annum* — and have been almost entirely free to follow my own tastes. If Fortune had filled only the measure of my expectation, I should to-day have been deeply in debt, if, indeed, I had been able to keep my place at all. But she has exceeded my expectations four-fold, and 'yet I am not happy.'

April 30

Went home [to Roxbury] to-day; got there at one
o'clock. Noted a different smell in the fields as I went up
across them, from that about here — the smell I knew in
boyhood. It whirled me back quickly to that long gone
time. The breath of the cattle was different, too, and the
odor of the ground.

May 19

I have discovered the secret of happiness — it is work,
either with the hands or the head — something to do. It
is the only safe and sure ground of happiness. The moment I have something to do, the draughts are open and
my chimney draws, and I am happy. The trouble is
generally that we do not know when we are happy.

May 25

A fine swarm of bees to-day. It made me prick up my
ears when I saw the queen amid the mass of bees. She is
a superb creature. Before you have seen the queen you
wonder if this or that bee which seems to be a little larger
than the rest is not she. But when you have seen the
queen, you do not doubt a moment. You know it can be
none other — long, elegant, shining, feminine-looking.
How beautifully her body tapers! The drones are large
bees, too, but coarse, blunt, broad-shouldered, masculine-
looking. They have a strident masculine hum. The
queen is not a sovereign in any strict sense, but the
mother of the swarm, and they cling to her as to life.
Among all those 30,000 or 40,000, she is the most precious
bee. [Compare with 'The Pastoral Bees,' p. 12, 'Locusts
and Wild Honey.']

May 27

Never help a chicken out of the shell; he will come to naught if you do. If he is a strong, healthy chick, he will get out himself. Moral easy.

June 14

Attended the funeral of Bryant to-day with Walt and Gilder. Walt and Bryant used to be old friends, and had many long walks and talks together before Walt wrote poetry — after that Bryant was cold and distant.

June 17

Oh! the strawberry days! who does not remember them? The smell of clover in the fields, and of the sweet syringa about the house. The first hot, moist days. The daisies and buttercups; the songs of the birds, their first madness and love-making over; the smell of the blooming rye-fields, and of the wild grape; the full, tender foliage of the trees. The bees swarm, and the air is strung with resonant musical chords. The time of the greatest milk yield, and of the sweetest and most succulent grass. Indeed, the strawberry belongs to the juiciest time of the year. [An earlier form of the fifth paragraph in 'Strawberries.']

Sept. 22

To-day is the funeral day of Charley Caswell; to-day they put his body in the ground, the ground that but a few weeks ago I saw him turning with his plow. Death has seldom despoiled the race of a nobler specimen of a young man. He was a young giant in strength and robustness. With his blond hair and fair skin he was like a Norse Viking. I had not known very much of him and yet I loved him. He was the ideal farmhand — worthy the muse of a Virgil or a Theocritus. He had the virtue and quality of all sweet rural things. How cheerful and happy! What a worker, what strength! But yesterday, it seems, Aaron and I saw him cradling on the hill, and remarked his fine, manly form and power. How he walked up to the grain and through it! It was a delight to see him pitch hay, but no fun to the one who had to mow it away. But perhaps his great mastery was best seen when he had hold of the ax. It was better than a play to see him make the white chips fly, and the big logs vanish before him.

They gave him a sweat one night when his disease (typhoid fever) first began to wrench his bones, and in the morning he was missing from the house. After a while they found him up in the orchard lying on the ground. 'A bad sign, a very bad sign,' Mother said, and so it proved. The last day he worked he ploughed up on the side-hill, but at eleven o'clock turned out and came with his team to the house. He could plough no longer. And there his work in this world ended. My heart is full of unshed tears for the lost youth. I will go walk over the hill and consecrate this day to the memory of him. [J. B. once told me that Whitman became so enthusiastic over his description of this superb youth that he made a picture of him in 'Leaves of Grass.']

Oct. 10

The feeling of fall comes to me very suddenly sometimes. There comes a day, the latter part of September,

or early October, when cold, grayish-blue clouds cover
the sky, the trees are shaken by a cold, raw wind, the
rarer birds are gone, and the more hardy are flocking,
and, as you walk or ride along, there suddenly comes to
you a vision of a fire in a grate, of nuts and books and
papers, and the charm of indoors beside one's own hearth.
The summer is gone and the sterner season makes itself felt.

March 12, 1879

A change to more crispness and coolness, but a delicious spring morning. Hundreds of snowbirds with a
sprinkling of song and Canada sparrows are all about the
house, creeping and lisping, and chattering and squeak-
ing in a very animated manner. The air is full of bird-
voices. Through this maze of fine sound comes the
stronger note and warble of the robin, and the soft
warble of the bluebird. Whatever else they may have in
Europe, I doubt if they can ever have such a morning as
this. A few days ago, not a bird, not a sound; everything
rigid and severe; then, in a day, the barriers of winter
give way, and spring comes like an inundation, and the
birds keep even pace with the flood.

April 1

At Fredericksburg, Virginia, [Ernest] Ingersoll with me.
A bright spring day. We walked over the battlefield and
through the cemetery where fifteen thousand of our soldiers lie.

April 26

These days I am happy. The days are perfection —
sweet, bright, uncloying April days — and then Walt

Whitman is here. He sits in the open bay-window, reading, writing, musing, and looking down upon Smith and me grafting trees, or ploughing among the currants, or upon me wheeling baby Julian about the grounds. His white beard and ruddy face make a picture there I delight to see. Occasionally he comes out and strolls about, or sits on the wall on the brink of the hill and looks out upon the scene. Presently I join him and we have much talk.

May 9

New book ['Locusts and Wild Honey'] came last night; like it better than I thought I should. The late pieces are richer in tone and color than the other books.

Dec. 3

A good time at the Holmes festivities.[1] Saw and spoke with Emerson. He is the most divine-looking man I ever saw; does not look like a saint, but like a god.

Jan. 30, 1880

How true it is that every person has his or her permanent water-level, like a mountain lake! We can hold only just so much happiness. A streak of great good fortune raises one for a short time, but we surely settle back again to the old water-line. So ill-luck, sorrow, the loss of friends and kindred, lower one for a season, but we recover and come back to the old measure, be it little or big. How much I love little Julian, and what a godsend

---

[1] The breakfast given in Boston by the *Atlantic Monthly* to celebrate the seventieth birthday of Dr. Oliver Wendell Holmes.

he is to me, and yet is not my water-level permanently raised.

Dec. 22

To-day Mother was buried. A bright, cold day, the air full of glistening frost particles, and a curious fog clinging to the mountain-tops. Mother looked as if wrapped in a profound calm. Her features wore a more severe and noble expression than they ever had in life.

After they had carried her coffin down and placed it in the sleigh, Father stood by the window and looked out after it, and I heard his agonized words, 'I shall see her no more, my dear wife! I shall see her no more!' Few men have ever loved a woman more. He clung to her more than she to him. Mother's heart and life were devoted to her children — she could not do enough for them; but she was often curt and unkind to Father. Not so with him; his children were secondary — she was first always. 'There was never a better mother,' he said, 'and never a better wife.'

Dec. 25

It is Christmas and I have but one thought, 'Mother is dead! Her toil-worn hands and aching heart are at last at rest. After life's fitful fever, she sleeps well.'

Dec. 30

Every hour in the day I see Mother's image and hear her voice. In the night I wake and my heart cries, 'Mother! Mother!' The saddest of all is that I can eat and sleep, and read and laugh, and go about my affairs cheerfully with Mother in her grave.

Jan. 6, 1881

Everywhere I turn, the image of Mother — her voice, form, features, ways, are all before me. She appears always a little withdrawn, a little in shadow, as in life. Mother was not a bright, chirp, smiling woman, though as happy, perhaps, as most persons; but her happiness was always shaded, never in a strong light. The sadness which motherhood and the care of a large family and a large yearning heart beget was upon her. I see myself in her perpetually. A longing which nothing can satisfy I share with her. Whatever is most valuable in my books comes from her — the background of feeling, of pity, of love, comes from her. [See 'Our Friend John Burroughs,' pp. 63–64.]

March 14, 4 P.M.

The ice on the river has just started. Presto! what a change, the dead is alive again — resurrected! Where was that white, rigid, death-like expanse but an hour ago, is now the tender, dimpling, sparkling water. All the forenoon I have noted the signs; the river stirred a little, put forth a little streak of water here and there; made breathing holes, as it were. At 3 o'clock, the ice was rent here and there, and shoved one piece upon another slightly; there was something alive and restless underneath them. Then, by and by, the whole body of ice began to move down stream very gently, almost imperceptibly at first, then with a steady, deliberate pace, till the whole expanse of the river in front of my house was dancing in the light again. The resurrection of the river! but the dead, oh, the dead! [Compare with 'A River View,' p. 185, 'Signs and Seasons.']

Two mornings since saw five swan flying over, in single file, the first I ever saw; they looked very large, spread out on the sky — like great geese. How gently their wings flapped — the tips of them apparently doing the most work! They went north. It was a noble sight — an express train bound for Labrador. The hens saw them first and asked one another curiously what birds those might be.

March 31

In some respects the city is more favorable to the production of literature than the country. There is more electricity in the mental atmosphere. But, offsetting this, is the life of the clubs, and the tendency of men to get together and chatter and chaffer, and talk and talk; and there is nothing that kills production like this incessant palaver and rubbing of your heads together.

April 10

The finest fox sparrow song I ever heard. How it went to my sad heart! Of all the sparrow songs this is the finest. Either I have never heard the full song before, or else this bird was an exceptionally fine songster among its kind. The song sounded strange and foreign to me, and I had to look sharp to be sure of my bird. It almost made me weep; it echoed in my heart, and the thought of it clung to me long and long. So plaintive, so bright, and prophetic — of what — sadness or joy?

July 10

Old Mr. Martin down at the dock told me this anecdote about Si Terpenning — a fellow not well stocked with

brains: He was hoeing corn for Mr. So-and-So, who told
him to leave only four stalks in a hill — all others were to
be pulled out. When, in the course of the day, Mr. So-and-
So came into the field, he found, indeed, only four stalks
in a hill, but they were the smallest — all the biggest ones
had been pulled out. 'That's the way to do it,' said Si in
explanation — 'pull out the big ones, and give the little
ones a chance.' 'There is a great deal of that kind of
philosophy in this world,' said old Martin, reflectively.

Sept. 21

We go down to Ocean Grove and spend one week by
the sea. The beach attracts me much. Its purity, its
odor, its elemental wildness, its rustling, liquid drapery,
the great white lace-like spreads which it is forever throwing, and forever withdrawing, from the smooth breast of
the sands. I never tire of it. Day after day I walk for
miles on the beach, barefoot, skirting the thin edge of the
waves, alone, soliloquizing with the soliloquizing sea.

Sept. 30

One's pleasure with a dog is unmixed. There are no set-
backs. They make no demands upon you, as does a child;
no care, no interruption, no intrusion. If you are busy, or
want to sleep, or read, or be with your friend, they are
as if they were not. When you want them, there they are
at your elbow and ready for any enterprise. And the
measure of your love they always return heaped up. Ah,
well! I cannot help but mourn — my daily companion
and comrade [his dog Lark] is gone. The door that opens
and shuts but once, to dogs as well as to men, has closed
behind him, and I shall see him no more, no more.

Jan. 13, 1882

The universe, eternity, the infinite are typified by the sphere. The earth is the symbol of the All, of the riddle of riddles. We speak of the ends of the earth, but the earth has no ends. On a sphere every point is a center, and every point is the highest point, and this explains the puzzle of time and space. There never was a beginning of time, and there never will be an end. Time always *is*. Any number of trillions of years hence, and any number of trillions, or quadrillions, of years past, and you are just as near the end, or the beginning, of Time as now, and no nearer. This moment is the center of Time; this instant is the highest point in the revolving sphere. The same with that other form of Time, Space. There is no end to Space, and no beginning. This point where you now stand, this chair, this tree, is the center of Space; it all balances from this point. Go to the farthest fixed star and make that distance but the unit, one in millions and sextillions of such distances, and you have only arrived at Here. Your own doorstep is just as near the limit, and no nearer. This is the puzzle of puzzles, but it is so. We cannot understand it, but we can see *why* we cannot understand it.

March 1

Finished my 'Signs and Seasons' [the essay, not the book] to-day, begun two weeks ago. Writing is like fishing: you do not know that there are fish in the hole till you have caught them. I did not know there was an article in me on this subject till I fished it out. I tried many times before I had a bite, and I did much better some days than others. Stormy days (either snow or rain, though snow is best) were my best days. I did not know I had that bank article [1] in me till Gilder told me I had, and commanded me to write. The same is true of the Thoreau article, and, indeed, of nearly all my articles; they have been discoveries, and have surprised me.

April 3

My forty-fifth birthday. Clear, crisp, and delightful. All day in the old sap-bush at home, boiling sap. How delighted I am again amid the old scenes and at the old occupations! Now, on my forty-fifth birthday, my hair is about half gray, beard ditto, mustache unchanged, except on close inspection, when three or four small gray hairs appear. Health good, and much of a boy yet at heart, but the boy is growing more and more sad with longer and more frequent retrospection. Indeed, the past begins to grow at my back like a great pack, and it seems as if it would overwhelm me quite before I get to be really an old man. As time passes, the world becomes more and more a [Golgotha?] — a place of graves, even if one does not actually lose by death his friends and kindred. The days do not merely pass; we bury them; they are of us, like us, and in them we bury our own image, a real part of ourselves. With what longing and regret we look back athwart this cemetery of the years, where our days, many of them so beautiful and happy and bright, lie hushed and still! They cannot rise; they cannot come back to us. They were the offspring of our loins. Many of them we have entirely forgotten the look and aspect of; we cannot recall what they were like, and this makes us sad. Occasionally

[1] 'Broken Banks and Lax Directors,' *Century Magazine*, March, 1882.

a word, a forgotten air, or a perfume, brings back for
a moment the buried past, and a mournful thrill goes
through the soul. [*See* 'Our Friend John Burroughs.']

April 28

Emerson died last night at 8.30 o'clock. At that hour
I was sitting with Myron Benton [1] in his house, talking
of [Emerson] and his probable death. With Emerson
dead, it seems folly to be alive. No man of just his type
and quality has ever before appeared upon the earth.
He looked like a god. That wise, serene, pure, inscrutable
look was without parallel in any human face I ever saw.
Such an unimpeachable look! The subtle, half-defined
smile of his face was the reflection of the smile of his soul.
It was not a propitiatory smile, or a smirk of acquiescence,
but the reassuring smile of the doctor when he takes out
his lancet; it was the sheath of that trenchant blade of
his. Behind it lurked some test question, or pregnant saying. It was the foil of his frank, unwounding wit, like
Carlyle's laugh. It was an arch, winning, half-playful
look, the expression of a soul that did not want to wound
you, and yet that must speak the truth. And Emerson's
frank speech never did wound. It was so evident that it
was not meant to wound, and that it was so true to himself, that you treasured it as rare wisdom.

April 30, Sunday

To-day Emerson is to be buried, and I am restless and
full of self-reproach because I did not go to Concord. I

---

[1] It was in company with Myron B. Benton and Donald G. Mitchell,
at West Point, in 1863, that J. B. first met Emerson.

should have been there. Emerson was my spiritual father
in the strictest sense. It seems as if I owe nearly all, or
whatever I am, to him. I caught the contagion of writing
and of authorship before I knew his books, but I fell in
with him just in time. His words were like the sunlight to
my pale and tender genius which had fed on Johnson
and Addison and poor Whipple.

I must devote the day to meditating on Emerson, the
greatest and most typical of all New-Englanders.

May 2

The last night in my little hermitage [the Bark-covered
Study at Riverby] before sailing. Every morning, if I
have slept well, I am glad I am going, and every night I
am sorry; thus does the day make and unmake us. To-
night the old ties draw strongly, and I am sad.

May 12

One of the first impressions [in the Scottish landscape]
is that the cattle and sheep have all got in the meadow,
and one's impulse is to go and drive them out. Then you
look farther and see that there are no pastures, as at home;
it is all fresh and green and meadow-like, smooth and
well-kept.

May 27

Again comes around the anniversary of Channy's [his
nephew Chauncey B. Deyo] death, and I am sitting here,
at 12 M., on the top of Ben Venue in Scotland, Loch
Katrine at my feet, and apparently a universe of mountains about me. On four peaks I can see snow or miniature

glaciers. Ben Lomond is eight or ten miles west of me, a little taller than this peak. If he were a little nearer, I should knock his cap off yet. Only four or five houses in view over all this stretch of mountain and vale. The nakedness of these mountains as regards trees is what one is not prepared for. The wind whistles among the rocks and hums in the heather, but at a distance they are silent. Two peaks in the distance the clouds are now just touching; their keels scrape the rocks, but they seem high above me. The atmosphere is filled with a white film, an effect only produced in our country by a fine mist. A certain tameness in the view, after all; perhaps because of the smooth and grassy character of the mountains — not solemn and impressive, like the tops of the granite mountains in Maine. These mountains are only very big knolls and sheep-ranges — no sense of age or power. The rock crops out everywhere, but it shows no great faces or walls, no cleavage, nothing overhanging and precipitous. The pass called The Trossachs is far less impressive than the 'Long Woods' of my boyhood, at the head of the East Branch of the Delaware [the Pepacton]. [Compare with 'Nature in England,' p. 24, 'Fresh Fields.']

[Undated]

On the way to Helvellyn. The hay-rakers in the fields of Grasmere plain seem to be rolling up a great sheet of brown paper, exposing beneath it another of the most fresh and delicate emerald green. The hay has probably been cut two weeks, and the grass has all the while been growing. Large, coarse ferns or brakes cover all the lower slopes of these mountains, with an underlining of fine grass which extends up and over the ridges, and affords pasturage for the sheep and cattle.

On the top of Helvellyn. Wind moderate, all the northern landscape in sunlight as far as Carlisle. A vast panorama of mountains about me, not quite so severe and savage as the Scotch mountains, but the view finer and more extensive than from Ben Venue. The mountains all covered, for the most part, with that wonderful green — the green of the tenderest, freshest April grass, yellow-green. The black tarns at my feet — how curious!

Away beyond Ullswater, what a sweep of country, flecked here and there by a cloud shadow! To the north, in places, the folds and backs and flanks of the mountains are voluptuous. One, in particular, seems covered with the most delicate lawn. Here and there the rocks crop out and puncture the green drapery, and here and there the mountain-side is covered with loose shale and washed earth and pebbles; but nowhere do I see great boulders strewn about. Patches of black peat here and there. The little rills, near and far, white like milk, so swift they run. On the more precipitous sides the green grass and moss are lodged like snow, and oh, so tender and fresh! All the lakes to the south in view, and the bay, and Preston. Sheep everywhere, loosely scattered; now and then I hear one bleat; no other sound but the occasional chirp of the mountain pipit (the wheat-ear).

These mountains are the South Downs pushed up a little higher, and the rock cropping through, here and there. One part, now in full sunlight, is wrinkled in the folds like the skin of a sheep, or a seal — so smooth and fat and sleek and fresh! But here is a vertebra, sharp and jagged, and strewn with loose fragments of stone.

What a spectacle now before me! All the near mountains in shadow, and the distant in strong sunlight! I shall never see the like of that again. In places the vestment of green grass is in tatters, so to speak, and barely clings to the naked mountains; then on others it is whole and complete; no heather in view. To the south the mountain-crests are rough and jagged, but to the north, smooth. The air filled with the same white, insensible moisture, or vapor, as in Scotland. When the sun breaks through the crevices in the clouds, there are the spokes of light. [Compare with 'In Wordsworth's Country,' p. 153 *et seq.*, in 'Fresh Fields.']

Aug. 6

Long sunny days upon the sea. The sea at times like burnished steel, the sky like a dome of glass; very hot. All to-day, to the south, a long line of soft, white-capped clouds, sometimes swelling into thunder-heads, and seeming to rise out of the sea, and to be quite motionless. Now, for some hours, the clouds have stretched along the horizon, their bases all in the same plane, making a line as straight to the eye as if they rested upon a substratum of masonry of uniform thickness, while above they rise into all manner of heights and irregular shapes, their white, fleecy forms reflected in the polished surface of the sea. All day this procession of clouds has been in sight like an army filing across a desert, while the sky has been clear in all other directions.

Sept. 1

A spider's web is a trap to everything but a spider.

The writings of Emerson and Thoreau drew readers to seek them personally. My books do not bring readers to me, but send them to Nature. I take credit to myself on this account. I always seek to hold the mirror of my mind up to Nature, that the reader may find her lineaments alone reflected there. I remember that this is one of the great merits of the 'gentle Shakespeare'; himself you see not, only the great world, compacted and idealized as in a Claude Lorraine mirror. Shakespeare, I take it, was really a gentle spirit who never obtruded himself; who made little impression upon those who knew him, so that the memory of him was quickly lost; far less of an egoist, say, than Ben Jonson, and with a less striking personality — all his vast power working in a kind of impersonal way — just the contrary, for example, of such a man as Carlyle.

March 2, 1883

If a man can live without God in this world, there is not the slightest doubt but that he can live without him in the next, and the next, and have just as good a time. How childish this talk is, that we can be nearer God, nearer heaven, in some other world, than we are here! what irreligion and atheism it is! The child in its mother's womb is no nearer its mother than you and I and all men are *at all times* near God. Does not the Book say, 'In him we live, and move, and have our being'? This is the literal truth, whoever says it, or denies it. The great embosoming Power and Life of the Universe — call it God, or call it what you will — we can no more escape from, or live independent of, than we can escape from the

air. Out of this mountain races and sects carve their gods,
make them in their own images, and set them up on
various pedestals, far or near.

April 10 [*Roxbury*]

These are the days of which I dreamed — bright, warm
days in the maple woods; the perfume of my sap-pan
upon the air, the flashing buckets upon the trees; the
clink of the slowly dropping sap; the tall naked stems of
the maples; the leafless woods; the sunlight pouring in,
bright and strong; the smell of the leaf-mould; the leaf-
strewn ground; the bubbling sap-pan; the slowly vanishing snowbanks, here and there; the distant mountains,
bristling with trees, with the lining of snow shining
through; the voices of birds — nuthatches, bluebirds,
robins, snowbirds, highholes, crows, chickadees, woodpeckers; the liver-colored butterfly, the first-born of his
kind; the claytonia and hepatica, just bursting the mould.

April 19

Back home [West Park] this afternoon. While at Roxbury I daily saw and heard the shore larks.[1] They were in
pairs and small flocks about the hill pastures. Above the
house, on the hill, they soared and sang. The flight and
manner on such occasions is like that of the skylark. The
bird mounts up and up on ecstatic wing, till it becomes a
mere speck against the sky, where it drifts to and fro
and utters, at intervals, its song — a mere fraction or
rudiment of the skylark's song — a few lisping, sharp,
unmelodious notes, heard a long distance, but insignifi-

[1] The subspecies known as the prairie horned lark.

cant — a mere germ of the lark's song; the first attempt, as it were, of Nature in this direction. After due trial and waiting, she develops the lark's song itself. [See 'Spring Jottings,' p. 164, in 'Riverby.']

April 22

A great bright day. Such days seem large, ample, high-domed, the sunlight is so strong, and no screens of foliage yet to shut it out. The few clouds float high, the crows fly high, the mountain wall looks high. The sailing vessels going by spread all their canvases. The eye takes in a long distance; space is clear; the altitude of all things seems exalted.

May 2

At sunrise this morning the river was like a mirror, duplicating the opposite shore perfectly. Presently a breeze came and tarnished it, or made it white like ground-glass. The river idealizes the landscape. It multiplies and heightens the beauty of the day and season. A fair day it makes more fair, and a wild, tempestuous day it makes more wild. The face of winter it makes doubly rigid, and corpse-like, and to the face of spring it adds new youth and sparkle. [Compare 'A River View,' p. 183 *et seq.*, in 'Signs and Seasons.']

May 6

Finished Mrs. Carlyle's Letters last night. Have hardly skipped a page. Why does one read them so entirely? Probably because there is not a dull line in them — not a false note in the matter of style or rhetoric.

A more clear, incisive, telling way of putting things it would be hard to find. Yet there is nothing in the letters — merely a record of her own ups and downs; not a ray of light cast upon anything but her own personal matters and feelings — very little upon Carlyle himself, and none at all upon his works and thoughts and genius. It is the sprightly and charming gossip of a lifelong invalid, to whom the great problem is, how she is going to live from day to day in this miserable world of nerves and kitchen-maids, and be as a buffer between her husband and every-thing that might, could, or would annoy him. Unless she can receive every blow upon herself; unless she can gather every shaft into her own bosom, she is wretched. When she cannot aid him, she is more worried than he is. When she hears him jump out of bed at night above her head, because the demon of sleeplessness possesses him, it brings her heart into her throat, and she agonizes until she hears him return to his couch.

May 11

Johnson and his boy [1] came to-day at two. Feel like a boy again; the face of Nature has an added charm. So much for this brief feeling of companionship!

May 12

Brilliant day with drifts of cherry blossoms against the fresh new green. We lounge about, listen and talk and admire, absorbing the May beauty at every pore. John-son says that the sugar-maple blooms — clusters of delicate, yellowish-green fringe, depending from little

[1] Robert Underwood Johnson and Owen Johnson.

canopies of just-hatched leaves — in some way suggest
oriental decorations. There is much more grace and
delicacy in the bloom of our maple than in that of the
European. The soft maples were loaded with bunches
of scarlet keys, a lovely mass of color against mingled
larches, spruces, and hard maples. The leaves but just
out and not yet showing on the soft maples.

June 10

Finished Carlyle's 'Cromwell' to-day in the shade of
my summer-house. No such histories as this man writes.
How omnipotent his eye, how keen and sure his scent!
that turn for the higher mathematics which he early
showed doubtless stood him in hand in sifting such a
rubbish-heap, and tracing and mending the threads of
meaning. He could solve the problem; could set the
equation upon its feet again.

The best thing about Carlyle's contempt is its perfect
sincerity and inevitableness. He cannot help it; it is
genuine, and has a kind of felicity. There is no malice
in it, but pity, rather, and pity springs from love. His
contempt is the negative pole, and measures the force of
the positive — strong as it is strong. Such quick love,
sympathy, tenderness, few men have had. He cannot be
indifferent.

June 27 [*Concord, Mass.*]

At Sanborn's in the evening. Much talk. Then to Dr.
Emerson's — worthy son of his father, stamped mentally
and physically with the Emersonian stamp — eye, voice,
mouth, all Emersonian. Talked well about Thoreau.

Said Channing drove away his family, then drove away
his dog. This last act angered Thoreau much.

June 28

A pleasant breakfast at Sanborn's. His new house the
most courageously plain, and, therefore, the most pleasing, of any recent house in Concord. No aiming at architecture in it. A combination of brick and wood. A great
success. Gilder and I walk to Walden Pond, much talk
and loitering by the way. Walden, a clean, bright pond,
not very wild. Look in vain for the site of Thoreau's hut.
Two boys in a boat row up and ask us the question we
have on our tongues to ask them. We sit in the woods and
try to talk about immortality; do not get very near together on such a theme — like ships at sea, we soon part
company.

I saw nothing in Concord that recalled Thoreau, except
that his ripe culture and tone might well date from such
a place. On the whole, Concord is the most pleasing
country village I ever saw. Nothing like it in England,
where only the poor live in villages. It impressed me
much. Its amplitude, its mellowness, its homelike air,
its great trees, its broad avenues, its good houses. Emerson and Hawthorne are its best expression in literature.
It seems fit that they should come from such a place.

Aug. 6

Finished Darwin's 'Descent of Man' this morning.
A model of patient, tireless, sincere inquiry; such candor, such love of truth, such keen insight into the
methods of Nature, such singleness of purpose, and

such nobility of mind, could not be easily matched. The book convinces like Nature herself. I have no more doubt of its main conclusions than I have of my own existence.

Aug. 17

Darwin's theory of the descent of man adds immensely to the mystery of Nature, and to the glory of the race. Man's greatness, then, was not thrust upon him, but is his own achievement. We respect him less who is set up in business, with a fortune at his disposal, than he who, from humble beginnings, achieves his own success. Then the theory so ties man to the system of things, and makes his appearance not arbitrary, or accidental, but a vital and inevitable result. Who has not felt what a mechanical, inartistic view of creation that which the churches have so long held is? But that all these vast, complex results and forms of life were enfolded in the first germ — *that* view makes the universe alive, the veritable body of God, the organism of a vast, mysterious, all-embracing, eternal power, impersonal, unhuman in its general workings, but manifesting conscience and beneficence mainly through the human race.

It is a new sensation to come to see man as an animal — the master animal of the world, the outcome and crown of all the rest. We have so long been taught to regard ourselves as something apart and exceptional, differing, not merely in degree, but in kind, from the rest of creation, in no sense a part of Nature, something whose origin and destiny are peculiar, and not those of the commonality of the animal kingdom, that this [newer] view shocks many. But it is full of the deepest meaning to the thoughtful and the impartial. The story of Adam and Eve is a beautiful myth. There is an Adam and Eve in Darwin's plan, too, but they were not set up in business on the home-farm, their garden ready planted. They made their own garden, and knew how they came by their acres. There was a long line of humble, and still more humble, progenitors back of them, toiling, fighting, breeding, sorrowing — Grandfather Adam, who ate his steak raw, and Great-Grandfather Adam, who had a tail, and lived in trees, and had a coat of hair.

Aug. 30

August is the month of the yellow-bird.[1] While most of the other birds have gone silent, their work done, their brood flown, the yellow-bird comes to the front and is the most musical, active, and conspicuous. It is his turn now. It is the first bird I hear in the morning, circling and swinging through the air in that peculiar, undulating flight, and calling out on the crest of each wave, '*Here we go, here we go!*' The rival males pursue each other about in the most courtly, high-bred manner, uttering the most conciliatory and cheerful, even gleeful, protestations possible. It has the effect of saying, with pleased and happy surprise, 'Why, my dear sir, this is my territory, permit me to salute you, and to escort you over the line.' While the other gleefully assures him that it is all right, and that he would not have any hard feelings aroused for anything in the world. Yet he does not always leave, and the two do not always separate amicably. Occasionally

[1] American goldfinch.

they have a brief sparring match in the air, and mount up and up, beak to beak, to a considerable height, but rarely ever actually come to blows.

Sept. 21

At Ocean Grove since last Monday, by the 'cradle endlessly rocking.' Alone, but pretty cheerful and well. Hardly speak to any one. Cannot herd promiscuously, like most persons. The lady who sits beside me at table, and who eats a pound of beefsteak at each meal, and nothing else — a consumptive recuperating on this beef diet — why have I not spoken to her? I can hardly say. It required an effort to do so, and I have not done it. Am I really unsocial, as these people probably think? No person can long more for companionship than I do, but I cannot mate right and left with this class of people. In fact, I generally separate from those of my countrymen such as I meet at summer hotels, and on ocean steamers, as oil separates from water. They leave me, and I leave them. I am not the least bit of a cosmopolitan. I am at home nowhere but in my own nest, and in my own thoughts. I am aware that I carry a shell; I have to, my meat is so tender. I cannot cross my thoughts except with a person much like myself; it must be a closely allied species.

Sept. 26

Finished Darwin's 'Origin of Species' last night. A true wonder-book. Few pages in modern scientific literature so noble as those last few pages of the book. Everything about Darwin indicates the master. In reading him you breathe the air of the largest and most serene mind. Every naturalist before him, and with him, he lays under contribution; every competent observer in every field. Only the greatest minds can do this as he does it. He furnishes the key to every man's knowledge. Those that oppose his theory unwittingly bring some fact or observation that fits into his scheme. His theory has such range; accounts for such a multitude of facts; easily underruns and outruns the views of all other naturalists. He is, in his way, as great and as remarkable as Shakespeare, and utilizes the knowledge of mankind in the same way. His power of organization is prodigious. He has the candor, the tranquillity, the sincerity, the singleness of purpose, that go with, and are a promise of, the highest achievement. He is the father of a new generation of naturalists. He is the first to open the doors into Nature's secret Senate chambers. His theory confronts, and even demands, the incalculable geological ages. It is as ample as the earth, and as deep as time. It mates with and matches, and is as grand as, the nebular hypothesis, and is in the same line of creative energy.

Sept. 27

Walt Whitman came yesterday, and his presence and companionship act like a cordial upon me that nearly turns my head. The great bard on my right hand, and the sea upon my left — the thoughts of the one equally grand with the suggestions and elemental heave of the other. From any point of view Whitman is impressive. The slope of the back of his head, and shoulders, and back, how suggestive! You would know that he was an extraordinary man.

Sept. 29

Long autumn days by the sea with Whitman. Much
and copious talk. His presence loosens my tongue, that
has been so long tied since I came here, in a remarkable
manner. I feel as if under the effect of some rare tonic or
cordial all the time. There is something grainy and saline
in him, as in the voice of the sea. Sometimes his talk is
choppy and confused, or elliptical and unfinished, and
then again there comes a long, splendid roll of thought
that bathes one from head to foot, or swings you quite
from your moorings. I leave him and make long loops off
down the coast, or back inland, while he moves slowly
along the beach, or sits, often with bare head, in some
nook sheltered from the wind and sun.

The grainy, saline voice of the sea. Shoveller of sands,
moulder and carver of coasts; grinder of shells and of
rocks, beating them up with a pestle and mortar; washer
and screener of soils; hoarder of silt, covering the sunken
floors deep with the earth-pollen; reservoir of all rivers,
fountain of rains, purifier of climes — the everlasting, in-
satiable, omnivorous, remorseless sea!

The crescent-shaped waves, reaping and reaping only
shells and sand; yet I seem to hear the hiss of steel, as of
some giant cradler fronting waving fields, the rustle of
sheaves, the pounding of flails, or whirr of cylinders, the
shovelling and screening of grain.

Sept. 30

Perfect days by the sea with Walt. A sort of realization
of Homer to me. No man I have ever seen cuts such a
figure on the beach as Walt. He looks at home there, is
ample for such a setting.

Oct. 10

The third of our matchless October days — the ripest, best fruit of the weather-system of our clime; the likeness of a thousand days of the kind I have seen — the perfect equipoise of the autumn. The early frosts are over, the fall heats are past, and the day is like a full-orbed mellow apple just clinging to the bough. The great moist shadows on the opposite shore I see through the tender medium of sunlit haze. The day broods and dreams. The hills are pillowed upon the mellow air. Chestnuts drop in the woods; their fresh, glowing coats show amid the leaves. The birds are social, gregarious, sportive, inquisitive. One by one the leaves drop from the trees. A sloop goes drifting by, part of her great sail in blue shadow. I can hear the ripple of the water about her bow. The day is retrospective, and seems full of tender memories.

Oct. 29

Go to New York to meet Matthew Arnold at Gilder's. Was cordially met by him; found he knew of me and was glad to see me. Liked him better than I expected to — a large, tall man with nearly black hair, black close-cut side-whiskers, prominent nose, large, coarse, but pure mouth, and muscular neck. In fact, a much coarser man than you would expect to see, and stronger looking. A good specimen of the best English stock. A wholesome coarseness and open-air look. They do not refine in looks as we do; they look like a bigger and more powerful race. Arnold's voice was husky, more like a sailor's, I thought, than the other voices I heard. But what is that look I see, or think I see, at times, or in certain lights, about his nose

and upper lip? Just a faint suspicion of scorn. I was looking for this in his face. It is not in his brow, it is here, if
anywhere — the nose sniffs a bad smell, or sniffs an affront,
and there hovers about it a little contempt. When he
talks to you, he throws his head back (the reverse of
Emerson's manner), and looks out from under his eyelids,
and sights you down his big nose — draws off, as it were,
and gives you his chin. It is the critical attitude, not the
sympathetic. Yet he does not impress me as cold or
haughty, but quite the contrary. He is too wise not to
know what cards to play. In his writing his simplicity
seems a little affected, at least conscious; but he knows
that there is no card like simplicity. [Compare 'Arnold's View of Emerson and Carlyle,' pp. 129–30, 'Indoor
Studies.']

Nov. 19

My best and truest friend among womankind, Mrs.
Fanny A. Mead, of Lansing, Michigan, is dead, since
October 25. Nearly all night, November 15, I lay awake
thinking of her. In many ways the noblest, most loving,
most discerning, most charitable woman I have known.
She visited me here the latter part of August, 1880. Her
death nearly blots out the West for me.

No matter how much learning, or force, or capacity of
any kind a man has, unless he has that something which
we call style — an apt and original expression and individual flavor of his own, he can make no permanent
contribution to literature. Style is the precious spice that
embalms thought. The iridescent hue of pearl is an effect

of style — the manner of arrangement of the particles —
not any new matter.

Jan. 5, 1884

To New York [to hear Arnold lecture on Emerson] last
night. A fine audience; lecturer introduced by Curtis, the
pensive Curtis, in a neat little speech. Curtis is the cosset
of the elocutionary graces; he fondly leans and sighs and
languishes upon their bosoms. Arnold put his MS. up
high on a rack beside him, turned to the audience, let off a
sharp glance in my direction, through his one cockney
eye-glass, straightened himself up, and, after a delay that
was a little too long, lifted up his voice and spoke his
piece — voice too thick and foggy — has none of the
charm and grace of his literary style; hence his lecture is
better in the reading than in the hearing. There is something almost like pudding in an Englishman's throat when
he speaks from the stage.

Jan. 21

Stern, rugged, winter days and the cold snows cover a
new grave beside Mother's. At rest at last, after eighty-
one years of life. The event he so long predicted and
waited for, and, I think, toward the last, began to long
for, came, and came as he had hoped. No suffering, no
lingering illness to make trouble in the house.

I went home on the 9th. Drove up from the station in
the moonlight in a whirl of wind and snow. How lonely
and bleak the old place looked in that winter landscape
by moonlight — beleaguering Winter without, and Death
within! Jane and Abigail were there with Hiram, and
some of the neighbors. Father had died at seven in the

morning, as I had learned at Kingston by telegraph. How the wind howled and buffeted that night, and the steady roar of the mountain, like that of the sea, came to me in my sleepless chamber! How often in youth I had heard that roar, but with what different ears, as I snuggled down in my bed while Mother tucked me in! Early in the morning I went quietly, and with composure, and looked upon Father's face. Never had I looked upon his face before in the morning, before he had arisen, without speaking his name; and I could not refrain from speaking his name now, and speaking it again and again. The marble face of Death! What unspeakable repose and silence there is in it! I saw, more clearly than ever before, how much my own features are like his. The nose the same, only, in his case, cut away more at the nostrils. The forehead, too, precisely the same. Head nearly as large as mine; feet and hands smaller.

It was his time to die; it is better so, and the reason said yes; but, oh, the heart! the time for its loved ones to die never comes. . . . Father knew me not. All my aspirations in life were a sealed book to him, as much as his peculiar religious experiences were to me. Yet I reckon it was the same leaven working in us both. The delight he had in his Bible, in his hymn-book, in his Church, in his creed, I have in literature, in the poets, in Nature. His was related in his thought to his soul's salvation hereafter, mine to my soul's salvation here.

Father made a great deal of noise about the farm, had great strength of voice, and could send it over the hills a mile away; was, indeed, a noisy man, hallooing to the cows, the sheep, the boys, and, in drawing rocks with the oxen, you could have heard him a great distance. He never went away from home, while I was a boy on the farm, without stopping out on the 'big hill,' and calling back to us some command, or renewal of some order, generally entirely superfluous, always to the annoyance of Mother, if she was beside him — his voice was so loud and harsh. Often he would call twice before he got out of sight. Even last summer he used to exercise his voice by starting the cows from the upper pasture, a quarter of a mile or more away.

Father had no enemies, no quarrels; never lied, or cheated, or stirred up strife. His word was as good as his bond. He had a kind of selfishness, but it was like that of children — thoughtless and uncalculating — and related mainly to appetite. He was a hearty eater, and at the table would always pick for the best. He would always take my biggest trout, and the next biggest, and the next — if I would give it to him, as I usually did. It never occurred to him to decline a thing on the score of manners. Mother used to say it was 'hoggishness,' and he would not gainsay her. I doubt if he ever said 'Thank you' to any person in his life; I certainly never heard him. I took him, and sent him, many little things, in his latter days, which he always accepted without remark. . . . He had no sentiment, and would snort at what you call poetry; and yet was much of a real poet himself. His faults were like those of children; and in his old age he became childish to a degree. His intelligence and judgment were yet good, when appealed to, but his will, his self-control, his force and authority as a man, were feeble. His curiosity was always great, and continued to the last.

Father never had much faith in me — the least of any
of his children. He saw I was an odd one, and had tendencies and tastes, from the first, that he did not sympathize with. All the other children, but me, he helped with
money when they began life. When I wanted help, as I
did twice or three times, in a pinch, he refused; and, as it
turned out, I was the only one of his children that could,
or would, help him when the pinch came — a curious
retribution, but one that gave me pleasure, and him no
pain. I was better unhelped, as it proved, and better for
all I could help him. He went according to his light; and
perhaps I loved him the better for denying me. I never
laid up anything against him, not even the fact that once,
when I was away to school and got short of funds, and
wanted five dollars to help me out, he would not send it,
though Mother berated him soundly for it. Hiram sent
me the money, and I worked in haying and paid him back.
Father did not like my tendency to books; was afraid, as
I once found, that I would become a Methodist minister
— his special aversion. [See 'Our Friend John Burroughs,' p. 59.]

Feb. 10

Finished yesterday Carlyle's 'Frederick,' begun in
December. What an experience to read such a work! It
colors one's days and all his thoughts. By far the most
striking and effective historical work I have ever read.
If all histories were as vivid and entertaining as this, I
should read nothing but history henceforth. A great
Carlylean poem, and a fit and artistic completion of his
career as a writer. Having preached so long and so vehe-

mently about the strong man at the helm, the divine
right, and the imperative need of government by the
ablest, he cast about him for an example; and, having
found the nearest approach to it in Frederick, he devotes
the rest of his days to portraying him; to showing his life
and his work, his obedience to the stern behests of duty,
and the love and obedience of his people to him. 'The
last of the kings,' he says. He makes one thoroughly love
and admire Frederick. In many ways he was the embodiment of the Carlylean ideals. [Compare with 'A Sunday
in Cheyne Row,' p. 213, 'Fresh Fields.']

April 3

My forty-seventh birthday — my first fatherless
birthday. I have lived to see Father and Mother grow
old and die and be buried from my sight. Well, it is the
order of Nature that the child shall look upon the grave
of his parents, rather than they upon his grave. I should
have been at the Old Home to-day but for this storm and
snow. But how empty and desolate that home is, I know
full well.

April 30

A ride to Coxsackie. Met Mary Hallock Foote and
her husband and children on the train, *en route* for Idaho.
A woman with a rare charm — full of genius, and full of
womanliness. Said my 'British Fertility' made her sad;
quoted Holmes's remark that 'grass makes girls';
thought instead of troubling ourselves about 'woman's
rights,' we better look to woman's health, and study
physiology, and the laws of life, a little more; all other
questions were premature.

A bright, lovely day. What pleasure to ride through the country at this time! — spring so visible upon the ground, but hardly discernible yet in the trees, as if the latter waited to give the earth a chance. How vivid the green here and there! The home feeling, the work of man in the landscape, is enhanced and brought out. Nearly every farmhouse has a more genial and expressive look than it will have by and by. How the green deepens all about the barns and rich moist places! How friendly certain nooks and slopes look, as if one would like to recline there, or walk there! Here and there a little meadow watercourse, golden with marsh marigolds. Here and there the bloom of the red maple shows vividly against the tender green of a slope beyond. The fresh-plowed fields, too, and the teams plowing or harrowing, the sower sowing, and pausing to regard the flying train — how it all pleased! O Spring, all thy sights and sounds are fresh and pleasing! The harvesting looks wearisome, but the sowing and planting, how attractive! There is nothing cloying in nature now, but all is appetizing.

June 3

As a writer, especially on literary themes, I suffer much from the want of a certain manly or masculine quality, the quality of self-assertion — strength and firmness of outline, of individuality. I am not easy and steady in my shoes. The common and vulgar form of the quality I speak of is called 'cheek.' But in the master writer it is firmness, dignity, composure — a steady unconscious assertion of his own personality. When I try to assert myself I waver and am painfully self-conscious, and fall into cu-

rious delusions. I think I have a certain strength and pos-
itiveness of character, but lack egoism. It is a family
weakness; all my brothers are weak as men; do not make
themselves felt for good or bad in the community. But
this weakness of the *I* in me is probably a great help to
me as a writer upon Nature. I do not stand in my own
light. I am pure spirit, pure feeling, and get very close to
bird and beast. My thin skin lets the shy and delicate influences pass. I can surrender myself to Nature without
effort. I am like her. That which hinders me with men,
and makes me weak and ill at ease in their presence,
makes me strong with impersonal Nature, and admits me
to her influences. I lack the firm moral fibre of such men
as Emerson and Carlyle. I am more tender and sympathetic than either, perhaps, but there is a plebeian streak
in me, not in them. This again helps me with Nature,
but hinders with men. [See 'Our Friend John Burroughs.']

June 19

It is a greater consolation to me to know that the universe is governed by unalterable laws than that it is subject to any capricious and changeable will. I like to know
that what we call God is without variableness or shadow
of turning. We know what to depend on. Strict justice is
and must be done to every creature, else Life and Nature
would miscarry. I ask but justice, yea, I demand it, and
let me not flinch and whimper.

July 22

How different the feeling and purpose with which I sit
down to read the Bible from that which Father and

Grandfather sat down to read it! I sit down to read it as a book, a curious and instructive legend, and to suck the literary value out of it; they sat down to read it as the autocratic word of God; to learn God's will toward them; and to feed their souls upon the spiritual riches it contains. It was a solemn and devout exercise with them; with me it is simply a search after truth and beauty, in a mood more critical than devout. Yet I cannot help it. I cannot read it otherwise. I cannot believe the Bible in the way that Father and his father believed it. It would be hypocrisy to pretend I could. This reading of it was the best for them, and is not my reading of it the best for me? There is perhaps more religion in the eye with which I read Nature, than there was in the eye with which they read it; and there was more religion in the eye with which they read the Bible than in mine. Father and Mother no more doubted the literal truth of the Bible than they doubted the multiplication table. They knew it to be true. Their own experiences told them so. Experience was their guide and test, not reason; and there is no more fallacious guide in such matters than experience. By experience people believed in witches, and spooks, and signs and wonders. When people began to reason about witches, belief in witchcraft ended. When you begin honestly to reason about the Bible, and to exclude all feeling, experience, sentiment, you cannot believe it other than a great primitive book — the greatest, perhaps, because the most human. The word of God, truly, as all good and wise books are the word of God, as every wise word ever spoken by man is the word of God. The Bible is naked, as it were; faces entirely toward God and eternity; whereas, other books face toward the world, or toward man. Its burden is God, righteousness, etc. There is no pride of letters here, no pride, only fear and awe and worship. It transcends all other books so much in this respect that we have come to look upon it as a record of God's word — an exceptionally inspired book. It is full of error, of course, full of human infirmities; but it is flooded with the sentiment of God, and the aspiration of the soul toward the Infinite; and this is the main matter.

Resuming my remarks upon Father's religion, and the religion of people like him: Experience was a safe guide for him to go by; no other guide was possible for him; the clear light of reason he did not have; for him to have seen the Bible and the Church with my eyes would have been disastrous in the extreme; it would have been like blotting the sun from heaven; he would have had nothing to lean upon, nothing to give him joy or religious satisfaction. The avenues through which my spiritual nature is ministered to were closed to him, or were never opened. To have robbed him and Mother of their hymn-book, of their faith, of their Bible, would have been the greatest cruelty. Their hymns, that are so flat and prosy, or else vulgar, to me, were precious beyond words to them. How quickly they could give the reason for this, quoting the Scriptures about the carnal mind; but of course this is not the true explanation. Their minds were much more carnal than mine. They had no taste, no culture, no ideality to satisfy (these they would have called 'carnal' and 'irreligious'), but only the one thought of their souls' salvation — meaning salvation from some threatened evil, in some future world. Their belief, their religion, was not disinterested. Yet I think of them with inexpressible love and yearning, wrapped in their last eternal sleep, the sleep of which they thought so often, and for which they tried to be so well prepared. And prepared they were: no harm can befall them; they had, for them, the true religion — the religion of serious, simple, hard-working, God-fearing lives. To believe as they did, to sit in their pews, is impossible to me; the Time-Spirit has decreed otherwise; but all I am, or can be, or can achieve, is in emulating their virtues. My soul can only be saved by a like truthfulness and sincerity.

July 31

Start for Phœnicia on the 6.45 train to meet Aaron [Johns] for a trip to the woods. . . . Reach Larkin's at I P.M. amid quite heavy rain. We bring up at the barn. Larkin comes out and invites us to the house, but Aaron prefers the barn and the hay-mow. Rain stops near night and I take enough trout for our breakfast. Mrs. Larkin gets us some dinner. We sleep on the hay-mow, and Mrs. L. does not feel complimented that we prefer the hay-mow to her feather-beds. In the morning fry our fish and make our coffee on her stove, and eat in the barn, in front of the ox-stall — the soldier in Aaron asserting itself once more. [Compare, pp. 57–58, 'The Heart of the Southern Catskills,' 'Riverby.']

Sept. 26

A day of great beauty. All the forenoon upon the hills bee-hunting. . . . The day not merely bright, but radiant, full of glory. . . . I have to pause and regard the day as one presses a rose to his nose; all the maple trees in the valley burning.

Nov. 4

Vote for Cleveland. Ah, me! a pretty bitter pill. Never before voted for a Democratic candidate for President, but shall do so again, if I live, and the Democrats take the stand on tariff for revenue only. High production has had its day. Let our manufactories sink or swim now; the people should no longer be taxed to buoy them up.

Nov. 9

The days bring but few thoughts to me; my thoughts have not begun to fly yet; probably there are not many to fly. I keep an eye on the horizon there, and seize my pen at the first indication, but the game is insignificant. Finished and sent off the chapter on Carlyle in my new book ['Fresh Fields'] yesterday. Chapter too long, and in many ways unsatisfactory.

Nov. 16

All the week in Poughkeepsie, examining the banks — a steady grind between the upper and the nether millstones of bank ledgers. I am not a good bank-examiner, and never shall be; I am very slow to see the points in such matters; it is all painful to me, and therefore is not my proper work.

Nov. 21

I am quite persuaded that my family is Welsh and pure Celtic. Much that Renan, in his recollections of his youth,.

says of himself comes home to me, especially his confessions of the family weaknesses. He speaks of his absolute inability to be resentful, or to appear so, as an inherited trait. It is a trait of my family, and of me. I cannot harbor resentment, and I often think it is one of my cardinal weaknesses. I cannot get mad and keep so. If a person called me a liar I probably should not feel half the resentment I ought to feel; and it is the same with the rest of my family. No slight, or neglect, or offence, indignity even, touched Father. The same with my brothers; we do not know when we have been insulted; and when we feel hurt, it is almost impossible for us openly to resent it. Is it a Celtic trait? Not an Irish one, certainly. Renan says if his ancestors engaged in any kind of trade, or commerce, they were sure to get cheated. It is so with us. We can never ask enough for what we have to sell. The fact that it is ours, seems to depreciate it in our eyes; it ought not to bring quite as much as other people's. We have no 'cheek' at all. He says also that his people lacked decision of character. That is a weakness of mine, and of my family. We are slow to reach a decision, and are easily turned.

I wonder if Renan is not too literary — too entirely under the sway of the literary and the artistic spirit. One seems to feel that the underlying master-impulse of all should not be literary, but moral, or scientific; in other words, should be entirely serious. Renan writes eloquently and suggestively, but, after all, one feels that the chief thing about him is his literary and artistic faculty — that he is not a great person, a great character; no deep conviction. One would hardly expect to be helped by him,

or be furthered in any direction. Probably all the charac-
teristically French critics, such as Renan and Sainte-
Beuve, seem to lack something to us who have fed on
English literature. Is it moral fibre, moral purpose, that
they lack? They lust after fine phrases; they revel in the
disinterested; their end and aim is the artistic.

Nov. 23

One important thing in writing is to divest yourself of
any false or accidental mood, or view, or feeling, and get
down to your real self, and speak as directly and sincerely
as you do about your daily business and affairs, with as
little affectation. One may write from the outside of his
mind, as it were; write and write, learnedly and eloquently, and make no impression; but when he speaks
from real insight and conviction of his own, men are always glad to hear him, whether they agree with him or
not. Get down to your real self — your better real self,
and let that speak. One's real self is always vital, and
gives the impression of reality. So much writing and
speaking is like machine-work. The Sunday sermon, and
the leading editorial, are generally pieces of machine-
work, as if you turned a crank and the discourse came out.
It is not the man's real mind, his real experience. He does
not know how to get at this; all is artificial, factitious; his
garden is upon the housetop instead of upon the ground;
his ideas have no root, no succulency, no flavor. He
speaks from art, from culture, from faculty, and not from
inspiration. How rare are real poems! poems that spring
from real feeling, a real throb of emotion, and not from
the mere itch of literary vanity!

The great mass of the poetry of any age is purely artificial; a *tour de force*, the sheer result of effort. It dates
from the outside; it is in the air, from the friction of much
reading, or a superficial knack at rhyme. No wonder the
public gets suspicious of poetry and refuses to buy it. It
is for the most part counterfeit coin. It is a kind of
masquerading. The poetic forms are masks behind which
the writers hide their real poverty of thought and feeling.
In prose a man has no such factitious aids; here, if he has
nothing to say, he is quickly found out; he must stand or
fall for what he is; he has not the cloak of Virgil, or
Spenser, or Milton, or Tennyson, to hide in.

Dec. 4

To Philadelphia to see Whitman. Found him and Dr.
[R. M.] Bucke at Green's Hotel. Walt looks as well as
usual, and seems to be so. The grain of him yet seems
sound and good; though perhaps a little more inclined to a
purplish tint, at times, than I had noticed before. Dr.
Bucke, a large man with a broad, long head, of choleric
temperament mainly; voice rather hard and harsh; brow
with a nervous pucker; whole look rather harsh and intense. Pass the night, all of us, at the Smiths', a Quaker
family in Germantown; a fine hospitable family. A long
drive next morning in the park; then to Philadelphia; dine
together, and part at 4 P.M. Walt says his opinion about
our poets fluctuates a good deal. He used to place
Emerson first, then Bryant, and Longfellow. Now he
puts them in this order: Bryant, Emerson, Whittier,
Longfellow. He has much to say in praise of Bryant,
though does not like his poem on Death; but praised the

'Winds,' and such poems. Walt is writing a long preface for his poems. Has many ups and downs about it. One day thinks it a good idea, and the next thinks it too much like a concession — that his poems should be taken as they are, without any argument or explanation, like the works of Nature. He seemed anxious to hear what I had to say about it. I told him it was a secondary matter; that the poems would have to stand or fall on their own merits; as time went on, his Preface would be dropped, if it had nothing important in it; but if necessary to the poems, it would be retained. I said, 'Write it, if you feel you have something valuable to say, and let it take its chances; it can neither make nor break.'

Dec. 25

Cold; river nearly covered with floating ice; good sleighing. In my hut [1] writing with indifferent success upon Arnold — find it very hard to encompass him and state and define him without praise or blame. The critic should confine himself to description and elucidation. He shall praise and blame only when his praise and blame throw light on his subject; when they throw light only on his personal likes and dislikes, they are not permissible.

Dec. 30

I have had to accomplish in myself the work of several generations. None of my ancestors were men and women of culture, knew nothing of books. I have had to begin at the stump, and rise from rude, crude things. I have

[1] Bark-covered Study at Riverby.

felt the disadvantages I have labored under, as well as
the advantages. The advantages are that things were not
hackneyed with me, curiosity was not blunted, my faculties were fresh and eager — a kind of virgin soil that
gives whatever charm and sweetness and spontaneity my
books possess; also seriousness and religiousness. The
disadvantages are an ineptitude for scholarly things, a
want of steadiness and clearness of the tone of letters,
the need of a great deal of experimenting, a certain thickness and indistinctness of accent.

Jan. 5, 1885

All night I skirted the shore of sleep and vainly essayed
to land. But just as I neared the low, tranquil beach,
some fiend would cry, 'There! there, you sleep!' when
back my shallop moved with a spring, and the lotus-land
would mock me in the distance. (One's anxiety to sleep
always stands in the way of sleep.) Then I said, 'I will
try no more,' and ceased all effort, when, I know not how,
I slowly drifted upon the shore, and presently found
myself, or did not find myself, in the land of dreams. I
knew I had been there only because the fragrance of the
land was upon me in the morning, and some memory of
what I had seen.

Jan. 11

The stages of an orb's life, say the astronomers, are
stages of cooling. So are the stages of a man's life. It is
a process of cooling and hardening, from youth to age.
The gassy, nebular youth, out of which the man is
gathered together and consolidated; fiery, stormy,
vapory, at first, then cold, hard, impoverished, at last.

The evolution of the earth from the early geological ages, when it was at most a hot, barren rock, to its present condition of deep, fruitful soil, wealth of grass and verdure, and animal life, is no more marvellous than the evolution of man from the lowest forms of life to his present high position.

Jan. 12

One can drink cold water, or hot water, but not luke-warm. Faint praise is lukewarm water. Give it to us either hot, or cold, my impartial reviewers.

Feb. 2

In reading Stedman's critical writings I seem, for the most part, to be trying to see objects through small chinks in the wall. A good broad glimpse, or anything like a total view, he never gives me. I admire this and that and the other thing he says, but they do not, taken as he gives them, make a picture, or give a total impression. The only thing large about Stedman is his generosity. This saves him from being a conceited prig. It was his generosity, his manly feeling, that inspired his superb poem on old John Brown.

Feb. 10

I have arrived at that point in life, for some years now, in which all things are seen as in the light of the afternoon sun. How different from the light of the first half of the day! A little faded or diluted by the vapors, and with a pensive tinge. It is perhaps in many ways the most trying period of life — this transition state from one's prime to old age. The latter has not yet come, but the former is clearly on the wane. Let us hope that the land of old age, when we have once really arrived there, will have its own compensations and charm. When the sun really begins to shade the hills, there is a new charm in nature — more color in the sky, more privacy and illusion on the earth. Let us hope it will be so in life.

Have finished Arnold, and am letting my timber season before putting it in final shape.

March 2

Shall I go West this summer? I carry such a burden of home memories and longings and regrets with me when I go abroad that I should probably not get as close to what I want to see as I ought, to make the seeing profitable. If I could only go forth eager and curious, and emancipated from all past ties, it would be worth while to go; but if I am to be mentally bed-ridden in the great, free West, better stay at home.

March 4

This great vital Nature, this life and power of the universe, is the cloth out of which we cut, to some particular pattern, our goods. Each cuts to his own pattern and rejects all that is left. Matthew Arnold cut out that 'Power not ourselves which makes for righteousness.' What is he going to do with what is left? with all that which does not make for righteousness? It is like selecting the Gulf Stream and calling that the ocean. What do you call the rest of the water? This is only one of the currents; there are many others. The sea, as a whole, does not flow to any particular point; it flows to all points, and in all directions; there are currents beneath currents. So in Nature: we cannot say what the end of Nature is. God is nothing less than the Whole. If he directs any, he directs all. If he is one power not ourselves, he is every power not ourselves. The sphere bends at every point; every point is at the top, and yet no one point is at the top. When we can grasp the sphere, or find the end of the circle, we can grasp this power we call God, and find where he begins and ends.

March 22

I shall live in the future just as I have lived in the past, namely, in the life of humanity, in the lives of other men and women. When the last man perishes from the earth, then I perish — to reappear in other worlds, other systems. No doubt that man has always existed on some of the myriad worlds of space, and no doubt he will always exist. So far as consciousness or personality is concerned, this life is all. We do not know ourselves again, we do not take form again, except in others.

March 27

A spring day at last, warm and sunny, the snow running fast. The old, old story, the old, old enticement and charm. The song sparrow has endeared itself to me afresh. Everywhere about the house and grounds, on every bush and fence, the sweet spring ditties arise. How touching, how mindful of home! and of the days that are no more! The robins and the bluebirds, too,

promptly are they here to play their parts, and they play
them with the same old charm. The red-shouldered
blackbirds, too, a tree full of them back near the depot,
all uttering their willow-brook notes. It is the voice of a
multitude, but March has no more welcome chorus — a
great sheaf of reedy bird-notes.

April 3

The thought uppermost in all minds is the death of
General Grant — a brave, resolute, patriotic, unimpeachable, common-sense man; not shrewd or sharp in a
worldly way; often victimized, but a noble, solid character. He held together and kept his head under circumstances which broke or scattered more brilliant men.
Much of pure adamant in him. How free from brag and
bluster! how taciturn! I have seen him many times in
Washington between 1868 and 1872, but I shall see him
no more!

June 1

Reading now and then in Stevenson's 'An Inland
Voyage' — very bright and very light. It does not pene-
trate the mind at all. What is the matter with it? So
much wit and fancy and good nature and good writing
ought to make a deeper impression. It has no proper
earnestness or seriousness. The author is constantly on
the stretch to be bright and entertaining. It is this that
occupies him, and not any serious purpose to give us a
vivid and truthful picture of the river and country. He
is occupied with himself, and not with objects about
him. Hence his fine things seem to have no root. His

thoughts are parasitical. You never know how much he means, or how much to believe. Indeed, the fault is a fundamental one. See that thou avoidest the like of it!

Sept. 15

What appears more real than the sky? We think of it, and speak of it, as if it were as positive and real a thing as the earth. It is blue, it is tender, it is overarching, it is clear. See how the color is laid on it at sunset. Yet what an illusion! There is no sky; it is only vacancy; it is only the absence of something. It is a glimpse of the Infinite. When we try to grasp, or measure, or define God, we find he is another sky — sheltering, overarching, palpable to the casual eye, but receding, vanishing to the closer search; the vast power or space in which the worlds float, but himself ungraspable, unattainable, forever soaring beyond our ken. Not a being, not an entity, but that which lies back of all being, all entities.

Oct. 3

On the beach [at Ocean Grove] the waves at times come wallowing ashore like a great flock of sheep; they break far out, and then comes that rushing line of tossing, leaping, woolly heads and shoulders; they are not steeds, but a wild mob of woolly-headed sheep.

Oct. 9

Apples dropping in the orchard, leaves slowly dropping from the trees. When a big apple falls, there is a sudden rustle amid the branches as it lets go its hold, then a mellow *thump* upon the greensward, and the King, or Pippin,

lies there in the grass, dependent upon the tree no longer;
its arboreal life rounded and ended; now it mellows and
mellows to make itself a tempting bit for man or beast,
and so ends.

Oct. 9

How much there is in race! Suppose Mexico and the
South American states had been settled by the English
and the Germans, instead of by the Spaniards and the
Portuguese — would there not have been a vastly different outcome? Spain begot these countries in the height of
her power and splendor, but the fatal germ of her decad-
ence was upon them; the race was spent.

Emerson says, 'No man ever stated his griefs as lightly
as he might.' There was at least one man who stated his
griefs as strongly as they could be stated, and that was
Carlyle.

Nov. 1

A baby, or a young child, has not, when danger threat-
ens, the instinct of the young of animals, or birds, namely,
to remain perfectly motionless till the mother makes a
move, and then to follow her. When the cow hides her
calf, you may almost run over the calf and it will not
move till its mother appears. The other day in the woods
I came upon a brood of half-grown partridges. As I stood
looking intently upon a certain point, my eyes gradually
made out the form of a partridge squat upon the ground,
not twelve feet away. The old bird did not even wink, so
motionless was she. A step forward, on my part, and she

was off in a twinkling, and, instantly, all about my feet, her young burst up. They were within reach of me, but not one stirred till the mother gave the signal.

Dec. 13

Prayer is practically a belief in miracles — a belief that the world is not governed by immutable law, but that God may be persuaded, or stirred up, to step out of his way to do what he would not otherwise do. Yet prayer is a good thing for those who can have faith and pray in all sincerity; they shall surely be blessed. All sincere belief tends evermore to fulfill itself. If I believed in ghosts, I should doubtless see ghosts; people always have. If I believed in answer to prayer, and could pray, my prayers would be answered — when I asked only for spiritual good. But if I prayed for victory over my enemy, on the eve of battle, and believed that God listened to me, and favored me, I should fight the better, and stand a better chance of winning. Whatever begets enthusiasm and warms the soul up, as sincere prayer often does, is a blessing. We think the dew comes down from heaven, but it rises from the ground; so the answer to prayer rises within the soul itself. The answer is already within you; the heat of prayer calls it to the surface and makes you conscious of it.

Dec. 18

Read to-day in the 'Academy' of the death of Mrs. [Anne] Gilchrist. Many a sad thought has it caused me. Just now I can see or think of no one in England but her; she is the principal fact over there, and she is gone. The only woman I ever met to whose mind and character I instinctively bowed. She was a rare person, a person of rare intelligence. I met her first in 1876, in Philadelphia, and saw her last in London, at her home, in July, 1882.

Dec. 23

It is no doubt inevitable that Whitman's poems, launched as they are in the midst of modern literature, should be adjudged and tried by the standards of such literature; but how different, how vastly different, they are from it! How the sacred books of a race, or a people, rise above the familiar songs and poems of that people! Whitman's poems are much nearer akin to the sacred books than any other modern poems. It will take ages to assign them to their true rank.

I suppose there are times when every cultivated person turns to literature for consolation, for strength, for spiritual refreshment, the same as our fathers turned to the Bible. What poets does he read then? Not the more literary poets — the third- and fourth-rate singers — but the real bards. I can read Wordsworth, Emerson, Whitman, but not Byron, or Shakespeare. I can read Tennyson and Arnold, though not when in my most serious moods. I cannot say that these poets help me, as certain others do. Swinburne and Rossetti I cannot read in any mood.

Jan. 14, 1886

Three remarkable days, perfectly clear and perfectly still, with the mercury hovering about zero; the purest of winter products, like brilliant frost diamonds. Apparently very uniform all over the country; little inequality of pressure or temperature, so that there is no motion of the air. The great aërial ocean has found its level and is perfectly calm — the serene content of winter. Yet out of the sunshine comes peal upon peal of soft mimic thunder, sometimes a regular crash, as if all the batteries were discharged at once; it is the thunder of the ice on the river. As noon approaches, and the power of the sun begins to be felt, the air is filled with a continuous mellow roar. The whoops or peals are as mellow as if made by a huge bee shooting past. The sound is like thunder in that it is in such swift motion; you cannot locate it any more than you can the hum of summer overhead; it is everywhere, and yet nowhere; there is a phantom character about it; the valley down there seems haunted with weird whooping voices. To the eye all is still and rigid and corpse-like, but to the ear all is in swift motion. The ice-cloud does not open and let the bolt leap forth; but, walk upon the ice, and you see its shining track through it, in every direction; the ice is shot through with crystal lines where the force passed. Sometimes I fancy the sound is like the strokes of a gigantic skater, one who covers a mile at a stride, and makes the icy floor ring beneath him. His long tapering stroke rings out in your front, and then, before you can think, is heard half a mile away. With what speed he goes! but that flash was not from his skate; it was the gleam of a huge frost-crystal. Not merely by day, but all night long, the ice thunders. It is then contracting under the cold, naked skies, as by day it is expanding. A variation of the temperature, either up or down, sets it going. A fall of snow and all is still, the icy thunder is quenched. [Compare with 'A River View,' p. 189, 'Signs and Seasons.']

Jan. 15

Dr. Holmes, as a writer, is like a stove that always draws well; the fire is very bright and lively, and the combustion is complete; but the heat is not great; often no more than the heat of rushes or straw. If his profundity and seriousness were equal to his wit and brightness, he would take rank among the great ones. No smoke in our genial Doctor, no smouldering embers, but always the clearest and quickest of flames.

March 7

Whole seasons pass and I make not one new observation, gather not one new fact; other seasons again I make many of them. It all depends upon your temper or frame of mind. If you are not in the mood for the new facts, you will not find them. The new facts are always there before you; the question is, will you, or can you, see them? Some conditions of the mind and heart attract facts as a magnet attracts iron filings; other conditions repel them, or pass them by indifferently. When I am intent upon any particular phase of natural history, I meet with new facts and confirmations everywhere. If a man thinks about arrow-heads in his walk, he will be surprised at the number he will find. Train your eye to pick out four-leafed clovers, and you find them everywhere.

March 17

The 'Westminster Review' praises my style, says language in my hands is like a violin in the hands of a master. But really I have no dexterity as a writer. I can only walk along a straight, smooth path. Of the many nice and difficult things I see done in prose by dozens of writers I am utterly incapable. What I see and feel I can express, but it must all be plain sailing. I do not know how to utter platitudes, if I wanted to, and the other things come only at rare intervals.

March 19

Finished Gibbon's 'Decline and Fall' this morning, begun last summer — my principal reading during all these months. Not easy reading to me. Gibbon's sentences are like spheres — there is only a smooth curved surface for the mind to grasp. Carlyle groaned over 'Frederick,' but how much more reason had Gibbon to groan over his task; and yet, he says it only 'amused and exercised twenty years of his life.' His work is like a piece of masonry of dressed stone. Every sentence fits its place; there is not a jagged line, or an unfinished spot, anywhere. And it is plain to see that he tore his material from the rocks and mountains, as it were, and set it in this smooth, compact order. A splendid bridge, as Carlyle said to Emerson, leading from the Old World to the New.

April 6

Another destructive and damnable rain from the northeast, one of the series of downpours that began last August, and have continued every two or three weeks since. Everything afloat; folly and excess on the part of the weather, like that of a drunken man.

A delicious day, warm as May. This, to me, is the
most bewitching part of the whole year. One's relish is
so keen, and the bites are so few and tender. How the
fields of winter rye stand out! They call up a vision of
England. A perfect day in April far excels a perfect day
in June. How busy the bees are to-day carrying pollen,
every bee in a hurry! The river crinkles and stirs slowly
and lazily, as if it, too, enjoyed the warmth and the blue
sky. How clearly and singly the bush sparrow's [1] song
is projected upon the fresh, warm quiet. Phœbe and song
sparrow building yesterday and to-day. Such days have
all the peace and geniality of summer without any of its
satiety and enervating heat. [Compare 'Spring Jottings',
p. 165, in 'Riverby.']

Always on the extreme verge of time; this moment
that now passes is the latest moment of all eternity.
New time always; the time we have lived and mellowed,
and that has been hallowed by the presence of friends, or
parents, or by great events, is forever gone; this we keep
only in memory. The day is always new, hence the
crudeness and rawness and prosiness of the present. We
can keep the old — all except the old time. The old
house, the old fields, and, in a measure, the old friends;
but the atmosphere that bathed it all — the past days —
these we cannot keep. Time does not become sacred to us
until we have lived it, and until it has passed over us, and
taken with it a part of ourselves. While it is here we
value it not; but the instant it is gone and become yester-

[1] Now called the field sparrow.

day, or last week, how tender and poetic it looks to us!
Oh! the power of the Past! How the days accumulate
behind us and turn their beautiful sad faces toward us!
Here we stand upon the marge of Time, with all that
growing past back of us, like a fair land idealized by
distance into which we may not return. The Future is
unknown to us, in fact does not exist, but the Past is a
part of ourselves. The days are our children which we
have for a little time, and then they are taken from us;
one by one they step across the line into that land from
which there is no returning, and not till they are gone do
we see how beautiful and pathetic they were, and how
deeply we loved them. If our friends should come back
from the grave, they could not be what they were to us,
unless our dead selves came back also. How precious and
pathetic the thought of Father and Mother, yet the
enchantment of the Past is over them also. They are in
that sacred land; their faces shine with its hallowed
light; their voices come to us with its moving tones.
Probably the last time you looked upon your aged father
and mother in life, you said, 'Now let me forestall the
grief which I shall feel when he is gone; let me feel it now;
I know it must come soon; let me look upon him as with
the eyes of the Future when he shall be taken away.' But
you cannot. You cannot anticipate the Past; you cannot
see the Present as you will see the Past; beyond that
impassable gulf all things assume new and strange features. [Compare 'The Spell of the Past,' p. 239 *et seq.*, in
'Literary Values.']

Sept. 12

'Come and do business for eternity,' says a camp-meeting pastor, and it struck the right note. Religion, with the masses, is a kind of business transaction in which they drive sharp bargains with God, and seek to cheat the Devil out of his due. It is not so much love of God that moves them, as fear for the safety of their own bacon. They invest in the heavenly securities because they expect big dividends by and by. It is a matter of worldly prudence and nothing more.

Oct. 11

At Lake Mohonk, for past three days, invited to be present at the Indian Conference; an enjoyable time. Meet President Gates of Rutgers College; like him much, a genuine fellow; has a quality which only those born and bred in the country ever have. President Gilman also, of Johns Hopkins; like him, but a man of less force than Gates. Meet Elaine Goodale, a very sweet and attractive face; serious, thoughtful, self-conscious, genuine. Expect great things from that girl.

Nov. 5

Religion is subjective, an emotion, a feeling, an aspiration of the soul; science is objective, and rests upon demonstration. When the objective, or reasoning mind, turns to religion, it makes creeds and dogmas, and seeks to prove the literal truth of the Bible. The subjective mind hates creeds and formulas, and seeks to live in the spirit.

Voltaire had no religion, Tom Paine had much, Goethe

had much, but Carlyle more; Schiller and Richter, more.
Plutarch was full of it, as are nearly all the antique
authors. Victor Hugo had it, Darwin had it, even Mr.
Dwight L. Moody has it. Ingersoll, I should say, has
very little. Newman is full of it, but in most theological
treatises it is absent. Lincoln was a truly religious soul.
Beecher is not. It is by no means common among the
clergy. The Biblical writers are the most full of it of all
others. Indeed, here is its great deep, its primordial
ocean. There is no religion in Swift; he is thoroughly a
worldly mind; there is more in Johnson, but not much —
not much in either of these writers that appeals to the
conscience, or touches it. Not a scintilla in such poets as
Swinburne, or Rossetti. Indeed, none of the new poets in
England, or America, possess a deep high seriousness
which goes with the religious sense. There is more in
Gilder than in any of his friends.

1887-1900

[DURING 1887 and the close of the century Burroughs was more actively engaged as a husbandman than heretofore. His bank-examining had ceased, and he had the more leisure for his vineyards and for literature. After extending his nine acres to eighteen, in 1888, he developed a keener interest in his avocation, and a keener relish for nature, the annual 'grape racket' or 'grape war' which he waged affording him just the needed zest for his intercourse with nature.

'Indoor Studies,' published in 1889, was followed by a long lull till 1894; then came 'Riverby.'

In 1895 he built his cabin, Slabsides, about a mile from his river home; built it in a wild, secluded spot in the woods, attracted there by the aloofness from much that encroached upon him in his more accessible home at Riverby. There, for many succeeding years, during certain months of the year, he kept house for himself and a homeless bachelor brother, going down to Riverby daily, however, to lend a hand in the vineyard work, and, on occasion, to filch from his wife's larder. John Muir was one of his early guests at Slabsides. From the beginning of withdrawing himself to that secluded spot, Burroughs found he had drawn others to it and him — the world quickly made a beaten path to the hospitable door of Slabsides. Nevertheless, he had many long forenoons to himself in that sweet solitude, and for years to come many of his essays were written there. Besides the silent companionship of his brother Hiram, he had, in turn, that of his dogs, Nip and I-Know, both of whom, like most of his other dogs, met with tragic deaths, leaving him bereft indeed.

During this period Burroughs did a little public speaking, at schools and colleges and before women's clubs, but never without perturbations which finally decided him to abandon that form of self-torture.

After Whitman's death, Burroughs immersed himself in Whitman for the four subsequent years, then published 'Whitman: a Study,' in 1896.

In 1899, after several months with the Harriman Expedition in Alaska, he wrote a chronicle of the expedition, 'In Green Alaska' ('Far and Near'), and several poems inspired by the new songsters that had endeared the strange scenes to him.

While spending some weeks in Cambridge toward the close of 1900, to be near his son at Harvard, he compiled an anthology of nature poems ('Songs of Nature'), the exposure to so much poetry, as he said, begetting in him a severe attack of rhyming fever. Then, and subsequently, he wrote many nature poems which came out in the magazines and were, in time, gathered into the volume 'Bird and Bough.'

The year 1900 saw the publication of 'The Light of Day,' although many of the essays contained in it had been appearing for some years previously in the magazines.]

Feb. 9, 1887

The books that come to me from their authors, why do I look upon them with an eye inclined to be cold and in-

different? and let them be so long untried upon my table?
It is because I did not seek them; and a book unsought is
generally a book unwelcome. We do not expect the men
we most value, and long to see, to hunt us up; those who
do so generally turn out to be of little moment to us.
Moral: Never send your book to a man whose good opinion of it you solicit. Let him find it out for himself. I
shall act upon this in future. I have sent my books to
many people from whom no response has ever come. I
flatter myself that they never looked into them, and
looked upon them as intruders.

March 6 [Washington]

Dined to-day with Hugh McCulloch. The old man not
quite so well and brisk as when I last saw him. Old age
is really upon him, and the end of life's journey not far off.
A large, noble, and lovable man; no public man to whom
I feel so drawn.

March 9

Find Walt sitting in a chair with a long, gray-bearded
goat-skin behind him, a shawl pinned about him, and
a chaos of papers, letters, MSS., books, and so on at his
feet and reaching far out into the room. Never saw such
confusion and litter: bundles of letters, bundles of newspapers, slips, cuttings, magazines, a cushion or two, foot-
rests, books opened and turned downward, dust, etc., etc.,
and, above all, the grand, serene face of the old poet. He
is, or seems, more alert and vivacious than when I saw
him in May; inquires anxiously about William O'Connor;
has a little too much blood, I think, and tell him so.
Walks out to supper without help, and tells the story of

the old woman who, when commiserated for her blind-
ness, said, 'But I have so many things to be thankful for!'
We have much talk, and it does me good to be with him
again. He talks affectionately about Beecher, just dead,
and says many things in his praise. The word 'miscellaneous,' he says, describes him. We sit by the firelight
till 9 P.M., when I go back to Philadelphia.

March 15

Beecher died on the 7th or 8th, while I was in Washington. A man of the times — large, coarse, multitudinous,
like the earth in spring when all the streams run full; a
man for the multitude — copious, eloquent, versatile;
touching our common American humanity at more points,
perhaps, than any other preacher of his time. He gave
forth no divine light and no divine warmth, yet he
amused and warmed and swayed the multitude. He was
peculiarly American in his freedom, his audacity, his
breadth, and in his secularization of the pulpit. The great
source of his popularity was that, after all, he represented
us so well; represented our better tendencies and possibilities. He was alive, and showed no tendency to become
a fossil. Expansive, copious, quick-witted, every leading
and formative idea of the times found lodgement and
reinforcement in his mind. He was as the sea, and could,
on occasion, exhibit the might and vehemence of the great
natural forces.

April 14

Go to New York to see Walt and be at the lecture. In
the 'Century' office ran upon Lowell and Charles Eliot

Norton. Johnson introduces me to Lowell. Lowell greets me heartily and says, 'You once said I did not know the difference between a dandelion and the buttercup, but as I was looking down upon them when I wrote the poem,[1] it did not disturb me.' 'Oh,' I said, 'I know you do know the difference, Mr. Lowell,' and turned it off with a laugh. Lowell is a pretty strong-looking man, more than a mere scholar; a man of affairs, and of the world, and able to hold his own in places that test men's mettle. Of his kind he easily ranks first of the New England writers. He said he once advertised me in a speech he made in England, at some dinner or occasion — I forget what — and that many persons afterward asked him about me. Of course I thanked him. Norton I found a very sweet, gentle nature — a man to make fast friends with and to love. He spoke warmly of the pleasure my books had given him. Something in his manner of talking reminded me constantly of an English woman I know (Mrs. Smallwood). We met again at the lecture, and I sat in a box with him and Lowell.

Found Walt at the Westminster Hotel, fresh and rosy and sweet as ever. The lecture [on Lincoln] went off finely. A distinguished audience and much sympathy with, and appreciation of, him. At the reception, in the evening, saw many new people. Walt looked grand and distinguished as he sat in his chair and received the callers. His is easily the grandest face and form in America. He stood it well; the little excitement was just what he needed — a wholesome human breeze that quickened his circulation and made his face brighter.

[1] 'Al Fresco.' See 'Nature and the Poets,' p. 105, *Pepacton*.

At 12 P.M. John Fiske, and some one else, came in and began to discuss the immortality of the soul. Walt said he would have given anything to get away to his room and to bed, and as some one else caught on to the discussion, he did so. In the morning at eight I found him dressed and resting after his bath, and as fresh as a pink. At ten he went to the photographer's with Jennie Gilder, and then to the studio of Miss Dora Wheeler for a sitting. Think Miss Wheeler will make a strong picture of him. I left him at 2.30 P.M. on his way to the ferry, brighter and stronger than I had ever expected again to see him.

May 11

Just now the leaves and branches of the young hickories are being born. They come into the world like young birds, or young puppies. The great hickory buds grow and swell and color up till they are often two inches long, when the fleshy sheath parts and the young branch, leaves and all, emerge. The leaves are folded up and pressed together like hands in prayer. The great flesh-colored membranous scales, or wraps — how curious they look! They turn back and surround the tender branch like a purple or crimson ruffle, and then, after a few days, drop off and perish. I do not know of any other tree whose branches spring from the parent bud so fully developed.

Sept. 15

Drove through Tongore, where I began my career as a young man thirty-three years ago, and where I had not been for twenty-seven or twenty-eight years. . . .

Yonder is the little red schoolhouse itself. With what

emotion I gaze upon it!   Here I made my beginning in the
world. Here I spent my first days away from the paternal
roof. Seems as if some beloved son of mine had taught
that school so long ago. How green he was, how tender and bashful, how homesick! How my heart yearns
toward him! How long the summer days were! Those
first children, or children of my first school, the faces and
ways of many of them are still vivid before me. Jane
North, delicate and fine-looking, about twelve (long dead);
Mary McClelland, fat and chubby and a little saucy; Ella
Terwilliger, large head and eyes and small body. Why
do these scenes make me so sad? Then Father and
Mother were in their prime, as I am now, and all went
well on the farm. It was the morning of life with me; now
it is long past the meridian. Oh, the past, the past!
Slowly I drive through the place, finding this house
smaller than I remember it, or that barn in a different
place, or a new house or other building, here and there.
I saw no person but a boy of eleven or twelve — the very
image of a boy that came to my school — Alonzo Davis
— doubtless his son; the same pronounced blue eyes and
short nose, and the same mischievous air and way. How
the sight of him carried me back! Here Sands Beach
lived, who told me spook stories; there Bloom Shout, who
kept me up at night till eleven o'clock, talking theology.
Here a road turned off toward the creek under the hill,
where a poor family lived, where I occasionally passed a
night. One night, as I rolled over in bed, the bedstead
gave a lurch and came down with a crash to the floor, but
I stuck to it till morning. Ah! how well I slept those
nights; how sweet and fresh existence tasted! I taught the

school for eleven dollars a month and boarded round. The next year, in August, I returned there on a visit, and they had had such bad luck with teachers that they hired me again, giving me twenty dollars a month. I taught from September till March or April, but remember less about this second term, except that some big girls came to me, attracted more, I found, by me, personally, than by desire to learn. Two of them had taught school.

During this second term I became acquainted with the girl [Ursula North] who later became my wife.

Oct. 1

No man's argument is invulnerable; it is just as strong as he is, and no stronger. A skilled man in dialectics, like a skilled man with a sword or a lance, is sure, in time, to be met by a man more skilled, or to be caught off his guard, and his argument overthrown. Great men are not much more likely to be right in their opinions than little men. What absurd beliefs and views of things truly great men have at times held! Their greatness is not so much in this as in their power, their grasp, their capacity to master and absorb a multitude of things. Of course I mean opinions upon abstruse or theological questions. In practical, verifiable matters the great man is nearer the truth.

Oct. 10

Encountered a large wolf spider in the path between the house and my Study. He seemed to charge upon me, and tried to climb up my leg. Black, 1½ inches long. When I brought him to bay with my lead-pencil he reared

up and leapt spitefully toward my hand, then presently
sprang upon the pencil and sank his (or her) fangs into
it. Two minute drops of liquid remained on the pencil
where her fangs had penetrated it. The largest and most
savage spider I ever saw, the wolf spider (*Lycosa fatifera*).

Nov. 10

A tremendous wind from the north; day like a raving
maniac bent on demolishing the world. It almost blows
the hair off a dog. The little steamer cannot make her
return trip from Poughkeepsie. The wind roared all night
so I could not sleep. Never have I seen the river look
rougher than to-day.

Nov. 24

Pretty busy the last few weeks in the vineyards. . . .
Just now a large flock of wild geese called me out of doors.
They went squawking southward. Winter must be close
behind them. No snow here yet. Pretty well these days,
but no thoughts.

I think it saves much confusion to regard religion as
quite distinct from morality, or the right conduct of life —
as having necessarily nothing to do with these, but as a
system of faith and worship, a belief in something extra-
natural. The Children of Israel had a marked religion,
but little morality, as we practice it. Indeed, the most
religious peoples are by no means the most moral. Hence
it is that religion so rarely changes the man, or makes him
practically any better. Let us keep things separated,
religion by itself, and morality by itself. Religion implies

a belief in the supernatural; in a personal deity who takes sides with or against us. A man may be pure, noble, virtuous, high-minded, spiritual, and not have religion. Religion and superstition are close akin. Hence religion may be dispensed with; the world is fast outgrowing it. (See passages in ' Goethe's Autobiography,' p. 114.) The world is saved by morality, and not by religion. Christianity lays great stress upon the virtues; makes them indispensable; makes right conduct the main thing; and yet right conduct is not Christianity. To be a good man is not necessarily to be a good Christian.

Jan. 1, 1888

Find myself reading over and over aloud a poem in the current 'Century' by J. W. Riley, 'The Old Man and Jim'; not great poetry, but meets one's hunger for something human and pathetic, something eloquent that makes the tears start. In the desert of 'Century' poetry, this is a green live thing, if only a weed.

Jan. 4

While eating breakfast this morning I saw, through the window, a fox run along over the hard snow, eight or ten rods below the house. He trotted out in the currant-patch and disappeared toward van Benschoten's. He did not seem at all frightened, and was in no great hurry. The sun wasn't yet up, but the light was strong on the white surface. It is the first fox I have ever seen in this place, though I have seen their tracks quite as close to the house. I love to think of that wild, cunning creature passing over my lawn and amid my currant bushes, just as if I were not near, or as if it were a remote mountain lot.

About my only reading these rugged winter days is Boswell's Johnson. Johnson's bearishness, his temper, his arguing for victory, his love of applause, were not traits of greatness — all these things are detractions. No great thoughts or view ever escapes him. How contemptible his hatred of America! his views of most foreign countries are narrow. He had a narrow mind, anyhow. But his conversation was remarkable. His mind was wonderfully discriminating, and was so instantly, quick as a flash. His sentences are like level deadly rifles; they do not go off vaguely in the air; they are aimed at the subject and hit it squarely.

He seems to have been pious and religious mainly from fear; just as he wrote mainly from want; fear narrowed and darkened his mind. He believed God to be another touchy and acrimonious Dr. Johnson; yet one comes, in Boswell's pages, heartily to love the old bear. He bowed very low and elaborately before all kinds of dignitaries. There was not a spark of poetry in him, that I can see. He did not make one verse or line that still lives. He said he had lived so long in London that he did not remember the differences of the seasons.

Still very cold; a blizzard for three days; at zero, or below, nearly every morning. A total eclipse of the moon to-night — the first I ever saw. The moon seemed to be covered by a piece of smoked glass. It hung there in the eastern sky, a dim, coppery ball that gave no light. It looked very strangely. It was bitter cold, but there was not a cloud in the sky. The shadow on its face seemed

thickest and darkest toward the top. By and by the lower
edge or limb began to shine out. Then it was very interesting to watch it slough off this dark, opaque skin. It
was like a bursting, swelling, developing process. The
bright, clean limb of the moon, how it protruded from
this confining shell or crust! It seemed to swell out till the
impression was precisely as if the luminous part was confined by a copper case, like a cork by a bottle, and was
slowly getting free. How surely an ignorant people would
have said the moon was passing through some crisis, was
being confined and held by some dark object which yet
was unable to keep it! It was like a bud in spring bursting
out of its scales. For this swelling, protruding effect I was
not prepared. When the eclipse was half off, the moon
looked elongated, and as if the freed part was much
larger than the confined part. By and by the shadow was
only a little round cap that sat upon the head of our
round-faced friend like the cap of an English soldier. One
half expected to see the cap burst, and the expanding
edges of the moon to show at the edges, but it did not;
it was slowly crowded off, and the large free moon again
rode the heavens in triumph.

March 22

At Gilder's on Friday night. Meet Miss Edith Thomas
and like her — a thin, nervous girl with dark hair and
dark eyes, talks in a curious feminine bass, the voice of
country solitude.

April 13

The 'Andover Review' says that 'in Christ God recon-
ciled the world unto himself.' How curious and absurd

this jargon of the theologian sounds to an outsider! And jargon it is. Theology, and the theological view of the universe, is precisely the antipode of the natural or scientific view. There is no sense or reason in it. It comes down to us from the dark ages. It ruled the minds of men before science or the rationalistic view of things was born. Think of what trouble poor God took to reconcile the world to himself! what a curious and intricate scheme he concocted — worthy a theologian! He got himself born of a virgin, then grew to manhood, then became an itinerant preacher, then got himself crucified by the Romans, and buried, then came to life again, and so on — all to reconcile the world to himself — to appease his own anger!

April 20

The death of Matthew Arnold, which came without warning the other day, has been constantly in my thoughts since. Does it give a sad tinge to this April, or does April beautify and render more significant his death? It does really seem to put a seal upon him as I think of him, as I go about my work and hear the happy birds, and see the grass springing. April can make even death beautiful.

I look upon Arnold as the greatest critic of English literature; such steadiness, directness, sureness of aim and elevation, we have never before seen. He had the best qualities of the French, and he had something the French have not. He was not at all a miscellaneous man; he stood for certain definite things; he was like a through train, always on time, and only fetching up at important points. His poetry is wonderfully good, only, for some reason, it

does not melt into one, and stick to his mind as it ought
to. As with all first-class men, his death leaves a vacancy
that no one else can fill.

April 27

A perfect day in April surpasses all others. Its sweetness, freshness, uncloyingness, and a sort of spirituality,
can be had at no other time. Still, brooding days, when
every sound strikes musically upon the ear. The highhole
now — his long, loud call comes up from the fields. At
night the full moon rises red and warm, and the toad
begins his long-drawn musical *tr-r-r-r-r-r-r-r-r*. Very
busy these days setting out currants. This morning the
river is like a great mirror. This labor in the fields gives
me a keener relish for Nature. I get such glances from her,
stolen glances. One may have too much leisure. But the
laboring man does not get sated with Nature. He has not
time. To him she is like a mistress who never fully
indulges him. [See 'Spring Jottings,' p. 165, 'Riverby.']

May 22

Still at work in the fields and quite well and happy. One
cannot keep his love for the land, the soil, without work.
Work brings him close to it; he embraces it and loves it,
and strikes his roots into it. . . . Every drop of sweat I let
fall into these furrows came back to me in many ways.
My sleep is restored, and my interest in things much
keener.

May 24

One reason why this country is uninteresting to the
cultivated foreigner, is that it is mainly the work of the

modern industrial democratic spirit, while Europe was
mainly fashioned during the age of poetry and romance,
the age of chivalry, of lords and ladies, before the 'average man,' with his industries and railways and prose, had
come to the front. All the vestiges of that previous age are
profoundly interesting to us, because we see them afar off;
the age belongs to literature, and poetry, and art, and
romance. Man had not then lost the perception of, and
the desire for, beauty. In this country the mass of the
people are entire strangers to the sentiment of beauty;
they deform whatever they touch. Will it always be so?

May 31 [*Roxbury*]

Warm and still. I walk up the road early in the morning to hear the bobolinks in the meadows; how they do
sing! and very nearly the song of my boyhood, only some
slight variations. But the song up there towards the sky,
above the hill-meadows, is new: it is the song of the shore
lark. Presently my eye discerns the happy singer, two
or three hundred feet in the air, flying round and round.
When he utters his crude, halting, lisping song, he flies in
a peculiar manner — tail spread and very conspicuous,
and wings slowly flapping. The song is only a faint copy
of the skylark's. The bird sings five minutes after I discover him, then nears the earth, singing at intervals till
within a hundred feet of the ground, when he plunges
straight down in true skylark fashion. . . . I go up to the
Old Clump and spend an hour on the top; three hermits
are in song as I go up. The spring beauty in bloom on the
summit. In the afternoon I go, attended by a throng of
memories, over to the stream below the school-house

and fish a little, and dream a good deal. Take three fine trout, which are as good as three hundred. I walk about the site of the old school-house, and in the field where we used to play ball forty years ago, and think of many things. I am tempted to go up to the spring, but I do not go. The spring is doubtless there, but where are the childish faces it used to mirror? Dead, many of them, and scattered far and wide, the others.

July 24

Digging our potatoes for market; prices high ($3.75) but yield poor, owing to dry weather. May get back the expense, and a little more, in which case the fun of the thing will not have cost me anything. All my hoeing, watering, killing of bugs, on Sunday and nights, will not cost me a cent.

In the potato patch a big spider with a young toad: body of toad about one inch long; spider has his fangs planted in the back of the toad's neck; toad soon succumbs; spider easily drags him along. When the toad is dead, he leaves him and retreats into the shade under a weed. Toad soon turns dark color. Did the spider suck his blood? He did not come back and claim his prey.

July 25

Think of the myriads of peoples that fill the past, the great ocean! There, in that sea of faces, I see Father and Mother. How precious they look to me! Oh, if they could only draw near and speak!

The little mouse I saw swimming in Balsam Lake did not get as wet as a domestic animal would have. It was quite dry, save on its legs and belly. Its fur shed water like a duck's feathers.

July 26

The July days go by and bring me little pleasure or interest. I pull weeds by spurts, read a little, and look after the farm-work. I crave and need, above all, some one to talk to — some comrade — and quite a different home life from what I have.

Aug. 5

While walking amid my vineyards, and lamenting the damage done by the rain, my attention was attracted by a strange bird-note, high in the air. Presently I discovered the bird circling around as if undecided which way to go. It seemed lost. After a moment I knew it to be an English skylark. Its size, flight, and strong, harsh call-note were those of the lark. It finally went northward. We have no bird that looks just as that did, as it flew swiftly across the sky. [Compare 'Lovers of Nature,' p. 210, 'Riverby.']

Sept. 8

The new book or essay must either add to our knowledge, or else tell us what we already know in such a way as to make us enjoy it afresh. If it is neither new in matter nor fresh in treatment, we do not want it. Can my books stand this test? I believe they can.

Sept. 20

In the evening I see Walt for a moment to say good-bye. He is partly undressed and ready for bed. He presses my hand long and tenderly, we kiss and part, probably for the last time. I think he has in his own mind given up the fight and awaits the end.

Nov. 2

Myron Benton comes at 4.30 P.M. Suddenly the world and life look different to me, so glad am I to see him. For a moment the atmosphere of long-gone days is over things again, and the old joy in life comes back.

April 11, 1889

How I delighted to see the plow at work this morning! The earth is ripe for it, fairly lusts for it, and the freshly-turned soil looks good enough to eat. Lew is plowing the currants, and Travis is plowing beyond them for grapes. I look after them and help mark out the grape-trenches. Plucked my first bloodroot this morning — a full-blown flower with a young one folded up in a leaf beneath it, only the bud emerging, like the head of a papoose protruding from its mother's blanket. ['Spring Jottings' in 'Riverby.']

May 11

While waiting for the train in Kingston, saw in the Tribune the notice of the death of William O'Connor, my old Washington friend, and co-defender of Walt Whitman. A man of extraordinary parts, but lacking the sanity or moderation of the greatest men. I cannot write about him now — it is too great a subject.

July 30

The hell of rain continues. A heavy shower yesterday at five, and a downpour this morning that set the whole

ground afloat. Washed my new vineyards badly. Almost
a cloudburst. No wind here, but probably a cyclone back
of the hill somewhere as, in the midst of the rain, shingles
and leaves and small branches of trees and vines fell
swiftly down from the clouds. It was a curious sight.
How long, O Devil! is this to last?

July 31

Rain continues, and the more it rains, the murkier and
nastier the sky looks. This morning the air is reeking with
vapor. Deluges yesterday all over the country. The very
sky seems rotten. Said to be the result of a huge air wave
from the Atlantic which has drifted in upon the coast.

Aug. 3

Still the rain comes down. . . . The earth oozes water at
every pore. Never saw my land so overflowing. Seven
days of rain, still the air is not relieved. . . . Flood and
devastation throughout the country.

Aug. 5

Rain takes up the tale where it dropped it last week;
air thick and murky; no motion, no wind, with a steady,
heavy rain from southwest. The destruction of all farm
crops is imminent. If this is not hell, what is it?

Aug. 14

Again the damnable rains are upon us. After nearly a
week's respite, and after we had all predicted fair and dry
weather at hand, the rain began again last night with such
thunder, and is still (at 9 A.M.) pouring. I am nearly

ready to believe in a *malignant* Providence at any rate. Looks like a deliberate purpose on the part of the weather-gods to destroy all the crops of the country.

Aug. 24

Dry, dreamy August days at last, no rain for ten days. Warm and tranquil.

Aug. 25

A bright cool day. Spent it on the hills and in the woods of Dutchess County. How delightful that long reclining upon the top of the pastoral hill in sight of the mountains! The slow sinking sun, the bleating sheep, the marsh hawk prowling up and down, low over the grass, and now and then dropping into it; then the sun setting in a notch in the Southern Catskills; then the glow of the embers as he went down.

Sept. 1

Hawthorne said it required a continued freshness of mind to write his sketches, and he could not keep up to the mark more than one third of his time. It requires the same continued freshness of mind to write my outdoor papers, and I fear it has gone from me forever. I cannot get up that keen fresh interest in things any more, I fear.

Nov. 26

A bright, mild day. Spent the afternoon up by the creek screening gravel. I had real enjoyment, almost happiness. The bright sun, the full bounding stream hasten-

ing along within a few feet of me, the trees and rocks, the
mild, secluded place; my dog, ' I-Know,' capering about,
the brisk exercise — it all went to the right spot. It dis-
pelled my gloom and almost made me cheery. The walk
home, too, near sundown, how it called up my many long
walks along this road in happier days! I came back to a
deserted house, but have eaten my supper with compara-
tive satisfaction.

March 6, 1890

Heard through Abigail of the death of Dr. Hull in
Olive. . . . When I first started out in the world, in 1854, I
went to his house. How much I have been there since that
time! How many letters we have exchanged! how many
miles I had ridden with him over that rough country! He
visited me in Washington, and has been twice here. He
was a very friendly, jovial man, but not profound. I once
studied medicine with him for two months. In his office I
wrote my one poem, 'Waiting,' in 1862. How many as-
sociations are connected with his name!

April 12

We plough the ground under the hill for the Moore's
Early. In opening the furrows for the young vines, I
guide the team by walking in their front. How I soaked
up the sunshine to-day! At night I glowed all over.
My whole being had had an earth bath. There was a
feeling of freshly-plowed land in every cell of my brain.
The furrow had struck in; the sunshine had photographed it upon my soul. [See 'Spring Jottings,' p. 167,
'Riverby.']

April 13

Such a sentiment of spring everywhere. The sky is partly overcast, the air moist, just enough to bring out the odors, a sweet perfume of bursting, growing things. One could almost eat the turf. All about the robins sang. In the trees the crow blackbirds called and jingled. Athwart these sounds, every half-minute, came the clear, strong note of the meadowlark; the larks were very numerous, and were love-making. Then the highhole called, and the bush sparrow trilled. . . . Then we went up on Reservoir Hill and gave the eye a wider range, and tried to drink deeper draughts of this April nectar. [Compare 'Spring Jottings,' pp. 167–168, 'Riverby.']

May 5

How curious it is that man in his enormous egotism has made himself believe that he is some exceptional product; that he has a special and extra, or supernatural, endowment — a soul — and that to bring him forth has been the aim and object of all creation! All other creatures, he believes, are mortal, but he is immortal. How he glorifies himself! But in the eye of science, he is part and parcel of the rest, just as ephemeral as summer flies, and no more the end and aim of creation than they are.

May 14

Heard my white-crown sing this morning. He sat in one of Atkins's cherry trees — *Fee-u, fee-u, fiddy, fiddy, fee* — with a pathos and tenderness about the long notes that no other sparrow song equals; not so brilliant and loud as that of the fox sparrow, but, oh! so plaintive and far away! A song in keeping with the rare beauty of the bird.

Sept. 21

The bee does not gather honey from the flowers; it is mainly her own product. What she gathers from the flower is sweet water — diluted grape-sugar. Out of this she makes honey by a kind of digestive assimilation. It is not honey till the bee has added something special and peculiar, herself. It is precisely so with the poet; he gets only the raw material of his poetry from nature — himself must be added, his spiritual and emotional quality, before it becomes poetry. Indeed, it is so with true literature of any kind. 'Tis what the man himself adds to his facts, or truths, or teaching, that makes it literature.

March 12, 1891

To my delight and surprise heard over by the station this morning my little sparrow of last year, him with the long silver loop of sound. What would I not give to know just where he passed the winter, and what adventures by flood and field he has had since last fall! But here he is, safe and sound. Of course it is the same bird. I have never before heard a sparrow with that song. Its chief feature is one long, clear, high note — very strong, sweet, and plaintive, which springs out of the trills and quavers, like a long parabola of sound. To my mental vision it rose far up against the blue and turned sharply downward again, and finished in more trills and quavers. It was the usual long, silvery note in the sparrow's song, greatly increased; indeed, the whole breath and force of the bird is put in this note, so that you catch little else than this silvery loop of sound. [Compare 'Spring Jottings,' pp. 169–170, 'Riverby.']

March 14

Since December I have written the following pieces:

3 for Youth's Companion	paid	$120
1 for McClure's Syndicate		40
1 on Wild Flowers for St. Nicholas		50
1 for Independent		15
1 ('A Hard Nut')		15
1 for Christian Union, 'Popular Errors and Delusions'		20
1 'Analogy'		50
1 'Points of View'		20
1 'Eloquence and Poetry'		25
Finished 'The Spell of the Past'		50
		405

April 20

Yesterday in my walk I sat down in the woods and said, 'There is nothing in the woods.' Then I lifted my eyes and, behold, a crow's nest on a hemlock! In a moment or two the water-thrush chipped smartly, and came and alighted on a branch above me. His *chip* is like the click of two stones struck smartly together in the water. I noticed that curious teetering motion of his body from which he has got the name of wagtail. The motion is not a wag; it is like the motion of a conductor's baton. The bird seems to be beating time for some invisible orchestra. It is a soft, gentle, graceful motion, up and down. [Compare 'Talks with Young Observers,' p. 312, 'Riverby.']

April 27

At 11 A.M. a fitful wind comes to my nostrils laden

with the perfume of cherry blossoms, a delicious bitter-
sweet or almond scent. I never remember it so noticeable.
Standing under the tree, it pours down upon you.

May 1

A visit from Douglas Sladen, a hearty, modest, handsome young English author and poet, an Oxford man.
Looks like Gilder, an English Gilder. Has lived in Aus-
tralia, and been to China and Japan. We have a long
talk and then walk to the woods and gather many wild
flowers.

June 4

Terrible thunder-shower last night from 8 to 9.30. The
heaviest rainfall I ever saw in this place, probably four
inches of water. Did irreparable injury to my vineyards
— tons and tons of soil carried away. The thirsty earth
could do nothing with such a deluge. A night of agony to
me; slept barely an hour. After the rain, the wind arose,
and I feared the young arms would all be stripped off the
vines. Wind continues to-day, and the havoc with the
arms is very great; some vines lose half. The worst blow
I have yet had. I fear the vineyards will prove the death
of me yet. Blessed is the man who has nothing!

June 9

Lovely June days, calm, warm, hazy. Clover and
daisies and wild strawberries in the meadows, young birds
calling, early grapes blooming, cherries ripening. It only
needs youth to make the world very beautiful and winsome.

Busy carting earth to repair damages done by the deluge; make but slow headway. Finished our third spraying this A.M.

June 16

In Central Asia, near the river Oxus, there is, according to travelers, a famous rock called the Lamp Rock, from a strange light that seems to issue from a cavern far up in the side of the rock. The natives have a superstitious fear of the rock, and ascribe the light to some dragon, or demon, that lives in the cave. Recently a bold English traveler climbed up the rock and investigated. The light was found, after all, to be only the light of common day. The cave was only a tunnel, and the mysterious light came through the rock from the other side, making a striking glow or nimbus at the mouth of the dark cavern. Nearly all our providences and mysteries will clear up in the same way, if explored. There is no light more mysterious than the light of common day. [See Preface to 'The Light of Day.']

July 23

Saturday we drove to the Platterkill Clove, Monday to the Mountain House. The scene here is a great surprise: You drive swiftly along a good road up an easy grade till you alight in the rear of a great hotel. You walk straight through the hall, and there lies the world below you, as if seen from a balloon. A young lady walked by my side, Miss Watterson, a New York journalist. After a moment I turn to her to make some remark and find her in tears. The grandeur and unexpectedness of the scene had overcome her. She wept like a child. I could hardly keep my own tears back, which an inward grief of my own had for days been brewing. We walked away from the rest and sat down on the brink of the precipice and gazed upon the wonderful panorama. I felt tenderly toward that girl during the rest of my stay, and think she did toward me. The night before I came away she found me in the sitting-room and, leading me one side, told me she was to be married in September, and was coming up to Onteora for a few weeks, and would be so happy if I could come, too.

Oct. 15

Very busy with the grapes till September 20. A fine season for shipping, for the most part. September, dry and fine. Shipped twenty-one tons, over four tons Delawares, over four tons Niagaras, five tons and over of Wordens, nearly five of Concords, etc. Brought $2100. Shipped mostly to Boston. Am convinced that small baskets pay best.

Oct. 29

Paused a while this morning, in returning from the post office, to see the stems of the leaves of the ash fall. The leaves were off some days ago, and this morning the stems were falling in the still air, coming down swiftly, one by one.

Nov. 6

Walk up to Terpenning's for butter in the afternoon. Pause in the cemetery on my return. I linger long about the graves. Consider whether or not I want to be buried

there. The old Baptist burying-ground at home is offen-
sive to me. So is this. No kith or kin of mine are here.
Had rather be buried beside my dogs, or else in one of the
old fields at home.

Nov. 27

Yesterday, Thanksgiving, I went to New York with
Anthony Gill, to see a football match between Princeton
and Yale. The spectacle fills my mind's eye yet: the great
well-dressed, well-behaved crowd, — 3500 people, mostly
all young, — the flutter of flags and colors, the cheering
and horning, and a glamour of romance or sentiment, in
some way, about the college youths, struggling there
against each other. Alas! that I have no college associa-
tions! It is a great loss.

Dec. 13

Prof. Du Bois's article on Immortality in last 'Century'
seems pretty conclusive. It is very ingenious and does not
assume the points to be proven. Yet why does it not pro-
duce conviction in me? Surely not because I do not want
to be convinced. Is it not because one cannot conceive of
the thing after it is proven? Life, and consciousness without the body, without the limitations of time and space!
It is unthinkable, and, therefore, incredible. We cannot
sum up nature; we cannot say, It is all for this, or for
that; we cannot say it is all a failure unless man is immortal. We think in straight lines, so to speak, from
point to point; but the universe is symbolized by the circle or the sphere. We think nature must have had a beginning, and must have an end; that it must have had a

creation; but when we look deeper, we see this is not true;
the sphere comes to our aid, and we see that we cannot
set bounds to creation. I am convinced there are no terms
by which we can express the truth of these things. Creation is infinite, and we cannot prescribe its ends or its
bounds without a contradiction. It is too large for the
mind to grasp. What is life for? Well, what, then, is immortality for?

Dec. 24

Go to Camden to-day. . . . Walt lies on the bed with
eyes closed, but he knows me and speaks my name as of
old, and kisses me. He asks me to sit beside him. I do so,
holding his hand. . . . Asks about my family and sends his
best love to wife and Julian. Gives me two copies of his
complete poems, just out. He tells me where to find them.
After a while I go out, for fear of fatiguing him. He says,
'It is all right, John,' — evidently referring to his approaching end.

Dec. 26

Walt had a bad night. I go up and look at him, long
and long, but do not speak. His face has steadily refined;
no decrepitude or breaking down; never saw the nose so
beautiful. He looks pathetic, but how beautiful! At
eleven I take a silent farewell. Reach home at night.
How green the patches of winter grain were in New
Jersey!

Jan. 2, 1892

What is my opinion about this religious business?
Well, it is that religion is a sentiment, like poetry or art;

that it is not a universal gift; that truly religious natures
are as rare as poetic and artistic natures; that there is a
gleam or touch of it in most persons, but that it is fully
developed in but few; that it belongs to women more than
to men, though the finest specimens of it are men, as in
every other field; that the great mass of the well-behaved,
church-going people are not deeply or truly religious; that
it is mainly a matter of prudence or thrift with them —
they join the church as they would take out an insurance
policy on their lives or property; they want to be on the
safe side; they want to escape hell; fear, and not love,
impels them; that in the great army of clergymen there is
only here and there a deeply religious nature. I think
Abbott is such. Mulford was such. Father Taylor was
such, and Elias Hicks, John Knox, and scores of others
one could name.

Jan. 10

My moral nature is not fruitful, as was that of Emerson, and Carlyle, if I may compare myself with these il-
lustrious men. It is not the source of my ideas, as was
theirs. The source of my ideas is rather my rational and
intellectual nature, or my emotional nature. I have few
reflections to offer upon life, or man, or society. I would
make a poor preacher. I am interested in things, in laws,
in growths, in Nature, more than I am in Man. The
platitudes of the moralist and the preacher are tools I can
never get the hang of.

Jan. 15

Cardinal Manning died yesterday. A good man and
worthy of remembrance. His last conscious hours of life

were spent in imploring God to have mercy upon him. He was firmly possessed with the Christian idea that he was about to go from a place where God is not, to a place where God is and abides; and that there was great danger that his God would be displeased with him, and would punish him. How curious, how curious! Poor man! why could he not have died in peace?

March 23

In General Grant there seem to have been two distinct men — a very great man, a hero, covered over, or wrapped about, by a common, ordinary man. During his life before the War this ordinary man seems to have been always on top. The strain of the War brought to the surface the hero, the great man, and, for the most part, kept him there. During his Presidency the vulgar, commonplace man shows himself frequently — the hero subsides again, sinks back out of sight. (Strange that he should have wanted A. T. Stewart to be his Secretary of the Treasury!) It was the ordinary man, too, that came in collision with Sumner, though Sumner was not a hero. Afterward, when Grant again became merely a citizen, the ordinary worldly man ruled. He ran after wealthy men; seems to have had a great itching to be one of them. But as the last crisis of his life came on, the hero again emerged. It was a great man that wrote those 'Memoirs,' one of the greatest. The cheap, worldly man and politician does not show himself there, nor ever again. Grant died a hero.

April 6

Again, dear Master [Whitman], I have bitten into this great apple of an earth with my plow and find it as sweet and appetizing as ever; the same old delicious smell; the same old fresh look; yet the new furrow is more eloquent and pathetic to me than ever before. Again the swelling buds and the sprouting grass; again the robin-racket in the twilight; again the long-drawn *tr-r-r-r-r-r-r-r-r-r-r-r* of the toad in the gloaming; again the tender ditty of the sparrow; again the water-fowl streaming northward; again the 'fields all busy with labor,' but thou, thou, in thy tomb!

April 24

To-day is buried in distant Chicago a man I loved, Dr. John C. Burroughs, son of my father's Uncle Curtis. He was one of the few men I have known of whom I felt 'He has walked with Christ' — so simple, sincere, gentle, charitable, and brotherly! A man of great activity and endurance, tall, thin, homely; his life was one of toil. He wasted his best strength on the old Chicago University, as its president — latterly was school-superintendent. Visited me in the year of the triple eights. A man whom all persons liked or loved.

May 18

The perfection of May days; bloom and perfume steep the senses. Again is the nymph Shadow born. I see her cool inviting circle beneath the trees.

June 3

An oriole this morning with a call like this: *Boys, boys, come here, boys!* Of course the words are not there, only the accent or inflection. One season an oriole called, *Set out your grapes, set out your grapes!*

June 14

Real and true culture can only come through the humanities. A man may be learned in the sciences, and still be uncultivated — coarse, obtuse, materialistic. Soul only can reach soul. Literature alone can reach and enrich and humanize the soul. The mere facts of natural science are like the inorganic elements.

Aug. 16

Bright, lovely August days. Ship first Champions to-night. Begin gathering Bartlett pears. Estimate grape-crop at near thirty tons. (Later turned out to be thirty-six.) Pretty well these days, but rather vacant. Beguile some of the time with Pierre Loti's 'Into Morocco.' Very graphic — just enough of everything.

Pride of style in writing is just as bad as pride of style in dress, or equipage. The best style is the absence of style, or of all conscious style. You must not think or know how well-dressed the man or woman is. Loti's style does not court your attention at all. It is a mirror.

Aug. 26

Just as we began to praise the weather and say, 'How fine! how seasonable!' it took a turn, and the rains began again. Rained nearly all day yesterday, sometimes heavy, and nearly all night; and, now the wind has shifted to the northeast, and a cold rain is falling. The weather-gods are the most exasperating of all the gods. Nine times out of ten they will turn a blessing into a curse. They are nearly always on a debauch. They will push the dry weather till we are parched and burnt up, and the

rain till it becomes a deluge. Finished the Champions to-
day in the rain, and many vines of the Moore's Early.

P.M. Rain very heavy; sets all the drains running and
the grapes cracking. I mutter my anathemas, but the
sulky divinities only raise the gates of the clouds higher.

Sept. 11

The war of the grapes has been hotly pursued the past
ten days. Weather cool, and bright, and dry; nights very
cool, suggesting frost; grapes ripened rather slowly;
shipped eleven tons past week; never more favorable
weather to work. Looks as if my crop might bring me
$3000.

Dear old Whittier died a few days ago. More of a real
countryman than any of the rest of our poets. Curtis,
too, has passed — the soul of gentleness and grace and
honor.

[Sept.] 20

On Saturday, the 17th, the bottom went out of the
grape-market, leaving me with two or three tons of Concords on the vines. These we are sending off slowly, and
getting low prices. For the first time in nearly a month I
can sit at my ease and look up at the serene sky. Have
lost near ten pounds in flesh during this grape campaign,
but am well and stronger than one year ago. Grapes over
31 tons; will probably bring me $3200.

Oct. 12

Golden October days continue. I spend the days looking into Tennyson and musing on various matters. A

mellow poetic spirit, like that of the dead poet, seems to pervade the air. All the woods and groves stand in their richest autumn livery.

Is there more reverie than contemplation in Tennyson, and is he, to that extent, weakening and dissipating? Does he sap the will? Longing, retrospection, regret — these largely make the atmosphere of his poems. He was the poet of the Old World, not of the New — of a rich, deep, ripe, refined civilization, not of a new fermenting, democratic era and land, like America. We enjoy him, but he is not of us. He is not always manly. He is much less, as a personality, than Whitman; much more, as a polished, conventional, orthodox poet. It is rarely that he gives one the impression of mass, of power, or makes you partaker in the universal brotherhood of man. Ripe and mellow always, but tonic and uplifting rarely.

Oct. 20

Again the maple in front of my window glows like a sunset cloud; it fills the room with a soft golden light. The autumn tints unusually rich everywhere. . . . The katydids and tree crickets still heard; birds holding their fall reunions all about. Titlarks flying south, uttering their shuffling, lisping notes. Health good these days, and life fairly sweet. Beginning to nibble at my pen again.

Nov. 5

All great poets are teachers. It is one test of the great poet. What does he teach us? He helps us to master life, to understand life. Arnold is right when he says poetry is a criticism of life. Tennyson was a teacher; so was Whitman. Was Lowell, Whittier, Longfellow? Poe and Swinburne certainly not. How much of life does the poet illuminate? Does he throw any light on the questions that vex men's souls? not solve them — because they are insoluble — but help reconcile us to them? help wont us to the planet? The great poet reflects back to us the spirit of the times in which we live. We understand the age, and ourselves, better through him. We see America and democracy in Whitman as we could never see them without him. We see the ripe, mellow civilization of aristocratic England in Tennyson, as in no other poet. Whittier and Longfellow help us understand New England. Our younger poets do not seem to me significant; they are not large enough to be representative. Stoddard, Stedman, Taylor, Lanier, were all men of fine gifts, but they have no tenacity of life as poets. Their poetry cannot compete or hold its own with the men of larger vision and stronger grip.

The mass of the literature of any age, and of ours especially, is the literature of pastime; it helps fill up the hour, and that is all the demand we make upon it. Our poetry is the poetry of pastime. Unless a man's outlook upon the world is wide and commanding, he can do nothing in literature that will last. Yet it is curious that the great poet or writer leaves the world just where he found it. We say he did this, and that; he cleared up this question, and let floods of light in there, and there; and yet it is all to be done over again by the new man.

Nov. 6

As I was out by the barn this morning I heard a continuous pattering sound above me, and on looking saw it was the leaves falling from the mulberry tree. The leaves of this tree do not seem to mature and ripen like others, but hang on and keep green till the frost cuts them, when they let go. Last night's freeze was making them let go. It was perfectly still, and the heavy leaves came down quickly like great green snowflakes. Not a second elapsed that several falling leaves were not in the air. I thought it was like the Tree of Life from which Death is constantly cutting down the leaves. Sometimes one leaf, in falling, would loosen others, and they still others, till a handful would come rushing down. The upper branches were affected most.

Nov. 13

I notice that boots and shoes standing alone always have a sad look, never a smiling or joyous one. The wrinkles about the instep seem to cause it.

How imposing and authoritative this verdict of the people seems — almost supernatural — a voice from out the depths. How the politicians heed it and trim accordingly, or bow their heads in reverence. We do not realize that it is only the voice of Tom, Dick, and Harry right around us, whose private, individual opinions we have very little respect for. If you multiply a foolish man's opinion by one million, or by ten million, is it any the less the opinion of foolishness? This is probably the way Carlyle would have viewed the matter. There is a fallacy in that statement. When the opinions of an ordinary man become widespread, and become the opinions of large masses, over a large extent of territory, it is very significant. It is like the voice of Nature; it is a matter of fate. Every era or age has its master-currents of opinion and thought. The master-current in the political field just now is in favor of less restrictions on commerce, and against home trusts and monopolies.

The voice of a multitude is more impressive than the separate voices of the individuals composing the multitude. There is a spirit and atmosphere in the forest that individual trees hardly hint. Is the social organism a real entity? Is there a general will over or under all the private wills? The country speaks — how portentous, how commanding! No doubt our imaginations have much to do with it.

Dec. 11

Spend the week in Boston; am interviewed and dined and put through generally. Twice on my feet trying to speak before gatherings of teachers. Meet Bradford Torrey, a fine-souled fellow — suggests a bird, with his bright eyes, and shy ways and sensitiveness. Meet E. E. Hale, a fine face — next to Whitman's among modern faces — ought to be a great man back of it. Call on Professor Norton at Cambridge — a fine man and gentleman.

Dec. 30

Vital literature is not made by the study of literature, but by the study of things, of life.

Jan. 3, 1893

On my way home from the post office to-night, something suddenly brought into my head a vision of the corn-shelling at home in my boyhood. The great splint basket with the long frying-pan handle thrust through its handles across the top, held down by two chairs on either side, and by my two brothers sitting in the chairs and scraping the ears of corn against the handle. I hear the kernels rattle, a shower of them falling in the basket, with now and then one flying out in the room. With the cobs which lay in piles beside the basket I build cob-houses, carrying them up till they topple over, or till one of the shellers hits them with a cob. Mother is sitting by, her tallow-dip hung on the back of a chair, sewing. Winter reigns without. How it all comes up before me! Soon will it be fifty years ago. Gone, all gone!

Feb. 5

Why should I have such an aversion to Swinburne? If I read him two minutes I am fairly gasping for breath; his page is a kind of intellectual vacuum — nothing tangible in it; neither thought nor feeling, but words, words, words. It is like a moonlight shadow-dance. His seems like a castrated mind and soul, or one of neuter gender. He is neither fish, flesh, nor fowl. I should think that certain brain diseases [conditions?], like hydrocephalus, might give rise to such a flux of words. I tried to read his poem on the death of Tennyson, and, though I went over it twice, I got not the least breath of meaning.

I suspect that Tennyson was unconscious of the softer, over-ripe, over-melodious character of his poetry. In reading it, they say, he took that element out, and made it wild and almost savage. As a man he seems to have been like a loaf with a rather hard bake on it — crusty, forbidding, curt and rough of speech, slovenly in dress, abrupt in manners, willful, ungrateful, and exclusive — not at all the melodious, conventional, slightly effeminate character he appears in his poems — the product of an old, rich, over-ripe civilization.

Feb. 14

The great artist is identified with his subject; it is *his* subject; he does not merely write about it; he *is* it; it fuses and blends with his personality. The lesser poets search for a subject; to the great poet, the subject comes; he stands in his place, and it finds him.

March 1

In New York. Attended the dinner of the Authors' Club last night. Spoke for the first time, and did fairly well. Papers say my speech and Joe Jefferson's were the speeches of the evening. With practice I think I could beat any of them. Two much chaff in the speeches — no serious word.

March 3 [*Washington*]

Walk up to my old house [1] on V Street in morning and stand as long as I dare at the gate, looking in. Place much neglected and in need of repairs. The brick walk I laid is still in good condition, as is part of the fence I built. What a host of thoughts and memories crowd in upon me!

March 4

Snow and cold. A villainous day for the inauguration of Cleveland. We start at eleven in a covered wagon.

[1] No. 1332 V Street.

See Cleveland and Harrison pass up the Avenue in a carriage; throngs of shivering people; slush on the streets, snow in the air. At the Capitol, after long waiting, we witness the ceremonies in front, jumping and slapping to keep warm. Then Cleveland steps forward and speaks his piece, with uncovered head. 'Grover, put on your hat,' we all feel like shouting. I only hear his strong, manly voice buffeted by the wind.

April 29

I have just been out digging rocks with the boys, and satisfying a sort of craving for rocks and soil that comes upon me in the spring. Father was a great rock-digger and rock-breaker. Every spring, till he got too old, he used to build a piece of wall with stone and rocks from a meadow or pasture, and thus make many spears of grass grow where none grew before. It is a keen satisfaction. In a few days now we have made room for several more grapevines by digging out the place-rock where it came to the surface. We broke the sleep of long ages of those rocks, sometimes with bars and wedges, sometimes with dynamite. Where the sun had not shone in some millions of years, we let it in. In seams, all but invisible, we find fibres of roots, and, now and then, a lichenous growth merely discoloring the stone. How life will squeeze into the narrowest quarters!

May 8

The greater a man is, the more distasteful is praise and flattery to him. If there were such a being as men call God, how sick and disgusted he must have got, long ago, by the cringing and abject attitude of mankind before

him — fulsome flattery and insincere praise, and all for
selfish purposes! As if I were to praise the President because I wanted an office of him. The attitude of the
Greeks toward their gods was far better. God must love
those who defy him.

May 11

As I sit here in the summer-house at 8.30 A.M., a soft,
moist, cool haze shuts down and veils all the distant objects. Beyond Crum Elbow all is a white obscurity. Why
do I think of Father and Mother so often such days?
Just such days came to them. How busy and eager they
were about their work! I see the cows hurried off to the
pasture, the teams started for the fields, or to haul out
manure. I see Father striding across the ploughed field
with a bag partly filled with oats slung across his breast,
from which he clutches a handful of seed and scatters it at
every step. The mountains begin to show signs of foliage
near their bases, but on their summits the trees are still
naked, or maybe a little snow gleams out here and there
amid the trees.

I remember, when I was a child of three or four years,
the girl threw my hat off the stone-work. I cried, and,
looking up on the side-hill, saw Father sowing oats. How
vividly and lastingly his image, there in the May sunshine! The white bag, the red soil, and all are imprinted
on my memory!

July 8

Doubtless one reason why the great men of the past
seem so great to us is because all other voices are silent,
theirs alone are heard. All the hum and roar and gabble

and racket of those days are gone, hushed, dead, and the few voices that reach us seem to fill the world of that time.

Nov. 30

Julian goes to Black Pond and in afternoon I join him, finish the blind, and then float down the stream in the boat, the water a perfect mirror. We gaze down into that reversed forest under the water, apparently as real as the one above. It is so still that a little Canada sparrow in the weeds and dry leaves makes a big noise. Reach home at dark. At night Venus and Jupiter play at see-saw, one going down in the west as the other rises in the east; never saw Venus more glowing — a great silver lamp in the western sky. [Compare 'A Sharp Look-out,' p. 4, 'Signs and Seasons.']

Dec. 5

Read some chapters in one or two of my books, sitting here alone by the fire, the other night. I could have wept over them — they were so fresh and joyous, so untouched by the fret and fever of the world. Where was the paradise I lived in when I wrote those books? Here, right here, where I now live. A kind of perennial youth breathes in those books. No merit of mine. I could not help it.

Dec. 31

In the Garfield–Conkling controversy, as related by Senator Dawes in the last ' Century,' there are the elements of a great tragedy, like the Greek plays. Here was this haughty, imperious, eloquent Conkling refusing to take the magnanimous part, refusing to believe in it at

all; refusing to credit the people with any love of magnanimity; believing in nothing but party, and in crushing
your rival; incapable of taking a large, disinterested
view of the situation; full of hate, jealousy, selfishness —
to rule and triumph with him being more than country
or duty or truth; seeing everything through the passion
of personal pride. Here was this man, at last, a victim of
his own selfishness and conceit, crushed by the popular
feeling of magnanimity, which he refused to believe in;
utterly humiliated and rejected by the party he had
placed before country and duty. What bitterness was his!
Did the Furies ever before so blind a man for his own
destruction? One of the proudest men who ever walked,
brought to the deepest humiliation by his own deliberate
folly. Every politician in this country who has presumed
upon the narrowness and meanness of the people has come
to grief. Conkling did, Blaine did, Hill did. No claptrap,
nothing theatrical, or that has the air of self-seeking, is a
success. Honors and victory come to the disinterested
man.

Feb. 10, 1894

Going over to the station last night, I said to myself,
Here have I lived in this place twenty years, and am not
yet wonted to it. Twenty years of youth here, and these
hills and valleys and the river would seem like a part of
myself; now I look upon them with alien, reluctant eyes.
I seem only a camper for a day and a night. So much more
plastic and impressionable are we in youth! As manhood
is reached we begin to harden, and by and by our affec-
tions will not take on new shapes at all.

Feb. 29

Milton's poetry, for the most part, is to me a kind of London Tower filled with old armor, stuffed knights, wooden chargers, and the emblems and bedizenments of the past. Interesting for a moment, but dead, hollow, moth-eaten. Not a live thing in one of his poems, that I can find. Yes, there is a nightingale, and there are a few flowers, and a human touch, here and there; but half a dozen pages would hold all that any man need read. The 'Samson' is said to be in the Greek spirit, but what business had he, a Puritan of Cromwell's time, writing in the Greek spirit? Why did he not write in his own spirit, or in the Puritan spirit — the seventeenth-century spirit? What business had he masquerading in this old armor? He put no real life under these ribs of death. His 'Paradise Lost' is a huge puppet-show, so grotesque and preposterous that it is quite insufferable. Milton seems to have been a real man, but he stands there in English literature like a great museum of literary archæology. He seems to have had no experiences of his own, and rarely to have seen the earth and sky, or men and women, with his own natural eyes. He saw everything through the classic eyes of the dead past. Who reads him? Professors of literature, I suppose. He was a great craftsman, no doubt; but he has been of no service to mankind, except a literary service; he has helped us to realize the classic spirit of letters, and the absurdity of the old theological dramaturgy. He spoke no word to any man's real moral or spiritual wants.

March 31

Wonderful aurora last night, beyond any I have ever before seen. Once while a boy I saw something approaching it. The wonder of this display was that it made a complete circle all around the horizon. We stood in the midst of a great tent of streaming aurora. The ghostly flame shot up from the north, east, south, west, and came to a focus just a few degrees south of our meridian. Never before have I seen it rise up from the south. The apex of this tent was the scene of constantly shifting and vanishing forms of light. It was an apocalypse. At times it seemed as if the heavens opened at this point, and troops of angels and winged horses came straight toward us. A pencil like Doré's would have caught many suggestions. Sometimes the electric clouds would gather at this point, like foam over the point of an escaping fluid, and whirl about. Sometimes there would be curious openings through it where the black sky and the stars would appear. A deep crimson flush would appear, here and there, near the horizon, and spread upward to the zenith. At 8.30 the motion of the streamers was hardly perceptible, but at 8.45 they were leaping up very rapidly, the subtle impulses traveling up precisely like flame; and such ghostly flame! Never was anything more spectral and unearthly than the whole display. It was a wild dance of many-colored, sheeted, ghostly forms. What an impression such a phenomenon must have made upon rude primitive man! I myself could hardly keep down an emotion of superstitious fear.

April 22

Notes for an April poem:

The soft maples are crimson, and the buds of the elm
swarm like bees in its branches.
The bee comes home with golden thighs from the willows,
and honey in her bag from the arbutus.

School-children pass with their hands full of hepaticas and
arbutus.

The newly ploughed fields glow like the breasts of robins.
I walk in the new furrow, in the strong sunlight, till it is
photographed upon my spirit.
The farmer strides across the brown field scattering the
seed-oats at steps alternate.

The sparrow, the robin, the jay, have nest-material in
their beaks.

The kinglet pipes his fine lyrical strain in the evergreens
— he flashes his ruby crown to his mate.

The white-throat sings on his way northward.
Long and long the highhole calls from the distant field.
The first swallow laughs down to me from the sky.
From the marshes rises the shrill, infantile chorus of the
piping frogs.
From the trees above them comes the *okalee* of the red-
wing.
The song of the toad — *tr-r-r-r-r-r-r-r-r-r-r* — is heard
in the land.

The first dandelion lies like a gold coin upon the greening turf.

Something delicate, prophetic, spiritual, is in the air.

The bud-scales are falling from the buds — some are fragrant and gummy.

The light shower fills the air with wild perfume.

The bluebird lifts and flickers to his mate his cerulean wing.

In the twilight the robin racket is prolonged and intense.

The cowbird sits beside his dusky mate on the top of the tree, and pumps up his liquid, glassy notes.

In the leafless woods the pedestrian partridge beats his drum — his own inflated breast.

Amid the alders, in the moist bottoms, the marsh marigolds have the effect of coined sunshine.

Here and there in the tree-dotted landscape, the greening rye-fields delight the eye.

Ere the month is ended the shad-blow makes a white mist, here and there, along the forest borders.

April 27

On the night of the 24th went up to Kingston to hear and see Robert G. Ingersoll. Much stouter and redder than when I saw him last May. Can drink whisky, he says, but not wine. Wine makes him throb and throb. He ate his supper in his room after the lecture; drank iced milk and iced water freely. Lecture full of telling points, much sound argument, and many eloquent passages. He said, in talking with me in his room, that he was by no means so sure that immortality was desirable; he would name conditions before accepting it — unconditional immortality he would refuse.

June 6

In the afternoon walk over to the weasel swamp. Find
three interesting things: The seventeen-year locusts coming out, all along the borders of the woods, some little
bushes loaded with them. Under certain trees find their
little earth-mounds, many of them yet sealed up, or with
only a peep-hole in them. Saw a little moth that evidently imitates birds' droppings on the leaves. When disturbed, it would fly a few rods and alight on a broad
green leaf, spreading itself out perfectly flat, simulating
the droppings of a bird. It was yellowish, with a faint
dark brown etched upon its wings. It would not move
till touched. I have read of a moth or butterfly found on
some islands of Oceanica that exactly mimics the excre-
ment of a bird upon a leaf — this, of course, for protection.
Found the nest of the worm-eating warbler beside the
path, in the edge of the woods. As I came along down the
path on my return, a small brown bird started up from
the ground a few feet from me. From the glimpse of it I
had, I took it to be the oven-bird. Looking to the spot
whence it started, I saw another bird, with a striped head,
standing on the edge of a nest in the side of the bank, with
the droppings of one of the young birds, whose heads I
saw beneath her, in her beak. My appearance upon the
scene was sudden, and the mother bird was surprised
while waiting upon her young. She stood motionless,
half turned toward me, and kept the white mass in her
beak. Neither of us stirred for a minute or two, when I
withdrew and sat down a few paces away. The male bird
now became quite uneasy, and flitted from bush to bush,
uttering his alarm *chip*. The mother bird never stirred. I

could see her loaded beak from where I sat. In two or three minutes she dropped, or otherwise disposed of, her unsavory morsel, but kept her place above her young. Then the male bird, seeing that was the game, quieted down also, and disappeared from view. After long waiting, I approached the nest and, pausing ten feet away, regarded it some moments. The bird never stirred. Then I came nearer, and when I sat down within four or five feet of the nest, the parent bird flew out upon the ground three or four paces from me, and began trying the old confidence-game of the birds upon me. She was seized with incipient paralysis; she dragged herself about on the ground; she quivered and tottered, and seemed about ready to go all to pieces. Seeing this game did not work, she began to use her wings and to scold sharply. The male now suddenly appeared, and, true to his name, had a worm in his beak. Their scolding brought a vireo upon the scene, which they seemed to regard as an intrusion. The nest was composed mainly of dry leaves. The young were probably a week old. I shall visit them again.

June 9

Met poor old Mrs. Green last night trudging down from Esopus to take train here for Newburgh to see her son, fatally hurt on the railroad. Poor old mother! I could have wept with her. Son a worthless fellow, a hard drinker, better dead than alive; but her mother's heart could not give him up easily. There were tears on her brown wrinkled face as we talked. It was very hard for her, she said, so old, so much trouble, so much hard work as she had seen: ten children, a drinking husband and

sons, poverty. And yet the old woman tries to keep up
a cheerful front, and has preserved a certain innocence
and sweetness.   The Methodist dominie went down and
prayed beside her son; went on purpose, she said. 'It was
showing him a good deal of respect,' she said, and she was
touched by it. Probably the first mark of respect the poor
devil had ever had. I have known her twenty years, and
yet she can't get my name right — calls me 'Mr. Burrell'
generally. As she stepped along alertly to get on the train,
I saw how pinched and crooked her old back looked —
between seventy and eighty.

Aug. 10

Perfect workmanship is one thing; style, as the great
writers had it, is quite another. It may go with faulty
workmanship — it is the use of words in a vital, fresh
way, so as to give the impression of a new and original
force and personality. When a man's writing is as distinct as his face, or his character, and could not be
mistaken for another's, he has the main element of
style.

Aug. 14

The ground aches with dryness. It seems as if the old
Earth must soon crack open in these parts, though east,
south, west, north, it has rained copiously. Many of the
grapes wilting — shall not have half a crop, at the best.
Not a drop of water has been added to the stock of
moisture in the ground since early June. The light
showers since then have only served to check evaporation
for a day or an hour.

Aug. 18

Threw water on vineyard to-day through Campbell's engine. Shall watch the result with interest. It was a great satisfaction, at any rate, to see the water flow, in spite of the weather. I enjoyed a real triumph.

Aug. 23

The hellish drought continues — a sky of brass and a sun of copper. No clouds in the sky for three days. In the South they are deluged, and have been for three weeks.

Sept. 7

Another week of smoke, heat, and drought. The woods look like middle of October — so many of the trees are brown and sere. Leaves falling from all the trees. A kind of torrid winter. All my maples look as if scorched by flame, red at the top. Never saw the like before; the hickory seems to suffer most, and the elms least. Peach trees have half dropped their leaves. People burning up in Minnesota by the hundred; whole villages swept away. The drought extends as far west as Nebraska. Nearly three months here without rain. Only a little water left in the well, half a bucket at a time. Grapes nearly off — eighteen tons, seven hundred. Dust six inches deep in vineyard.

Oct. 9

Just heard of the death of Holmes. No news of warning sickness had reached me. Even his cheer and vivacity have at last yielded. The last star of that remarkable constellation of New England authors. I owe him entertainment, and more or less stimulus, but probably no deep service. A brilliant talker; in letters gifted with both wit and humor, and the poetic temperament — an open fire to warm your hands by. He had the gift that makes literature — something direct and immediate — his mind touched yours. One of the best of the discursive writers.

Oct. 13

Never a morning does Julian start off for school but I long to go with him, to be his mate and equal; to share his enthusiasms, his anticipations, his games, his fun. Oh! to see life through his eyes again! How young the world is to him, how untried, how enticing!

Oct. 29

New book ['Riverby'] came to-day. Doubtless the last of my outdoor series. I look it over with a sigh. For a quarter of a century I have been writing these books — living them first, and then writing them out. What serene joy I have had in gathering this honey! and now I begin to feel that it is about over with me — my interest, my curiosity, are getting blunted.

Nov. 5

Start for Lawrenceville, New Jersey. Speak there at night to the boys. Not very well satisfied with myself; do not speak easily and freely, though the boys seem deeply interested.

Nov. 29

Are the men of the hour ever the men of the eternities?

Jan. 4, 1895

I ought to go to the Stevenson memorial meeting in New York to-night, but shall not. His death fills quite a space in my thoughts. He seems nearer to me than any other contemporary British man of letters — of the younger school. Some one has said, 'Be an artist, or prepare for oblivion.' Stevenson was an artist, and he is safe from oblivion — for a time, at least. Yet he is not one of the great ones. His literary equipment surpasses his more solid native human equipment, as with so many of the late school of writers. He was not a man of mass and power, any more than I am. We are all light-weights, and try to make up in cleverness what we lack in scope and power. Stevenson is not one of the men we must read; we can pass him by; but he is one of the men who fills the hour and relieves the tedium of life. He inspires love, and the thought of him, gone from life, and sleeping there in far-off Samoa on a mountain-peak, fills me with sadness.

Jan. 11

⸻ Why is F. Harrison far less persuasive and convincing as a critic in the same field than Arnold? Is it because he seems to have less root in himself? that his great talent is less a vital part of his personality? He is more like a flower without the stem and leaves; we do not see where all this richness of language and illustration comes from.

Jan. 19

Finished the fifth play of Ibsen last night. Have read 'The League of Youth,' 'Pillars of Society,' 'Ghosts,'

'An Enemy of the People,' and 'A Doll's House.' Do not think I shall read any more of them. There is nothing in them for me. Ibsen is not a sky-shaker—shakes the doors and windows a little, that is all. Nothing inspiring or prophetic in him. Nothing for the soul, no poetry, and not much philosophy. He is interesting; manages the dialogue well; his language is vigorous and direct; now and then a happy and telling comparison; but never breathing the atmosphere of the great creative geniuses.

Feb. 6

Why will artists, in painting naked women, so often give them the same expression of face that they wear when clothed and in their right minds in society? Think of the face of a society girl upon a nude figure! One feels sorry for her; how ashamed and awkward she must feel without her clothes! Sometimes one sees the face of a pretty schoolmarm upon these nude figures. The face and the body should be one; there should be no contradiction, as there is none in the Greek figures.

July 27 [*Roxbury*]

A little rain to-day from the southwest. [Rudolf] Binder and I lay in File Corbin's old barn on the hay and looked out into the broad fields and the dripping clouds. At that moment my vineyards were being devastated by a terrible storm of hail and rain. While at supper, a few hours later, a telegram was handed me which said: 'All your grapes destroyed. Come home at once.' It fairly took my breath away. What a cruel, brutal blow! I had all I could do to stand up under it. Little sleep that night.

Cannot put the thought from me. One prolonged agony till I reach home, at 7 P.M. on Sunday, and find it not so bad as reported. May save half of them, or more, though probably half their market value's gone. Vineyard terribly washed also. Probably three inches of water fell in less than a half-hour. Two clouds, or storms, met and fought it out just over my vineyard. Each cloud apparently gutted the other, and one came down as hail, the other as rain, all in a heap.

Aug. 12

Nearly every day I walk over to my muck swamp for a taste of the wild and unfamiliar. The walk through the woods, the glimpses, the vistas, the sudden revelation of the bit of prairie surrounded by gray rocky arms, Amasa swinging his bogging-hoe in the solitude; the fat marrowy soil; the sitting on a fern-hassock, and the talk and gossip; then the spring, and the long, delicious draught, repeated again and again; then the Scotch-caps and blackberries; then the slow loitering and browsing about — how sweet it all is! I look away to the west and north, and there is the distant landscape, with farms and woodland, and, beyond all, the blue curves of the Catskills. Then I come back refreshed.

Feb. 19, 1896

Go to New Haven to speak before the Phi Beta Kappa Society on Whitman. Am dreadfully scared and worried, as usual, as I sit in my room at the hotel; it seems utterly impossible for me to read that lecture. I could fly to the Moon easier. But when the hour strikes, and I find myself face to face with the enemy, my courage and confidence mount, and I acquit myself entirely to my satisfaction. I speak about one-third of it and read the rest. A fine audience, and appreciative.

April 15

The days are sweeter and sweeter, and warmer and warmer. What an appetite I have for them! I sit this morning with my door open and let the sounds and odors come in — the drumming of the highholes, the call of Phœbe, the trill of the bush sparrows and song sparrows, and all the other bird-sounds. The river shimmers and glints through the haze. The morning is like a nude woman veiled by her own hair. April is in heat; she is pairing with the Sun. She yields herself to his embraces all day. I can see the union taking place even in my vineyard.

April 18

Hiram and I move over to Slabsides.

June 22

John Muir came last night. Julian and I met him at Hyde Park. A very interesting man; a little prolix at times. You must not be in a hurry, or have any pressing duty, when you start his stream of talk and adventure. Ask him to tell you his famous dog story ['Stickeen'] (almost equal to 'Rab and his Friends') and you get the whole theory of glaciation thrown in. He is a poet, and almost a seer; something ancient and far-away in the look of his eyes. He could not sit down in a corner of the landscape, as Thoreau did; he must have a continent for his playground. He starts off for a walk, after graduation, and walks from Wisconsin to Florida, and is not back home in eighteen years! In California he starts out one morning for a stroll; his landlady asks him if he will be back to dinner; probably not, he says. He is back in seven days; walks one hundred miles around Mt. Shasta, and goes two and one half days without food. He ought to be put into a book — doubtful if he ever puts himself into one. He has done many foolish, foolhardy things I think; that is, thrown away his strength without proper return. I fear now he is on the verge of physical bankruptcy in consequence. Probably the truest lover of Nature, as she appears in woods, mountains, glaciers, we have yet had.

July 24

Why do the critics hesitate to call Mrs. Stowe an artist, and her 'Uncle Tom' a work of great literary merit? I suppose it is because, first, she never produced another work that approached it in general interest; her subsequent books fall far below it; second, it seems to have been the result of moral and humanitarian fervor, rather than of esthetic and artistic fervor. The subject mastered her. A man may make an eloquent speech at some crisis in his life, who is not a great orator. But the true orator is eloquent on many occasions and on many themes. The great artist does not commit himself as Mrs. Stowe did; his work has a flavor, a quality, which hers has not. Tolstoi, though he wrote with a purpose, and with as deep moral conviction as Mrs. Stowe, is much more surely an artist. He is not confined to one theme; his range is vastly

greater. Mrs. Stowe plays almost entirely upon our more
common, external, or animal feelings, as pity, mirth, fear,
anger. The deeper and finer chords of the soul she is not
master of, and no Beecher ever was. The pure literary or
artistic quality, which can stand upon its own ground
without the aid of voice, manner, or any laughter- or
tear-provoking circumstance, was not among the gifts of
this gifted family. They had the eloquence of passion,
action, earnestness, but not of the still, small voice, the
deep inner voice of pure Art. No one can read 'Uncle
Tom' without tears, laughter, indignation; it is one of the
books that lays strong hands upon the common emotional nature; but no one, I fancy, would ever get that
deep, tranquil pleasure and edification from it that works
of pure art give. Mrs. Stowe's inspiration was from without rather than from within; when she took a subject or
a field that presented less violent and tragic contrasts,
and that did not make the same appeal to her sense of
wrong and injustice, she was far less effective. If Hawthorne had written the book, how much less exciting and
arousing to the average man it would have been; how
much less animal heat there would have been in it, but
how much more of the pure gold of true literature it would
have held! Something as deep and calm as the light of
the sky. Nothing can take high rank as a work of art
that does not touch and thrill the soul. To excite the
feelings, or to enlist the moral nature, is not enough; the
man within the man, who sits calm and impartial, who
sees more in the silent stars than in the roaring tempest,
more in limpid brooks than in raging torrents, must be
reached and moved.

What constantly strikes me in Howells is the workmanship — the cleverness with which the thing is done. His
people make little impression. It is like exquisite carving
on very ordinary material. Am just reading his Saratoga
Novelette. It is like a photograph, and lacks just what a
photograph lacks — charm, illusion. But how clever!
He is a master in painting ordinary people. Can he paint
the extraordinary? I doubt it. Does he increase our love
for men and women, and for things? No. A talent so
fine that it is almost genius.

July 28

The fashion of fun passeth away, as do all other fash-
ions, whether in dress, art, or letters. Where is Doesticks?
How long will Artemus Ward, Mark Twain, Josh Bil-
lings be remembered? The great humorists have no
fashion and no trick. The new great man in any field is
only a new fresh growth of the same old traits.

Aug. 3

Visit the graves of my dead in the old churchyard. Our
country cemeteries are perhaps the ugliest in the world.
At least I saw nothing abroad that compares with them
in this respect. I laid my hands upon the marble slab at
the head of each grave in silent greeting and farewell.

Nov. 26

Hiram leaves me to-day to be gone several months —
thus closing a curious and interesting chapter in my life.
He leaves me pensive and vacant. He never looked into
one of my books lying here on the table, while here. When

the Whitman book came, I said to him, with the book in my hand, 'Hiram, here is the book you have heard me speak about as having cost me near four years' work, and which I rewrote about four times.' 'That's the book, is it?' said he, but never showed any curiosity about it, or desire to look into it.

Dec. 16

On my way over to Slabsides to-day was arrested by a great hullabaloo among the chickadees and nuthatches on a hemlock tree. Such a chorus of tiny voices I had not heard for a long time. The tone was of trouble and dissent, if not of alarm. The nuthatch, I think, was the red-bellied. I gazed long and long up into the dark green mass of the tree to make out the cause of the complaint. The chickadees were clinging to the ends of the sprays, as usual, very busy looking for food, and all the time uttering their soft plaints. At last I spied the cause — a little owl on a limb looking down intently upon me. How annoying such exposure and hue and cry on the part of the birds must be to the little lover of quiet and privacy!

Jan. 9, 1897

I wonder if there is another so-called literary man who spends his time as I do—in the solitude of the country, amid the common people. Here I sit, night after night, year after year, alone in my little Study perched upon a broad slope of the Hudson, my light visible from afar, reading an hour or two each evening, and then to bed at nine. No callers, no society, no proper family or home life. Not in years has a person dropped in to spend the

evening with me. Occasionally Julian comes in, after his
return from school, and we talk awhile. (Julian is developing a very quick, keen, and eager intelligence.) Up
in the morning before daylight and lend a hand in getting
breakfast, and then the furnace and a few chores; then
fifteen minutes' walk to the post office and back; building
a fire in the Study; a little reading, and then, at nine, to
work with my pen till noon. Then dinner, and a few
chores; then sawing and splitting wood for the next
twenty-four hours; then a walk to Slabsides, or elsewhere;
then a little reading and dozing in my Study; then supper
and darkness again. Every day; and every day in winter
the same. What long, long thoughts I have! What constant retrospection; what longings for the old days and
people! The world goes by me afar off. I hear its roar and
hubbub, but care little to mingle in it. It is mostly vanity
and vexation of spirit.

Jan. 18

In Dr. Johnson's talk, you touch the real man; in his
essays, you touch only his clothes, or his periwig. In
letters, too, people are apt to give us their real selves,
women especially. [Compare 'Style and the Man,' p. 76,
'Literary Values.']

Feb. 7

When I see in the local paper that a child has been
born to some one in Roxbury, why should I think of
Father and Mother, and feel a nameless pang? I do not
know, but so it is. I can hardly analyze the feeling. Their
last baby was born there over fifty years ago. I think of

the joy they had in their children, and of all their outlook upon life, and how it is all past and hushed so long ago. I see myself as a little boy rocking the cradle again, minding the baby, while Mother bakes or mends or sweeps or washes. I hear her voice singing. I see Father pushing on the work of the farm. Then there is another feeling: it seems late for babies to be born into the world; the show is about over; the curtain will soon fall; what can remain now of interest compared to what we have seen? It does not matter that one's reason tells him that the world is old and played out only to him; that Grandfather at his age probably felt the same; and his grandfather, and his, and his, felt the same; that to the young the world is young and untried and full of promise, as it was to us in youth — it does not matter — the actual, concrete feeling remains the same, and life is a tale that is nearly finished.

May 5

Mrs. Hale and her friend come Monday. Two very interesting women. The New Woman is a great improvement on the old. She loves the open air like a man, and is nearly as unconventional. There seems to be more poetry in her soul than in the man's.

Yesterday morning when we first got up, at five, Hiram called my attention to some large black object about midway of a tree near the top of the ridge back of Ingersoll's. It seemed as large as a turkey. Hiram said he bet it was a coon. I felt sure it was an eagle. We kept an eye on it for near an hour; then we saw it move; presently I saw a gleam of white as the bird bent forward to preen its plumage; then it stood up and lifted its plumage and wings, and shook itself — a bald eagle, and no mistake! Had he passed the night there? I hope so. By and by, having fixed himself for the day, he launched into the air, and flew directly over the cabin. The thought of him lingered all day. What attracted him here, attracts me — the wildness and seclusion, the precipitous gulf. Noble lodger, I hope you will come nightly to my craggy retreat! It is an inspiration for all day to look out of the window as I get up and see thee upon thy perch.

Sept. 27

Julian starts for Harvard. He goes off cheerfully, but my cheerfulness is only put on. I wheel his big trunk over on the wheelbarrow. Thus he starts for College, I serving as his porter. The dear boy! How youthful he looked! Oh, if I could go with him and be his chum! Well, he comes into the Promised Land for which I longed, but of which I never got a glimpse. How late in the day it seems to me! but not to him. . . . Had I gone to College, it would have been forty years ago. But I shall see him again soon, yet how sad the autumn fields look! Think of all the Harvard boys who had that life so long ago! And soon my experiences and his will be of the long ago.

Nov. 9

How much more valuable to a man is an instinct for the truth than any special gift or accomplishment! If he craves the truth alone, he will not be disturbed if his theories and systems fall in ruins about his head. Then I must find a larger and deeper truth, he says. What an instinct for the truth had Darwin! when facts appeared to be against him, how he welcomed them! then they became his friends. How often we see men of brilliant parts who achieve nothing of permanent worth because they have not this instinct for the truth! A man with a system or theory to uphold is handicapped, unless, like Darwin, he has this instinct for the truth. Taine's criticism is less valuable than it would be had he no system to uphold. They are free, indeed, whom the truth makes free, because the truth finds them free.

Nov. 16

The day inevitably comes to every author when he must take his place amid the silent throngs of the past; when no new work can call attention to him afresh; when the partiality of his friends no longer counts; when his friends and admirers themselves are gathered to their fathers; when the spirit of the day in which he writes has given place to the spirit of another and different day. How, oh how will it fare with him then! How is it going to fare with Lowell, with Longfellow, with Emerson, with Whitman? How will it fare with poor me? [See page 1, 'Literary Values.']

Nov. 28

I see that the success of my little poem, 'Waiting,' is not on account of its poetic merit, but for some other merit or quality. It puts in simple and happy form some common religious aspiration, without using the religious jargon. Persons write me from all parts of the country that they treasure it in their hearts; it is an anchor to windward. A celebrated New York preacher writes me that it steadies his hand at the helm. A woman died the other day in Poughkeepsie with these verses in her hand. They had been the consolation of her life. Pure poetry never affects people in this way, but poetry, alloyed with religion, does. Burns's best poem, 'The Jolly Beggars,' is not so popular as 'The Cotter's Saturday Night.'

The old people had their favorite hymns in the hymn-book — some verse or verses that spoke to their particular case, or experience, or aspiration. But the impartial, disinterested reader would be compelled to judge the hymns by their poetic quality alone, because this alone is permanent and universal. This we never outgrow as we do the religious views and feelings of the past. The religious thrill, the sense of the Infinite, the awe and mystery of the universe, is, no doubt, permanent in the race, but all expression of it in creeds and forms addressed to the understanding, or exposed to the analysis of the understanding, is transient and flitting, like the leaves of the trees. My little poem is vague enough to escape the reason, sincere enough to go to the heart, and poetic enough to stir the imagination.

Dec. 5

Finished Macaulay's 'Life and Letters' to-day. A great, omnivorous, partisan mind — not fine, but solid and strong — oratorical, always pleading or arraigning, or eulogizing; alternating from invective to panegyric. Coarse, like British oak, and loyal and strong. His style antithetic, lucid, sweeping. Indeed, he is always the orator, never the poet, or the true critic. One of the strange things in contemporary history is that he and Carlyle should not have seen and known each other.

Dec. 20

It is curious that Wordsworth should have liked only Burns's serious poetry, like 'The Cotter's Saturday Night.' His 'little amatory songs,' he said, we must forget. Tennyson, on the other hand, could not tolerate his serious poetry, but liked immensely 'the little amatory songs.' The moralist chose in Wordsworth, the artist and the true critic, in Tennyson.

Dec. 28

Julian goes up the river in his boat after ducks. At 3 P.M. I go down to the river and am alarmed at the condition of the ice — vast masses of it grinding on the shore; seems impossible for a boat to live in it. So I start up the river-bank, hoping to see him coming back. The ice roars louder and louder and jams and grinds harder and harder, and I become more and more alarmed. The farther I go, the more anxious about the boy I become. My imagination begins to work, and I am soon wretched indeed. At last I reach Esopus dock, but no Julian in sight. But a man here tells me he saw him go up about 2 P.M. It is now four. The man, who is an old river-man and duck-hunter, says the ice makes it dangerous: he was himself afraid to go out on such a day. I worry more and more. Darkness will surely come on and the boy, with his canvas boat, will be ground to pieces, or frozen fast in the ice. I tear up the river and reach Pell's dock, a mile further up. Then I fancy I see him in an open canal of water near the quarry dock. He does not seem to be rowing, and the ice is shutting up the opening south of us, faster and faster. Bill O'Brien joins me, and we look, and speculate, and try to put in his boat and go to the rescue. But it is too heavy. Then I tear along the shore again, and, when within a quarter of a mile of what seems to be his boat, shout to him. Just then his gun goes off and I see he has been stalking a duck, and is not alarmed, and in no hurry. I shout to him, and he rows along, much amazed to see me. No danger, he says, and laughs at my anxiety. The sun is down, and the tide nearly slack. I try to persuade him to put the boat ashore at Pell's, and come home with me on foot, but he refuses, and says he can beat me home, says there is open water all along shore, as, indeed, does seem now to be the case, and as, indeed, he found.

Nip and I take the road for home; the good level walking is such a change from our scramble along the riverbank, that I am less tired than I thought, and make good time. At ten minutes to six we are home, and, a few minutes later, Julian reaches the dock. I go down and am greatly relieved to see him safe back again. All my worry was vain, but I got a big walk, and ought to be better for it for days.

March 14, 1898

My outdoor and bird papers could only have been written by a countryman and a dweller in the country. But probably my literary criticism and essays suffer from this very cause. They should have been written by a dweller in cities, a mover among the throngs of books and men. This would have helped to give them snap, decision, brevity, point. The intellect, the judgment, are sharpened in the city; the heart, the emotions, the intuitions, the religious sense, are fostered in the country. (Is this true?)

March 18

Hazel-nuts in bloom two days ago — a great display of masculinity, and a feeble display of femininity. How modest and shy, as it were, all female blossoms are! — the hazel, the hickory, the alder, the oak, the butternut.

The fields and open spaces have a sudden new attraction. My thoughts go and scratch with the hens amid the dry leaves; I pick up as much as they do; they nip the short new spears of grass with the geese; they follow the migrating ducks northward; they hover about the farm and garden fires; they career away to the sugar-maple woods, where the sap is making music in the tin buckets. I have trouble to keep them here at my prosy tasks.

April 3

We shall probably have to class Henry George with the men of one idea — or men with a hobby. It is to me evidence of how narrow and limited his judgment was that he should have believed that there was a panacea for the ills of modern society — that he should have thought the disease so simple that the remedy could be named for it, and was within easy reach; or that he should have thought it a disease at all, instead of a crudeness, an immaturity. Go in the woods, in the fields, anywhere, and you see the same struggle, the same 'injustice' — the strong oppressing the weak — failure, defeat, starvation, imperfection. It is the law of Nature, and is as operative in societies as among plants and animals. There are two ways to abolish poverty: abolish inequalities of talents and opportunity, or run society on the plan of a hospital, or poor-house, or penitentiary — regulate everything, and see to it that all share and share alike.

July 3

Very hot, 100° at Slabsides, from 12 o'clock till 4. Dry air, like the breath of a furnace. The hottest day I have ever seen here. Our boys in Cuba fighting in much greater heat. My thoughts run that way constantly.

July 19

A nest of young robins in the maple in front being fed by a chipping sparrow. The little sparrow is very attentive — seems very fond of her adopted babies. The old robins resent her services, and hustle her out of the tree whenever they find her near the nest. She watches her chance and comes with food in their absence. The young birds are about ready to fly, and when the chippie feeds them, her head fairly disappears in their capacious mouths. She jerks it back as if she were afraid of being swallowed. Then she lingers near them on the edge of the nest and seems to admire them. When she sees the old robin coming, she spreads her wings in an attitude of defence and then flies away. I wonder if she has had the experience of raising a cow-bunting.

Aug. 10

There is no such thing as chance in the world. All events are determined by law. But with reference to my will and purpose there is chance. If I cast a stone in the dark, so far as my will is concerned it is a matter of chance where it strikes. I may chance to be on a train when there is a smash-up; inexorable law controls the event, and brought me there, but, to my will and conscious purpose, it is a matter of chance. Where the seed borne by yonder floating thistle-down will fall is not a matter of chance. If we could see all the forces that act upon it, and will act upon it, we could tell accurately where it will lodge. What seems chance to us is the result of our ignorance and impotence — our incomplete knowledge.

Aug. 20

No echo of the War in my Journal, yet what an absorbed spectator of it I have been, and, now that it is ended, I feel a great strain taken off me. I no longer rush for the newspaper in the morning, nor tarry impatiently at the station for it at night. I shared the popular feeling about it, and wanted to see Spain kicked out of the Western hemisphere. The Spanish blight and mildew have rested upon those fair islands long enough. If the races there are not worthy of liberty and self-government, we will put a race there that is. What a brilliant spot the War has made in our recent humdrum history! Out of a corrupt Mammonish time emerge these heroes, plenty of them, vying with one another, courting Death as a bride. How their example has electrified the whole country! has fused us and made us more completely one! It makes us realize that we are a country; it has begotten an enthusiasm of nationality; henceforth we are a worthier, nobler people. This heroism at Santiago is enough to leaven the whole lump.

Oh, War! so cruel, so mad, so destructive, yet how can
a nation be knitted and compacted and expanded with
thee? It is like the heat that helps make iron into steel.
It transforms the baser metals. So selfish, and yet so
unselfish! It is the plow and harrow of God. It tears and
destroys, yet a quicker and fuller life follows. A battle
between men is brutal; a battle between nations is often
divine — not from the personal point of view, but from
the point of view of history. Spain will ultimately be
better for this War, as well as this country.

Sept. 20

Julian starts for Harvard again to-day. Again I wheel
his trunk over to the station, filled with the old sad
thoughts and retrospections. He is not very well and this,
too, troubles me. How well it is that children think less of
their parents than parents of their children! If it were
not so, sons and daughters would never leave home;
families would never break up and scatter, as Nature
meant they should. The old cry to the young, 'Oh, do
not leave me!' But the young are full of hope and courage, and the future, not the past, sways them. Not until
they have become parents themselves, and tasted the
pathos of life, do children know how their parents suffer.

Nov. 1

I spend part of the day at Slabsides, trying to write, the
thought of Nip constantly hovering about my mind.
Men of my temperament make much of their griefs. It is
another form of our self-indulgence. We roll the bitter
morsel under our tongues and extract the last drop of bit-

terness. It is probable that I make the death of Nip the occasion to gloat over the past, and that which can never return. This is my disease; it is in my system, and the loss of the dog brings it out afresh. It gives it an acute form. But I was deeply attached to him, and the thought of him will always be precious to me.

Nov. 2

Of all the domestic animals none calls forth so much love, solicitude, and sorrow as the dog. He occupies the middle place between the other animals and man. Our love for him is below that for our fellows, and above that we have for any other dumb creature. How many men there are now in the world, millions of them, whose love for their dogs is next to that they have for their friends and families! and their grief at their loss, next to a domestic bereavement!

Nov. 25

Go to Boston in P.M. to hear Zangwill — a discourse full of point, wit, and sense. A hatchet-faced man with hair that suggests a wig; it seems to sit upon his head, rather than to grow out of it. Voice not big or strong, but agreeable. One of the coming leaders in literature.

Dec. 30

Yesterday lunched with Scudder and met Higginson. H. was very agreeable and complimentary — a fine, scholarly, accomplished talker and diner-out; looks ruddy and well, though his voice begins to show his seventy-five years.

Jan. 5, 1899

We go to Salem. I stand for some time on Gallows Hill, where the 'witches' were hung, among them an ancestor of mine, Rev. George Burroughs, over 200 years ago. A typical New England landscape, barren and rugged, low broken rocky waves [?] with a ragged covering of turf — a body of rock with a tattered covering of soil. Nothing to mark the site of the hanging. If I had the means I would put up a monument there.

March 1

Unless you can write about Nature with feeling, with real love, with more or less hearty affiliation and comradeship with her, it is no use. Your words will not stick. They will awaken no response in the reader. There are two or three writers now making books upon outdoor themes that I find I cannot read. The page has no savor; it is dry and tasteless. The writers have taken up these nature themes deliberately, as they might any other; they have no special call to write upon them. I have tried hard to be interested in Gibson's work, but I cannot. It lacks juice, unction. There is feeling in his drawings, but not in his text. Bradford Torrey is the only nature writer at the present time whose work I can read.

March 12

Reading Lockhart's 'Life of Scott.' Read Scott's Journals while in Poughkeepsie in February. A prodigious man; prodigious worker, player, eater, drinker (on occasion). Copious, fluent, abounding in all good feelings and instincts. He wanted a great deal of everything —

money, friends, retainers, land, dogs. He was a prodigal nature — prodigal of himself, of his time, of his means. Lived his life fast and under pressure, and was used up at sixty. Not fine, or delicate—dull of nose, obtuse of palate, heavy of ear — but all but inexhaustible. He has no style, or, rather, his style is that of the great average mass of mankind — ready, fluent, transparent, but nothing in and of itself; lacks individuality and delicacy. Nothing is felicitously said; but all is well said. The words have no aroma; there is no intellectual pressure; none of that kind of heat and intensity that turns carbon into the diamond. No suggestiveness; no phrase that lingers on the tongue. Akin to Southey, but greater by far. The finest, best work can never be done with such rapidity — some of his novels written in six weeks! 'The Bride of Lammermoor' written during great and acute bodily pain. A wholesale writer. One has no purely literary or artistic pleasure in reading him, but the pleasure of companionship, of health, of a flow of animal spirits, of content with a copious brotherly nature. What saves him from oblivion, then, and makes each succeeding generation turn to him for entertainment? Is it his humanity, his atmosphere, his geniality, and a kind of perennial youth in him — the same as in Homer? He does not savor of art, but of life. He was so canny, so copious, so ardent — a world by himself. He does not appeal to a select circle, but to a great multitude. He has great magnetism, and the kind of attraction that great bodies always have.

April 10

Since last November I have finished and written the following pieces:

$100 'The Vital Touch in Literature' (Atlantic)
  75 'Recent Phases of Literary Criticism' (N.A. Review)
  25 'Nature with Closed Doors' (Breeder's Gazette)
  25 'Nature Study' (Outlook)
  50 'Winter Bird Life' (Youth's Companion)
  80 'Bird Talk' (St. Nicholas)
175 'Wild Life Around My Cabin' (Century)
  80 'Criticism and the Man' (Atlantic)
125 'Literary Values' (Century)
150 'The Art of Seeing Things' (on hand)
  25 'A Walk in the Fields' (The Independent)
  75 'Thou Shalt Not Preach' (on hand)
——
985

April 11

Brilliant day, not a cloud in the sky till sundown. I walk to Black Pond and get Travis's boat; enjoy the walk through the fields and woods in the strong sunlight. Enjoy drinking at the springs by the path in the woods. How beautiful to get at the fountain-head of anything; to see the beginnings! I wish I might always drink direct from the spring. Such a drink is relished by something more than the tongue. My whole mind drinks. To stoop down, or lie down, and draw a life-giving draught directly from the earth — how satisfying!

April 19

Perfect day. A slight veil of smoke and vapor. With my glass I see the farmers plowing all about. We start the plow in the vineyard. Burn brush all forenoon. To Slabsides, to plant peas, in afternoon. Dick's man Charley sowing onions. Amasa planting celery.

May 23

Join the Harriman expedition to Alaska to-day in New York. Pass my place on the Hudson at 4 P.M. Look long and fondly from car window upon the scenes I am to be absent from till August. The sun is shining warmly. I see the new green of the vineyards. Wife is waving her white apron from the summer-house. I sit alone in my room in the Pullman car and am sad. Have I made a mistake in joining this crowd for so long a trip? Can I see nature under such conditions? But I am in for it.

May 26

Here this chronicler, with Dr. Morris, took a ride on the front of the engine from Harper to Amara, twenty-five miles; a bit of experience not soon to be forgotten. We strike two birds — shore larks — and frighten a big hawk till he drops his prey — a prairie dog, I think. For hours we seem approaching the Elk Mountains, which stand up sharp and white against the horizon. Our approach is very circuitous and cautious. At many points the velvet carpet holds little patches of snow; they lie in the wrinkles and folds of the slopes.

On the whole, nature here, along the crest of the Rockies, looks much more genial and friendly than one expects to see it. The face of the plains in Wyoming looks like our Eastern meadows in fall — the light gray of the stubble with a tinge of green beneath. All the lines are gentle, all the tints are soft. They look as if they must have fattened innumerable herds. Probably the buffaloes, grazing there for centuries, have left their mark upon them. They are almost as gentle and muttony in places as the South Downs of England.

Aug. 9

Returned from the Alaskan trip to-day, in much better condition in every way, in both body and mind, than when I left. Two months upon the sea — June–July 30.

I have written up my impressions from day to day in the Harriman Book, and in the three poems.

What joy to be back again and once more at my ease! No news from home till I reached Portland, August 1. All is well. Fine crop of grapes, and vineyards in good shape.

Dec. 14

To be remembered in art or literature, or in almost anything else, you must do something unique, that no one else could do. The secret of your power lies in the breadth of your relation to mankind and to common nature; in the richness and fullness of your human endowment; but immortality is the result of something above and beyond all this, something which is your own, and must suffuse and color and shape all the rest. The universal and the special, the general and the particular, must be blended and harmonized.

Jan. 1, 1900

Good-bye, 1800 and all thy progeny. We have grown old together; thy end has come, but I stay a little longer. I have looked upon thy face all my life. My father looked upon it all his life, my grandfather more than half of his. Now the door is shut and we shall see thee no more. Welcome to thy successor! But he is a stranger, a newcomer, and it is hard for the old to make new friends; we become acquainted, but not wedded. The new days can never be to us what the old were. In youth the days become part of us; they mingle with our blood; they take on the very color of our souls. But in age they hardly touch us; they come and go like strangers.

Jan. 8

Over in the woods by the roadside I stopped to observe a flock of crossbills. They came down to drink through holes in the ice on a little pool by the roadside. They were quite tame. All did not come down at once, but took turns, while the others sat on the trees and bushes and kept a sharp lookout. They were going and coming for some minutes, only seven or eight being on the ice at one time. It is at such times that a hawk would like to surprise them, and they seem to know it, and are very alert. What a pretty patch they made there — mingled red, white, and drab — upon the leaves and ice! One of their call-notes was very liquid and sweet; another reminds of the goldfinch. I have seen and heard flocks of them every day since October. Almost every hour in my walks I see or hear them. Never saw such numbers before.

Jan. 11

Literature may be defined as that which we read for its own sake. That which we read for the sake of something else — knowledge, science, fact — may or may not be literature. We read a poem, a novel, an essay by Lamb, or Stevenson, or Thoreau, a work by Renan or Carlyle — for its own sake, or for the sake of the personality behind it. I read a criticism by Arnold or Scherer or Sainte-

Beuve, not because I want his judgment upon the work
in hand so much as I want him, his spirit, his point of
view, his kindling and illuminating touch.

Every writer of genius expresses a truth of his own, because he sees things from a particular, individual point of
view. We can make his truth ours only so far as our point
of view coincides with his. Of course this is not so in
science or mathematics, but it is so in esthetics. There are
no canons of criticism that can be passed from hand to
hand, and that I can use as well as you. Criticism is the
application, not of rules, but of mind to mind. It is an
art as much as any other branch of literature. Truth is
always the aim — the truth of style, of sentiment, of
spirit; the truth as seen by a free and vital mind.

Jan. 19

In my walk in the woods saw where a small flock of
quail had passed, six of them. They crossed over from
Brookman's swamp to mine. What a pretty trail they
made in the thin snow! In places where the woods were
densest, they seemed to huddle close together like scared
children. I could almost fancy them taking hold of
hands — real babes in the woods. How alert and watch-
ful they have been! Owls, foxes, minks, cats, hunters —
all had to be looked out for. In the more open places they
scattered more, no doubt looking for food. In the fall
there were twelve or fifteen of them, now only six.

Jan. 29

The British reverses in South Africa make me gloomy.
I am more than willing that British arrogance and super-

ciliousness should get a good slap, but my final interest
is in the higher type of civilization and the better race.
The Boer was a Boer 200 years ago, and he is a Boer still;
he will never be anything else. He is a kind of human
woodchuck. He fights well; so will a woodchuck; there is
no fear in his prototype of the fields.

Jan. 30

I suppose that one reason why, during my Alaskan trip,
there was all the time an undercurrent of protest and dis-
satisfaction, is the fact that I have passed from the positive to the negative side of life, when we begin to take in
sail; when we want less and not more; when the hunger
for new scenes and new worlds to conquer is diminishing;
when the inclination not to stir beyond one's own chimney
corner is fast growing upon us. The positive side of life
lasts till fifty or sixty — differs in different men; then
there is a neutral belt, when we don't care whether we
go or not; then the ground begins to slope the other way,
and we begin the great retreat.

Feb. 14

Staying at Slabsides, blessed Slabsides! Thank the
Lord! a house of refuge.... Here I am safe. How sweet,
how peaceful! a homeless cat has sought refuge here, too.
We are good friends. She sits on my lap and purrs so
contentedly, and gets under my feet when I do my
housework.

April 11

The crow blackbirds are again assembling at night in
my spruces by the house. Every spring they do this, and

after a few weeks disappear. Their notes make one want
to blow his nose and clear his throat. Of all bird voices,
theirs is the most wheezy, rasping, catarrhal, asthmatic
— voices half-obliterated by an influenza. How dry and
husky their throats must be! I wish they would grease
their whistles. Besides their call-notes, they have a kind
of rude, splintering, rasping warble or whistle, which
they evidently mean for music.

April 17

Sat here last night and read Emerson's oration on
Literary Ethics, delivered when I was one year and five
months old, and first read by me in 1857. I bought the
volume containing it and the essays in Chicago, in the
spring of that year. All that summer, while at the Old
Home, I lived on those volumes. I steeped myself in
them. After all these years of life and thought, I still find
pleasure in this oration, and in the others. I see, I think,
how it all must sound to the trained European man of letters — a little futile, a little provincial and American —
the gospel of Individualism and self-reliance, the brag,
the crowing over the present, and so on; it is all rather
intemperate and unclassical. It is by a man trained as a
New England clergyman, and not as a man of letters. Its
crudeness belongs to a crude people, and its courage and
inspiration to a young people. The quiet, restrained
moral buncombe of Emerson is one of his leading traits.

April 19

Warm and humid this morning with breaking skies.
A typical moist April morning; warmth and humidity

reign. Sit for some time in my summer-house. A meadowlark, on the top of the sugar maple over my head, gives
forth her clear, piercing, memory-stirring note; then a
highhole strikes up under the hill — a call to all things to
awake and be stirring. He flies from point to point and
repeats his call that all may hear. It is not a song, but
a summons and declaration. It is a voice out of the heart
of April — not a sweet voice, but, oh, such a suggestive
and pleasing one! It means so much; it means the new
furrow, and the seed, and the first planting; it means the
springing grass and the early flowers, the budding trees,
and the chorus in the marshes. It is warm and moist with
the breath of Middle April. '*Wick, wick, wick, wick, wick,*'
he says. Come, be up and doing! Air your house, burn
up your rubbish, scatter your compost, start your plow!
The soft maples are blooming; the bees are humming; the
robins are nesting; the chickadees are hatching; the ants
are stirring; and I am here to call the hour. '*Wick, wick,
wick, wick, wick, wick, wick, wick!*' Then the bush sparrow
sang her plaintive, delicious strain beyond the currant-
patch, while the robins laughed and *tee-heed* all about.
Oh, April! month of my heart!

The soil never looks so inviting as in April; one could
almost eat it; it is the staff of life; it lusts for the seed.
Later one wants it covered with verdure and protected
from the too fierce sun. Now his rays seem to vivify it;
by and by they will bake it. Go and dig up some horse-
radish now, and bring in some crisp spinach, and the
sweet and melting roots of the parsnips. Let us taste
the flavor of the soil once more — the pungent, the crisp,
and the sugary. Beware of the angle-worms this morning

as you walk in the yard and on the roadside; they are crawling abroad now. Beware of the newts, too, where they cross the road from the woods to the marshes — you may tread on them.

In the twilight now the long-drawn trill of the toad may be heard — *tr-r-r-r-r-r-r-r* — a long row of vocal dots on the dusky page of the twilight. It is one of the soothing, quieting sounds, a chain of bubbles, like its chain of eggs; a bell reduced to an even, quiet monotone. They are the only jewels she has about her, these jewels of sound. [See 'The Song of the Toad,' 'Bird and Bough.']

Aug. 21 [Ampersand Creek, Franklin County]

Here I stay till the last day of August with real enjoyment. A jolly lot of people, mostly graduates of Cornell. I fish and tramp and loaf. On Sunday we climb Mt. Seward, a hard climb, but a grand view; six women and ten or a dozen men. I stand it well. I gain in hardiness every day, and can make long tramps without much fatigue. Spend a day and night at Ampersand Lake — unforgettable; the gem of all the Adirondack lakes. . . . Maybe some day I can write it all up as an illustration of the pluck and hardiness of the New Woman. She could tramp and climb with the best of us.

Oct. 17

A grand meteor between eight and nine: a light suddenly came in my window [at Slabsides] like that of the full moon, followed, in less than a minute, by a deep rumbling like that of thunder; the rumbling lasts half a minute and dies away in the distance. Booth and Lown did not see the flash of the meteor, but heard the report and went out to see what it was. Others saw the meteor and heard the thunder. There can be no doubt but that the meteor caused the sound. Its course was north in the western heavens.

Oct. 21

Hiram leaves me again in afternoon. I watch him through a crack in the door till he disappears behind the bushes, and say to myself, 'We may never meet again.' A little nubbin of a man, with a very small mental horizon, but very dear to me. He has been with me at intervals since the 6th. Almost every moment while in the house, he was drumming with his fingers on his chair, or the table, and whistling a low tune to himself, in a sort of brown study. His drumming and whistling became quite a nuisance at times.

Oct. 26

Just found a hibernating mouse here where the men were working on the road. Van dug him out of the bank. He was cold and motionless. I brought him to the house in my pocket, and made a nest for him in a tin bucket upstairs. He had nearly come to — was warm and had his eyes open — when I put him in the nest.

Oct. 27

My mouse was active all night trying to get out of his prison. He disturbed my sleep. During the day he has been very quiet, deeply hidden under the rags in his prison-house.

Later. Concluded to liberate the mouse. He scampered away very briskly and hid beneath a rock. It keeps so warm he can easily make another nest and begin his winter's sleep again.

Nov. 10

Of course Higginson cannot endure Whitman. Higginson is essentially aristocratic; he tends to the elegant, the polished, the refined; he aspires to the scholarly, the witty, the distinguished; while in Whitman there is something rankly common, like freckles and sweat; he is democratic through and through; he makes no account of the social and elegant ideas; he is larger than they, and includes them.

A relative in Chicago writes me that she attended a Presbyterian church the other Sunday and heard a sermon on love, and that the human illustration of it used was myself. How curious! a hater of churches [1] and rarely seen within their walls, yet illustrating their doctrine of love! Well, no doubt love *is* my ruling emotion — love and longing. How I have loved the birds, the fields, the woods, the Old Home, Father and Mother, and all my days! Out of this love I have written my books, out of this love and joy in Nature.

---

[1] This gives a wrong impression: he means he is one who does not frequent churches and is, if a hater of anything, a hater of their dogmas.

1901-1913

[In Cambridge, Massachusetts, the Diarist begins the new century by finishing a poem on the bluebird, and by taking a long walk with Dr. Samuel Cleghorn. The keen pleasure he had in meeting him, and Dr. James, Professor Shaler, and many another of that group, was not the least of the pleasure he derived from his son's student life at Harvard.

The productiveness of Burroughs's later years is attested by the steadiness and rapidity with which he put forth his later books — 'Literary Values' and 'The Life of Audubon' in 1902, 'Far and Near' in 1904, 'Ways of Nature' in 1905, 'Bird and Bough' in 1906, 'Camping and Tramping with Roosevelt' in 1907, 'Leaf and Tendril' in 1908, 'Time and Change' in 1912, and 'The Summit of the Years' in 1913. That there was no abatement in his joy in the universe, or in the quality of his literary work, these books abundantly prove.

Early in this period he was called to mourn the death of his favorite sister, Abigail, and his favorite brother, Hiram, and also that of Myron B. Benton, his close friend for forty years.

Many flittings and some momentous journeyings marked these years — brief sojourns in Jamaica and Bermuda, several winters in the South, and two in California. Out of the trip to Jamaica grew his essay 'A Lost February' in 'Far and Near.'

One of the outstanding events of this period was the

appearance of his essay 'Real and Sham Natural History,'
in the 'Atlantic Monthly,' March, 1903. Its immediate
effect was to bring him an invitation from President
Roosevelt to accompany him into Yellowstone Park the
following April, but subsequent and most significant effects were seen in the controversy started among nature
writers, which raged for several years, a controversy
which was, on the whole, productive of much good. Many
essays by Burroughs which were the outgrowth of these
and allied questions are found in 'Ways of Nature' and
'Leaf and Tendril.'

'Camping and Tramping with Roosevelt' grew out of
the Yellowstone experience and other outings with the
President. Visits of the President and Mrs. Roosevelt to
Slabsides, and of 'Oom John' to Oyster Bay and to the
White House and to Pine Knot, Virginia, were pleasant
echoes of it also.

In 1908 Burroughs went back to his native hills, where,
in an abandoned farmhouse on the homestead farm, he
established a summer home, which he named Woodchuck
Lodge. Henceforth he spent less and less time at Slabsides. There amid the old scenes, a half-mile from his
birthplace, the remaining summers of his life were happily
spent. Most of the essays which came from his pen there-
after were written at his Haybarn Study, up the road from
the Lodge, or in Bush Camp under the near-by apple
trees.

For three memorable months in 1909, John Burroughs
and John Muir, with others in the party, traveled in the
Southwest and Far West, seeing the wonders of the Petrified Forests, the Grand Canyon, and Yosemite Valley.

Later the Burroughs party went to Hawaii. Essays in 'Time and Change' grew out of these happy journeyings.

The shadows deepened around Burroughs again in 1909 with the death of his long-time friend Richard Watson Gilder, and of his sister Jane and brother Curtis, and, in 1913, that of Francis Fisher Browne.

Three universities — Yale, Colgate, and the University of Georgia — conferred honorary degrees upon him, which he accepted rather reluctantly. Reluctantly also he posed to many artists and a few sculptors during these years, the most noteworthy results being paintings by Orlando Rouland, and Mathilde de Cordoba, and a bust, two statuettes, and an heroic sitting statue by C. S. Pietro.

A memorable event for Burroughs, after having steeped himself for years in Henri Bergson's 'Creative Evolution,' was the meeting with M. Bergson in 1913 and hearing him lecture. His essay 'A Prophet of the Soul' reflects his admiration for M. Bergson and his work.

A stimulating and helpful friendship developed between Burroughs and Mr. Henry Ford in 1913, and Burroughs celebrated his seventy-sixth year by learning to drive a Ford car, not without many hair-breadth escapes which he humorously records in his Journal.

He rounded out this eventful period of his life by the publication of one of the books his readers could least spare, 'The Summit of the Years.']

Cambridge, Mass., Jan. 1, 1901

Finish Bluebird poem in morning. Lunch with Dr. Cleghorn. We walk to Boston and back. A good start on the new century.

March 23

In the morning a meadowlark alighted on the top of the maple over my Study, and sent forth, again and again, his wonderful spring call. In the forenoon I worked on 'The Life of Audubon,' and in the afternoon boiled sap — six pails. The best sap day yet. The white gulls go up the river, their images reflected in the water beneath them.

April 24

The pretty musical festival of the goldfinches continues this morning in the rain. The air is filled with a fine spray of bird-notes. The finches have held their reunions there in the same trees for several springs. Many of the males already have their summer plumage. No other bird has so pretty a way of matchmaking. Where others fight and scratch, the goldfinches apparently all join in singing one another's praises.

May 12

The matchless old blue sky again from the west — the gift of a high barometer. The peculiar blue of the sky, a translucent blue — not the color of *something*, but of empty space — an unfading, immortal blue. As Homer and the prophets saw it, we see it to-day.

May 16

Days of great freshness and beauty. A sort of luminous greenness everywhere; the young leaves seem to let the light through them — a green transparency. The youth of Nature, when we almost see the blood in her veins, her integument is yet so delicate and thin.

May 27

How one's mind has its beat, a sort of round of thought, as a bird its particular range of trees and field where it spends most of its time — its *habitat*. The things upon which my own mind dwells most, of late years, are, first, the Old Home and Father and Mother, and all that past of my youth — not a day, or hardly an hour, that something does not send my mind back there; then the Nature about me; then Julian; then literature; then women; then death — more and more I think of death, and how incredible it is that I must really exchange this fair world for the silence and darkness of the grave; then of the mystery of the universe. I think often of Walt, and all that Washington life. I still dream, at times, of being a clerk in the Treasury, and also of teaching school. I think but rarely of politics, and of the great blundering world.

July 9

During the great heat of last week unfledged birds leaped from their nests in desperation.

July 10

Warm, tranquil summer days. The yellow butterflies dance and zigzag along the road before you; the call of the quail comes up from the fields; the meadow lilies ring their colored chimes above the grass; the bird-songs, grown a little languid, still fill the morning air; the landscape dreams under a soft, shining, milky haze.

July 26

A hermit thrush singing divinely this morning in the clover-lot woods, apparently for his own edification. His

young must certainly have flown long ago. A true poet,
he. Most birds sing for mate and young, and cease when
these are grown, or before. This is true of the nightingale.
But the hermit sings for the song's sake.

Aug. 4

August notes:
The teasel head with its band or zone of bloom,
Vervain with its creeping plume,
The spreading burdock shows its hundred brown and
    purple heads above the fences,
The crimson cap of the bee-balm (*Monarda*) above the
    ranks of bushy weeds,
The urn of the thistles afoam with purple bloom,
Every morning the evening primrose renews its canary
    yellow above its purple stalk,
The clematis begins to hang its white wreaths upon the
    wayside bushes,
The stubbly meadows are touched again with green.

Aug. 6

Go to Abigail's to dinner with Curtis and Ann. In the
afternoon a tall, gray-bearded man of gentle manners appears at the door and asks for me. I know him at a glance,
— James Oliver, my old teacher of fifty years ago. We
had not met in all that time, but had corresponded, and he
had sent me his picture a few years ago. Greatly pleased
to see him and his son and daughter, who were with him.
He lives in Kansas. He seemed hale and vigorous, though
near eighty. I was not one of his favorite scholars; I was
eclipsed by Jay Gould, and Andrew Corbin, and others;

and his appreciation now was very pleasing. My old master had at last said, 'Well done!' He was the best teacher my youth ever knew.

Aug. 20

Elbert Hubbard here yesterday. Looks like a man of genius, with his intense black eyes and long hair and smooth face — a little too intent, probably, to look thus. Called me 'John' and 'brother.' I like him.

Oct. 1, 7 A.M.

After breakfast, burdened with the thought of sister Abigail's death, I walk out the road and over the hill. Still, clear, cool, a resonant October morning. Fog in the valley, creeping up toward the heights. Every sound very distinct to the ear, as objects are to the eye in the Far West. The rumble of a wagon comes across the mountain from the head of Hardscrabble. The caws of the crows almost echo as if in a great hollow dome. Up in the clover-lot woods I hear one uttering that loud, peculiar, authoritative caw. Chipmunks chipping and clucking in the Deacon woods as I knew [them] in my youth. The air streaked with the plaintive autumnal calls of wandering bluebirds. I count twelve in one loose flock. The fine threads of flying spiders glisten upon the road and stream from the tops of bushes by the wayside. They show the direction of the currents of air. The woods all touched with the flames of autumn — many maples all ablaze — yellow, orange, crimson, and green paint the mountains. A thin blue mist or haze over the hills. Nuthatches and jays calling in the woods.

[Only those who realize his brooding cast of mind, and his instinctive going to Nature at all times, but especially in his sorrow, can approach an understanding of the above. There, three miles away, lay his best-loved sister, dead. In the night, when the summons had come that she was dying, he did not respond. He does not say why. On the face of it, it looks unfeeling. Was it a kind of self-protection? He knew himself so well. It was not the physical exertion of getting up and going down across the hills the three miles to the village, in the darkness — it was the dread of the emotional strain of going there and seeing his sister breathe her last. He was not equal to it. And on this morning, a day later, probably while waiting till the farm chores were done, and he and his brother could drive down to the village, he sought the hills, he scrutinized the face of the day; he let no sound or sight escape him. And he even wrote it down! Yes, he went to Nature as another might seek consolation in prayer. His sister gone, but in the midst of these evanescent sights and sounds of this never-to-be-forgotten day, he is actuated by the desire we so often see in him — to catch and keep what of it he can. In the midst of impermanence he will seize and preserve the day; and ever after it will be blended in his soul with thoughts of the sister who is gone. Always, in any of the significant moments of his life, when his heart is deeply stirred by joy or grief, blended inextricably with memory of it all, is the particular phase which Nature, at such times, showed to him. He was more with Abigail on the hillside, and, later in the day, on Old Clump, far more, than he would have been sitting around in the silent house, with neighbors and relatives coming and going and speaking in subdued tones.]

Oct. 2

I grieve less than I should. I grieve because I cannot grieve more. Why am I so insensible? Abigail was very dear to me, and yet my eyes are dry.

Oct. 15

Now is the time of the illuminated woods; they have a sense of sunshine, even on a cloudy day, given by the yellow foliage; every leaf glows like a tiny lamp; one walks through their lighted halls with a curious enjoyment.

Oct. 30

The sun came up red as blood this morning — a dense veil of white vapor over all. Here and there a maple still turns a flushed cheek to the sun. The leaves of the dogwood are red and ripe like Japanese plums. The light comes through certain oaks, as through red stained glass.

Jan. 11, 1902

One thing Nature — God — seems utterly regardless of — pain and suffering. In many ways they help forward her scheme, but she has made no effort to confine them, or to limit them in this respect. She has let them go at loose ends and grow like tares in the wheat. Her plans are forwarded by some of the pain — no matter about the rest, let it spread.

The needless suffering that attends childbirth, for instance — no utility in that. My poor cat, Silly Sally, got blind as she got old, and would have died of starvation had we not put an end to her life. What suffering the poor thing would have undergone! Most of the wild creatures that die a natural death probably undergo great suffering. Think of the sum total of physical suffering in the world at a given time that subserves no good!

Nature has taken pains to bestow pleasure where her interests are at stake, as in the propagation of the species, in taking food, etc., but she has made no effort to eliminate useless pain. Indeed, the universe is not run upon any system of economy that man can conceive of. Waste, suffering, delay, defeat, failure — all make up the whole. I can see no intelligence, or love, akin to our own, at work in the universe. Yet where did man's love and intelligence come from? He, too, is a part of Nature.

March 5

My last day by the purple seas of Jamaica. Hot, a light breeze, a few lazy clouds, the cocoanut spears rattling and quivering like quills. Every day and every day the same, except slight changes in the course and force of the wind. Yesterday a little squall stalked along over the sea. . . . Rainbow seas on one side, emerald seas on the other. The mountains with great cloud-shadows on their sides, and clouds dragging across their tops.

April 12

A curious phenomenon in the afternoon: the air filled with a thick, white haze; the clouds all seemed to dissolve and come down; then there was a sprinkle of muddy water; it soiled clothes on the line, and fouled the window-panes; the sediment it left looked like cement. Was it meteoric dust? It seemed to affect the whole body of the air.

May 12

Hiram was found dead in his bed [in the morning]. He did not get up when called, and when Eden went to his room, he lay dead. Apparently he had not stirred since he lay down at night. He had been around on Sunday, had eaten as usual, and at nine had taken his lamp and gone to bed, and there his journey in the world had ended. . . . I found it impossible to sleep that night more than two or three hours. I was in a strange excitement. My Hiram, my boy Hiram! as I so often called him, was gone — the dearest one of the family to me, and how could I compose myself to sleep in the room above his dead body? . . . Oh, the calmness and repose of death! I can no longer keep back my tears. Oh, if I had only done more for him; if I could only have another chance!

May 14

Hiram played a larger part in my life than any of the rest of the family. He was the one brother who always stuck to me, came to see me wherever I was, and wrote me regularly. He brought to me the Old Home, Father and Mother, and my youth on the old farm more than all the others. He had no intellect or judgment; was a mere child in many things; never read one of my books; but I loved him all the same. He had all my infirmities and little of my strength; he was a dreamer, an idealist; but he had no firm grip upon real life — was one of those men who are always crowded to the wall in the scramble of the world — no push or self-assertion in him.

We have camped and tramped together; we slept together as boys, and we have lived together as old men. He was the first-born, and, in the Old Home, stood next to Father. The work of his hands shows all over the old farm — in the walls that he laid, in trees and orchards he planted, in the buildings he helped erect. He was always handy with tools; he made the sleds, the stone-boats, the hay-rigging, the churning-machine; he made garden, and grafted the apple trees; he loaded and pitched off all the hay for near forty years, and built all the stacks; he drilled and blasted the rocks when I was a boy; he made sugar, and always headed up the butter in the fall; he cut and salted the pork, and did a hundred other things in the old days on the farm. . . . His death greatly enhances the burden of the past to me. It makes it all bleed afresh. It is like losing Father and Mother over again.

June 8

The bobolink seems the least rustic of our song-birds. There is something almost metropolitan about him. The tone, the quality of his voice, is like that of a great orator, its articulation is so clear and vibrant. His dress and manner, too, are not a bit rustic or rural. His voice has the polish and distinction of the town. All the field and meadow birds and ground-builders are inconspicuous in their colors — male and female alike — except the bobolink. His presence in the meadow seems accidental and capricious.

June 19

I think Browning has more ardent women readers than men. At least this is my observation. His bounce and vigor and rigid muscles seem to complement the women. They like this rubbing and chafing. He stimulates and excites them. Never a soft or feminine line in him, but a kind of procreant thrust and pressure. Tennyson is much more flowing and melodious, at least in his art, and is less passionately liked by women.

July 13

The boiling cauldron of the woods is afoam here and there with the chestnut bloom. In the meadows the orange lilies hang their bells. What secret have they that they hide so carefully from the sun and sky?

July 24

This summer will be remembered all over the country for its unprecedented downpours, from the Rocky Mountains to New England, and from Texas to Canada. A regular drunken debauch of the rain-gods.

Aug. 11

Some of my pole beans refuse to climb, and go grovelling about the ground, embracing weeds, and coming to naught. About one in ten are failures. There are some degenerates in every family.

Aug. 25

At Keene Valley [son's wedding]. Ceremony at three in little rustic chapel trimmed with ferns, mountain-ash berries, maple branches, etc. Emily's grandfather (eighty to-morrow) officiating — a pretty and affecting sight. With what long sad thoughts I witnessed it all! Age and youth, face to face, under such significant conditions — the evening greeting and encouraging the morning, the fall congratulating the spring. My father and mother were married over seventy-five years ago; I was married over forty-five years ago; and now Julian and Emily begin the same journey together.

Oct. 3

As soon as we have invented a word for a thing, then that thing seems to come forth and take shape and to have a reality. The soul, the reason, the fancy, the imagination — how these words seem to separate and fix these things! Are we in many things the victims of our words? No sooner do I hear the term 'subconscious self' than I see this under-self as distinct from the *I* as the cellar to a house, or the strata under the hills!

Nov. 6

Why do women seem to put on good looks with good clothes? Dressing her up certainly has a more marked effect upon her face than it does on a man. She lives in her clothes more than a man does — thinks more about them; and a new suit often makes a plain face look beautiful. It kindles the soul behind it.

Nov. 25

News of the death of Myron Benton this morning, my oldest and best friend among men. Friends and correspondents since '62. I dreamed vividly of him night before last — was with him somewhere; his cheeks were flushed, but he looked feeble. Before getting up this morning I planned a letter to him. Then came word of his death, yesterday A.M.

He was one of the few farmers of real culture—a man of fine literary taste, but a born countryman and lover of the soil. Tall, quiet, canny, lingering over the flavor of things, dwelling upon the quaint, the beautiful, the picturesque, fervently attached to his old home, always adding something to its beauty — a man with the virtues and charm of rural things, keeping their traditions and legends, making much of them; lover of the old poets and dramatists; a man with an atmosphere — gentle, genial, mellow, unobtrusive; his own native, meandering Webutuk in human form. I shall see him no more. Farewell, my beloved Myron! How often we have wrestled with the great problems together, all but breaking our teeth upon them in vain! His faith in immortality was stronger than mine. May he find it well-founded! The last letter Thoreau ever wrote was to him.

Dec. 31

Lovely winter days. Universally well this winter — nothing tires me, neither writing, walking, nor sawing and splitting wood. Have written more the past six weeks than ever before in same length of time.

Jan. 28, 1903

I see that Higginson, in his Lowell Institute lectures, continues his efforts to belittle Whitman. . . . Think of belittling Whitman because he did not enlist as a soldier

and carry a musket in the ranks! Could there be anything more shocking and incongruous than Whitman
killing people? One would as soon expect Jesus Christ to
go to war. Whitman was the lover, the healer, the recon-
ciler, and the only thing in character for him to do in the
War was what he did do — nurse the wounded and sick
soldiers, Union men and Rebels alike, showing no prefer-
ence. He was not an athlete, or a rough, but a great
tender mother-man, to whom the martial spirit was
utterly foreign.

Feb.

So poor, untidy, dishevelled, the land looked in South
Carolina — endless pine and scrub-oak barrens on a
yellow, sandy, infertile-looking soil — no country homes,
no thrifty farms; here and there a negro cabin raised up
from the ground on piles; at long intervals a scattered,
ramshackle village about a railway station; here and there
a measly-looking cotton-field dotted with stumps.

A dense fog enveloped the land. Out of this loomed the
most hag-like, weird-looking dead pine trees I ever saw;
such an expression of woe! almost Dantesque; as if they
had perished in the agony of some great cataclysm, like
the eruption of Mt. Pelée; yellow paths and roads leading
off, here and there, into the scrub.

From Columbia, S.C., to Jacksonville it is almost an
uninhabited and uncultivated country — torn and ruined
pitch-pine woods, half of them dead or lying upon the
ground; here and there vast areas of standing water
amid the trees — forbidding, unwholesome — the muddy
rivers out of their banks and flooding the woods for miles.

In Georgia the live-oaks begin to be seen, and the moss-draped cypresses. Occasionally in the woods a low tree of delicate pink bloom; then masses of the red bloom of the swamp maple; but apparently no end to the loose and torn pine barrens.

[In the South, without date, on separate sheet]

The scenery repels me. Nature here is too crude and watery and harsh; has not been subdued and tamed, but torn and mutilated and singed by the hand of man. She is wild, but not beautiful. She has not yet wholly emerged from the water. She is yet half-saurian. Some of her vegetable forms suggest reptiles (the palmettos and mangroves).

The soil I walk on plays an important part in my life. I strike roots into it. I draw sustenance from it. I sympathize with it. But I never could strike roots in this sand-heap. My life would stagnate in this flat country, probably in any flat country. The most beautiful things here are the live-oaks with their long gray beards of swaying moss. They suggest Walt Whitman.

March 15

Many letters of congratulation and approval anent the Long article [1] in March 'Atlantic,' one from President Roosevelt ending by asking me to go with him to the Yellowstone Park in April.

March 24

This morning the air is streaked with that wild, delicate,

[1] 'Real and Sham Natural History,' March *Atlantic*, 1903.

pungent odor, the origin of which has so often puzzled me
in the spring. How delicious, almost thrilling, it is — the
first odor of bloom! I am now convinced it comes from the
elm bloom. I could trace it this morning to the elms. A
soft maple, here and there, is opening, but the elms are
greatly in the majority. No soft maple near my Study,
and the odor is here.

June 8

Real observers are as rare as real poets. So few people
know or can tell exactly what they see; so few people can
draw a right inference from an observed fact; so few
people can help reading their own thought or preconcep-
tions into what they see. Only a trained mind can be
trusted to report things as they are. What did or does
the Indian really know of the wild life around him — except as it is related to his personal wants? What does the
farmer know of the wild life around him, except that the
crows pull up his corn, and the skunks and minks and
foxes destroy his poultry? He will kill every hen-hawk he
can, under the delusion that the hen-hawk kills his poultry.
He does not know from actual observation the relation,
beneficial or other, of the wild creatures to agriculture.
Hunters and trappers and woodsmen generally can tell
you the ways and habits of the particular game they
pursue, but of disinterested observation they are not, as
a rule, capable. They see certain things accurately —
what it concerns them to see — and draw just conclusions
along certain lines, but of the real life-history of their
game they know little.

July 10

President and Mrs. Roosevelt come to-day. A great day. Wrote it up for Dr. Barrus.[1]

Oct. 20

To me much of Jefferies' writing about nature is cloud-like — vague, formless, highly-colored masses of vapor. No tangible thought or fact. He is poor in ideas, poor in science, but rich in feeling and in fancy; no intensity or pungency of phrase, but a diffused kind of gladness in nature.

Let me define God in my own terms, as the active vital principle of the universe, without which nothing is, or can be, then I agree with the God-makers. Everything is of God, and for God, and by God. Not a sparrow falls, or can fall, to the ground without his cognizance, not a bud unfolds, or a seed sprouts without his ordering. You and I are a part of God in a literal sense.

Aug. 8, 1904

Read with keen intellectual pleasure William James's essay on Herbert Spencer in July 'Atlantic.' The most satisfactory discussion I have ever read of Spencer's claims.

Sept. 6

The thought that has quickened my pulse all summer is the thought of the Japs. When I begin to read the morning paper my heart hits it up from 70 or 72 to 85. What a

[1] See *Life and Letters of John Burroughs*, Vol. II.

wonderful people! May they break the last bone in the
body of the Russian bear!

Nov. 22

Go to the John Morley dinner at Carnegie's. Morley
a pretty strong man — large, fine head; fresh color; beard-
less face. A man without vanity or affectation. Spoke a
moment with Secretary Root; like him much; an able and
a sincere man. My seat at table is between the presidents
of Yale and Columbia.

April 14, 1905

Burn over Neighbor Allen's field this afternoon and
enjoy it much. If the world is ever to be burned up, I
want to be allowed to set the fire.

April 20

South wind. Smell my wild perfume in the air to-day.
Is it from the elms? A few branches of the pussy-willow
to-day gave out a marked odor, suggesting that which I
have attributed to the elms. But there are not enough of
them in this locality to so perfume the breezes.

May 9

A day of sunshine and apple bloom at the foot of Storm
King: fragrance, color, warmth, and a vast river prospect;
mossy boulders, a dripping ledge; the milk of the black
birch; the fragrance of the early meadow-rue; the spicy
ginger-root, with its 'dusky floral bell'; trilliums, and
many other sweet wild things — a May day not to be forgotten.

June 4

My little bush sparrow sings five times a minute. I timed him at 8 and at 11 A.M. on different days. And he has sung since April! He does not sing much in the afternoon. He probably sings 300 times an hour, for 7 or 8 hours, or 2000 times each forenoon. And yet he shows no hoarseness or falling off in his song! The red-eyed vireo sings all day till past midsummer. His is a continuous warble, or a string of ejaculatory notes, interrupted only while he is devouring the worm he has just caught. He is hunting all the time he is singing; he is like a boy whistling at his work.

Aug. 7

To Tyringham Valley to see the Gilders. Spend three enjoyable days. Gilder one of the best souls in the world, like a child in many ways — unselfish, unworldly, generous, devoted to any and every good cause; does not spare himself; flutters about too much — like a bird, from branch to branch; lacks continuity and concentration of effort, yet carries out what he undertakes; lacks system and organization in his life, it seems to me. A real poet, fluid, lyrical, with fine, deep touches now and then — the nearest to Keats of all our singers.

Jan. 25, 1906

I have no doubt but that back of, and working through, these visible, palpable forces and objects, is a whole universe of forces of which we only now and then catch glimpses. There are sounds too fine, and sounds too coarse for us to hear; there are material substances too fine for us to see; odors too delicate for us to smell. Would not analogy lead us to believe that there are forces and influences and presences that we wot not of? There is occasionally a person who by some subtle sense becomes aware of a cat hidden in the room; others seem to have the power to detect hidden veins of water in the earth; others to read the thoughts in your mind.

Feb.

Off for Washington.

Go at once to Harvey's for steamed oysters, as of old. Then to Cosmos Club. Put up at the Club by Dr. Howard. A quiet, homelike place.

Lunch at the White House. Meet Elihu Root, Dr. Merriam, Major Pitcher, and others. The President calls me 'Oom John,' and tells me of his affection for me. Mrs. Roosevelt very cordial.

I remained in Washington from the 5th to the 21st, part of the time at the Cosmos Club, and part of the time at Aaron Johns's and Dr. Baker's. Dined at Dr. Merriam's, Dr. Howard's, Mrs. Bailey's, Mrs. Gardner Hubbard's, Mr. Coville's, Mr. Gannett's. Lunched twice at the White House; met Root, Taft, and Moody. Moody a small, rather important man; able, but not great; opens his eyes too wide. Taft, big, fleshy, judicial.

Among these men, Roosevelt is of a different stamp. The imprint of the machine is not upon him. He touches life at so many more points; he is so alive all over. I liked Root the best of the Cabinet I saw.

Walked with the President on Tuesday for nearly two

hours, along Rock Creek and Piney Branch — a red-hot walk, through mud, water, over ice and snow, along paths, along the highway, across fields, driving ahead as if for a wager. I could follow him easier than I feared I could; a four-mile gait most of the time, with much talk.

April 12

Saw a female bluebird making love to a male and meeting with a spiteful rebuff each time. She followed the male about, lifting her wings, and calling to him in her most endearing tones, when he would dash at her viciously. I could hear the snap of his bill. She would utter a little scream of pain and protest, dart away, and then, as the male retreated, follow him again, pleading amorously.

Time after time I saw the angry male dash at her with clicking beak, and, as often, she recovered and followed him with her softest warbles and most winsome gestures. The female bluebird is the only bird I have ever seen make advances to the male. The hen sparrow always resents the advances of the males. I have seen a hen sparrow seize a male and hold him over the edge of the roof a moment, and then let him drop. The hens always tweak the feathers of their admiring suitors.

May 1

I often think of Lincoln's and Everett's speeches at Gettysburg; one of them has become a classic, of the other not a word has survived in the popular mind. But Lincoln had greatly the advantage: he had been through the fiery furnace and the pure gold in him had been brought out. He had had Gettysburgs of his own. Events had brought him close to the pith and marrow of

things, and to the hearts of the people. The fearful responsibilities that had been put upon him, and the ordeals
to which he had been subjected, had brought out the
nobler and more heroic lines of his character. He had a
depth of seriousness that Everett could not have. Had
Everett been through the same trials doubtless his
speech would have struck a deeper and more lasting
note. Atlas with the globe upon his back will speak
words of deeper wisdom than Atlas without the globe.

Off to Atlantic City with Periodical Publishers' Asso-
ciation. Meet Grover Cleveland on the train. Like him.
Kindly, serious, unaffected, humble.

Sept. 1

How important it is to keep in some vital, active relation with things! through one's hands, or head, or feet!
How much better and sweeter my life is when I have
some work that I like to do, or that makes demands
upon me! The vital currents of the universe seem to
flow through one the moment he is well employed.

The other day, in my walk through the fields, I came
upon a sap-bucket that had been left beside a maple tree.
It was full of rotten water or sap. It was unspeakably
loathsome; there were remains of birds and mice in it; it
reeked with corruption. How could innocent rain-water,
or maple sap, become so foul? It had been cut off from
the vital processes; it had been idle; it had taken no part
in the work of the seasons. I kicked the bucket over and
had to hold my nose. It seemed as if the very ground
would cry out in protest. But a few days of the active
chemistry of nature, and all will be pure again.

Dec. 21

Am reading some of Huxley's letters these days, or evenings. What a contrast to Emerson [whom he had also been rereading]! Another order of mind — the clear, logical mind, but destitute of charm, of suggestiveness, of poetic illusion, and of other things that make literature. Often a ringing eloquence, keen wit, apt and telling illustration, but wanting in color and the kind of warmth color implies. His sentences are like burnished armor or burnished weapons. How they flash and turn and make their way through all opposition! What precision, what directness, what motion, each locked to the other like soldiers in a Roman phalanx. Huxley brings everything down into the clear, strong light of the reasoning mind. 'You have been looking upon this thing in the light of tradition, or of sentiment, or of your moral nature, or of your hopes or fears, or of your prejudices and prepossessions,' he seems to say; 'now let us see it in the calcium light of the intellect, and know exactly what is what.' It is a fine discipline to read him. He clarifies. It is like going out in the morning and washing at the spring. The poetic, emotional mind moves me more, but how I love Huxley! what courage, what brightness, what gayety! what a lover of the truth! Scientific literature has no other such knight-errant as he.

Jan. 7, 1907

In my youth how many large and picturesque characters I knew. Now there is only the second growth of timber there — tamer, inferior men, trim and hustling and business-like, but so much less interesting than the shaggy, gnarly, primeval men. I can think of a dozen men of my youth that you could not begin to match now in that community for force, size, picturesqueness, — old Jonas More, Deacon Scudder, Elder Jim Mead, old Ed Burhans, Allen Whipple, Ira Hicks, old Nate Higby, Colonel Pratt, Abe Schultz, Pete Buckout, Eri Gray, Tim Corbin, Eli Bartram, Avery Bouton, John Gould, Henry Shout, and others, — all men that suggested primitive forest trees; many of them mean, hoggish, bullying, but all strongly stamped, whom you could not easily confound with any one else.

The old preachers, too, what a contrast to the flippant, scholarly, polished men of to-day! Men let themselves go more in those days, were not so timid and conforming. They could raise hell as their descendants cannot. They were more social, had races, and 'bees,' and shooting-matches, and raisings, and balls. I have heard Zalmon Bouton pray in the schoolhouse so that he could be heard on a still night a mile. . . . There is one picturesque old character still left here in my neighborhood, Rube Palmateer, whose type we shall not see again. He can neither read nor write; he does not believe the earth is round and turns around; and he believes, if he lives long enough, he can solve the problem of perpetual motion. He is eighty-three, and is still at work on such a machine. One day I saw him laying a stone wall by the roadside. 'Fifty years ago,' he said, 'I laid this wall. Now I am doing it again. Next time they will have to get some one else.' The Rube Palmateer of the future will know more, but he will not be half so racy and interesting, nor so picturesque in speech or figure.

April 23

Mrs. Dickenson is said to be dying, and I am hoeing my strawberry bed. This is life: we hoe and plant, while our neighbors are dying, or their graves being dug. Poor woman! I have not seen her for years, though she lives not five minutes away!

May 10

While home [at Roxbury] in April I saw in the sap-bush a bird I never before saw on the old place — the log-cock. In Chase's woods I saw, for the first time, leather-wood in bloom.

May 17

Heard and met Governor Hughes, whom I much admire. Heard and met Speaker Joe Cannon, whom I don't admire. I wish I knew the exact number of dandelions I saw blooming between Albany and West Park. Never saw the fields and meadow slopes so gilded with them.

Oct. 8

The smothered fires of the woodbine are beginning to burn in the cedars. I was interested in seeing that the sycamores that lost their leaves early last June did not develop new buds on the wood that held the dead leaves, but that they put out new shoots from the wood of the year before; that is, all last year's twigs were killed, and the whole work had to be done over again. The tree could evolve a new shoot, but not a new bud.

Oct. 24

To treat your facts with imagination is one thing, to imagine your facts is quite another.

Oct. 30

A pretty sight this morning on the road: figures of
leaves everywhere — elm, maple, and sycamore — not
mere imprints in the mud, but raised figures of the leaves
on the coarse gravel. It appears that the continued heavy
rains separated the fine particles of the soil and collected
these under the heavy leaves, making a perfect cast of
each leaf — a clay model, executed with great beauty and
precision. As soon as the leaves dried they lifted up and
revealed this model beneath them.

Nov. 9

Ernest Harold Baynes comes. Like him much, a sincere,
truth-loving man. His information very accurate. We
have much talk.

Nov. 10

Nothing can be lost. Of this I am sure. Just as surely
as all the elements of my body, and all the forces of my
mind, existed somewhere, in some form, before I was born,
just so sure will they exist somewhere, in some form, after
I am dead. But the consciousness, the *me*, how about
that? All analogy points to its cessation.

Motion is not a thing, an entity; it is an effect of a thing.
The flame ceases, goes out, as we say; a process is stopped;
but the elements that took part in the process still go on.
Was the flame an entity apart from the process? Is consciousness an entity? What remains after it ceases is the
capacity for consciousness in matter. Material things do
not cease, they change; but ideas, or our impressions of
material things, cease. In fact, I find it impossible to
corner consciousness and keep it.

The iridescent hues of a bird's feathers are not in the feathers, are not fixed colors, but only the effects of the play of light through the feathers. The rainbow fades, and yet nothing is destroyed. Our sensation of it ceases, and the conditions that make that which makes the sensation, cease.

We fade from life: a process is arrested; a motion is stayed; we have become only a memory in other minds. And when these other minds are gone, and the last element of our bodies has found its place in nature (where it was before it formed a part of us), where are we then? Is our identity a thing that can be added to, or taken from? Is consciousness a part of the universe? or only one of the phenomena of matter? If it ceases, is anything lost? Life ceases, as we well know. Is anything lost then? When a bubble bursts, what is lost?

Nov. 11

Cool, fair. Still at Slabsides. At night sit before the open fire with my dog and read James on Pragmatism, a stimulating and delightful philosophical argument — good literature, and good logic.

Christmas

Eat roast duck at Riverby. At Slabsides, my dog and I, since the 11th. A good time, writing each day, and getting 'Leaf and Tendril' ready. Much enjoy the quiet and the living close to the bone.

Jan. 22, 1908

Who has not observed how an inanimate object, caught and held by counter currents of water, or air, simulates a

thing of life struggling to escape, watching its chance,
turning uneasily, edging this way, then that. Try to re-
move a speck from your tea with a spoon, and the thing
seems to know your design at once, and eludes you, or
rushes away when cornered in the strangest manner.
What a panic it is in when nearly caught!

Feb. 26

To Washington to-day. The sight of the dome of the
Capitol against the blue, as I have so often seen it, makes
me both glad and sad; the sadness predominates. And
all the familiar scenes — how pathetic they all seem to
me!

Stay with the Bakers till March 2. Lunch with President Roosevelt on 27th. Find him looking as well and as
unruffled as I ever saw him. He told me that President
Murray Butler had written him a letter strongly con-
demning his famous message to Congress — said the message made any American hang his head with shame. The
President seemed astonished that Butler should look at it
that way, but said nothing in his own defence. Said he
was glad I liked the message. It was not an academic
document — that is why Butler could not stand it. There
was no stage thunder in it; it was full of the real thing;
and the elegant academic mind of Butler recoiled from it.

March 9 [*Orange Park, Florida*]

Glad to be with Trowbridge again. We walk and ride
and sit together. He is well and hearty. Doubt if I can
ever carry eighty years so well. Many people, much

pleasure, a little too many social demands, but beautiful hospitality.

Oct. 24

Yesterday, while my dog was eating his dinner, I started off hurriedly for the post office. As I was starting up the drive, my dog overtook me, jumped up against me and whined. I hurried on. When I looked around, he had gone — he had hurried back to finish his dinner. In a few moments he overtook me again and went with me to the post office. Now, most persons would say that my dog asked me, in his dog way, to wait till he had eaten his dinner. But I do not suppose there was any process in his mind akin to that which would go on in our minds under similar circumstances. This is my explanation of his act: He wanted the food, and he wanted to go with me. For the moment the latter desire overcame the former, and he started to follow. Then he remembered his food, and rushed back. The whining was expressive of his discomfort at being pulled in two ways at the same time.

To formulate an idea like 'Wait for me' — I doubt if even a dog ever does that.

Nov. 14

One trait I envy my dog: he never finds a walk or a run over the same route tiresome or uninteresting. The moment we start he is all alertness and expectation; the old and familiar become new and strange at once; adventure lurks on every hand; he is sure something exciting will happen around that corner, or behind that rock, or over that knoll.

Christmas at the Old Home. Twelve of us at dinner.

Glad to be at the old place again and see the winter landscape.

In the morning Chant found a woodchuck on the snow
above the orchard; brought him home in the sleigh. Slow
and dull, but apparently well. I found the hole in the
orchard where he came out, and followed his wanderings
about the fields. Had his sexual instinct awakened him
prematurely, and sent him forth in quest of a mate? He
seemed looking for something.

Jan. 13, 1909

Do we not recoil from the explanation of life and mind
in the terms of physics? Why should we? I know not. Of
course physics and chemistry and mechanics enter into
the problem, but are they the only or chief factors? Well,
when we invoke physics, we must accept the result of
physics; when we invoke metaphysics, we seem to be in
freer and more spiritual regions. Physics can explain the
phonograph; how simple the mechanism of it! but the
wonder, the marvel of it, is not diminished by [under-
standing?] its physics.

Probably the soul, and all that pertains to it, has a
physical or physiological explanation, but how inadequate
it seems in face of all we feel and think and dream and
aspire to! For the origin of those tones and harmonies and
living voices of the phonograph, we can only point to
these waving lines of the records. Yet think what sleeps
in those lines!

Feb. 25 [*in New Mexico*]

Many of these table-mountains or mesas have a sort
of cornice along the level line of the top — a broad band

of fluted or scalloped rock (trap?) that has the effect of
an architectural finish. At their bases, and on their
sides, there is often an effect of piers and columns, high
and massive, with deep shadows, that is very pleasing.
Abrupt perpendicular walls in the rocks and in the soil
are the order here. Something about it all suggests
Egyptian ruins. None of our Eastern mountains suggest architecture or architectural ruins, but here in the
West such suggestions come to you on every hand.

Reached Adamana, Arizona, Thursday night, February
25. John Muir met us at the train, and his voice sounded
familiar and good out of the obscurity of the night.

'How are you, Johnny?' and my reply was, 'By
thunder, Muir, I'm glad to see you!'

I introduced him to my two traveling companions [1] and
he said, in a jocose way, that he was surprised that there
were not six instead of only two women in my train.

We passed the night at the little inn at Adamana. In
the morning, February 26, we drove to the North Forest,
across an undulating plateau, and saw our first jack
rabbits scurrying among the low bushes, their big ears,
tipped with jet, always being conspicuous. They ran with
so little effort that they, in some way, gave me the impression of the motion of a bicycle.

After a ride of two hours we found ourselves on the
brink of the broad valley in which lie the petrified trees.
The spectacle of the Painted Desert in the distance moved
C. B. to tears. We descended into the dry river-bottom,
and, after a walk of two or three miles, came to the trunks

[1] Mrs. M. C. Ashley and Dr. Clara Barrus.

of the petrified trees, lying scattered about over the red
and gray clay mounds. Everywhere were trunks or fragments of trunks of enormous trees, some broken into
fragments, and others whole, and partly covered by the
soil.

We saw trees 100 feet and more long, straight as a
candle, apparently lying where they had fallen, as in
many cases the stumps and roots were still visible. We
spent several hours wandering about amid these ruins of
the foreworld. One could not look without emotion upon
these silicified trunks of trees that had been growing
millions of years ago, probably in Carboniferous times.

[His impressions of the Grand Canyon are given in
'The Divine Abyss,' in 'Time and Change.']

April 25

On the hills above Santa Barbara with Bradford Torrey
— A memorable day.

April 27

Go to Charlie Keeler's at Berkeley and meet interesting
people in afternoon and evening, connected with the
University of California. . . . Made the acquaintance of
the artist William Keith, whom I like much.

April 28

Went to Mount Tamalpais and the Muir Woods with
Keith and Keeler and several others.

May 1 [Yosemite]

Tramped to Vernal and Nevada Falls with Muir and
[Francis Fisher] Browne, and C. B. and Mrs. Ashley. A

glorious day, full of the exhilaration of those wonderful scenes — a walk of about thirteen miles.

I cannot stop to give my impressions of Yosemite here, further than to say that, as contrasted with the Grand Canyon, one could live in Yosemite and find life sweet. It is like a great house in which one could find a nook where he could make his nest, looked down upon by the gods of the granite ages. The floor of the Valley really has a domestic, habitable look, with its orchards and ploughed lands, its superb trees, and its limpid, silently gliding river; and, above all, its waterfalls fluttering against the granite precipices. The ethereal beauty of waterfalls, and the genial look of the pure streams, make almost any place habitable.

June 2 [*Honolulu*] [1]

Sitting here, in this land of perpetual summer, I think of the coming of June in my own land — the sparkling river, the new-born leafage of the trees, the first daisies and clovers just opening, the lush grass, the long, tender shoots of the grape-vines, the eager nesting birds, and of all the suggestions and enticements of early June. How it all comes back to me! How I wish I was there! These all-the-year-round summers get rather tame and humdrum, while the coming of our fresh, coy summer is like a new bride to one's arms.

Nov. 19

Am much shocked this morning at news of Gilder's death, which occurred yesterday, of heart disease. An old

[1] His impressions of Hawaiian scenes are given in 'Holidays in Hawaii,' *Time and Change.*

and true friend of mine. Not a great poet, but a real one
— very delicate and spontaneous; wrote too easily; lacked
force and intensity. Wanted too many things in life, I
think. Would have written greater poems had he wanted
fewer, and wanted them more. Of course I am trying him
by my own standards. A few of his poems will probably
live in anthologies. Peace to his ashes!

Nov. 20

Attend Gilder's funeral. Reach the church just before the close of the services. Meet many old friends and
acquaintances, mostly literary men. Saw Gilder's coffin
borne out on the shoulders of four men. A sad day for me.

Mr. Howells and James Lane Allen call upon me Sunday afternoon. Howells looks well, but his head begins to
settle down between his shoulders like an old man's. Allen
large, straight and dignified, with almost a military air.
Rouland brought out Garland's portrait which he had
recently painted. 'Yes,' said Howells, 'that is Garland
— Garland overtaken by civilization.' Ruth McEnery
Stuart also called. A very bright woman. Such people
cultivate their wits all the time; they ought to be bright.
The chief end of man, to them, is to be witty. (We who
have no wit avenge ourselves by such remarks.)

Feb. 18, 1910

Joy in the universe, and keen curiosity about it all —
that has been my religion. As I grow old, my joy and my
interest in it increase. Less and less does the world of
men interest me, more and more do my thoughts turn to
things universal and everlasting.

What a pathless wilderness the question of man's origin leads one into! All is veiled in mystery. The imagination even is baffled. One only knows that the wilderness is not limitless; that there is another side to it. But how to get there? There are many clues, but they lead but a little way.

March 23

How the knowing faculties of man have come to the front during the last hundred years! Time was when his religious faculties or emotions led all the rest, and his artistic powers went hand in hand with them. But now it is his understanding, or scientific faculties; now his desire above all else is to know things as they are, in and of themselves. He is less religious, less artistic, less superstitious; his emotions take a back seat; his exact knowledge leads.

The change has its unhandsome side. Life is in many ways less attractive. We have less veneration, less humility, less virtue than our fathers. Large, loving, picturesque personalities are becoming rarer and rarer, both in private and in public life. I sometimes think we cannot believe the things our fathers did because we are not men enough. We lack the heroic strain.

June 22

[At Yale University.] Put on cap and gown at nine and join the procession, and sit on platform in great hall and receive my degree of Doctor of Letters. Then to dinner at 1 P.M. Then to New York, and to Sherry's, for the Roosevelt dinner at seven. A fine affair, but hot, hot,

in my heavy swallow-tail. Roosevelt speaks over half an
hour. I leave before speeches are over. Henry Watterson
makes a characteristic speech. A pretty strong man.
Peary speaks well, but not very wisely — at the last.

July 6

Go to Oyster Bay. Roosevelt very cordial. Looks fine;
full of his African hunt. Two politicians there from Indiana; rather talk with me about birds than with them
about Indiana politics.

July 17

Read Darwin's Voyage Round the World, my third
reading. First time, on general grounds; second time, for
natural history points; this time for the geology. The
book is a storehouse of natural and biological science.

Oct. 9

Blue sky in the west all day. The first blue sky that
appeared above the earth — think of it! There must have
been a time when the vapors above the earth opened and
let the blue sky shine through for the first time. The
primal bad spell of weather was clearing up.

Nov. 8

Election Day. Vote the Republican ticket on account
of Roosevelt, but feel defeat in my bones. He has made
his first grand political mistake, I think. He should have
kept quiet and let the defeat which was bound to come
fall upon the Old Guard. Now it falls upon him.

Nov. 9

The Republican party has suffered a bad knock-out.
Serves them right. But the (Democrats) will be sure to
make a mess of it, if they come into power. The Democrats are fools, and the Republicans are hogs.

Nov. 30

To the Mark Twain Memorial meeting in Carnegie
Hall. Hear Choate, Watterson, Twitchell, Cable, Cannon,
and Clark. Cannon did best, a man I expected little from.
Champ Clark a disappointment. I think I could have
done better than any of them, if I could have spoken at all.
Howells presided in his usual happy way.

Jan. 10, 1911

[At the Grand Canyon.] Sun lights up the Canyon at
8.30. Walk down to Bright Angel Trail with Mrs. Burroughs. See the tourists go down on the mules. In afternoon drive to Hopi Point. The view overpowering. Mac-
Donald, editor of Toronto ' Globe,' and his wife, with us.
The Divine Abyss, indeed. The Book of Revelation
written in the red Carboniferous sandstone. Such order,
such tranquillity, such strength; such a well-swept house
of the gods! I find I have not exaggerated its beauty and
sublimity and unearthliness in my 'Century'[1] article.
No words can measure up to the reality.

March 2

Go to Los Angeles in afternoon to see my old school-
mate of sixty years ago, Anna Gould Hough. Find her
not so much changed as I had feared; eighty-three years

[1] 'The Divine Abyss,' *Time and Change.*

old, but I could see the schoolgirl of my boyhood. We
talked almost entirely of our school days. What an opening of the book of the past it all was!

March 13

[At Lamanda Park.] The chatter and giggle and *tee-hee*
of the house finches all about me; many of their notes like
those of English sparrows — the same loquacity, the
same busybodies. A hummer comes to the roof over me,
and to the sides of the house, for spiders' webs and lichens,
while the rat-colored brown thrasher is digging in the
garden with his long hooked beak. This beak is a regular
pickaxe. He runs as swift as a squirrel. His song I do not
know.

March 19

I cannot write about the birds till they have entered
into my life. I cannot write of anything well till I have
lived it.

April 25

An ideal April day. Julian working with his shovel in
the vineyard, and whistling as he works, just as he did
twenty years ago. It is his vineyard now, not mine.

June 21

Colgate confers upon me the degree of Doctor of
Humane Letters.

July 15

The rainbow hangs in the sky, though the drops of rain
through which it is formed are constantly falling; not till

the rain ceases, or the sunlight is hidden, does the bow
fade. The drops fall, but the bow which is formed by them
does not fall. The band of color, therefore, is not a part of
the rain; it is a function of the rain; the raindrops know it
not. It springs out on the rear of the retreating storm, but
the storm knows it not. It is in no sense a part of it.

No two persons see the same bow; there are as many
bows as there are beholders; the rainbow is truly an ap-
parition; you cannot approach it; you cannot grasp it, or
find its end. It has no end, and no beginning. It is also
born of the spray of cataracts, but sways not as the spray
sways. It is one of the oldest and most striking phenomena in nature, and one of the most subtle and elusive.
It is not an entity, but the radiant shadow of an entity.
What use has it? One of the most lovely and wonderful
things in nature, and yet it serves no purpose in nature; it
has no use. It pleases the eye, but it is much older than
the eye.

Is it not the only perfect arc that Nature draws —
mathematically perfect? Born of the most changeable
element, itself as ephemeral as a breath, yet its form and
color as fixed as adamant. It is unearthly in its beauty
and precision, like a vision from Heaven. Fugitive, unreal,
inaccessible, yet constant and eternal. The one permanent
illusion in the common nature about us. The sunset is
afar off, painted upon the distant clouds, but the rainbow
comes down to earth; it hangs between us and the next
field or hill; it spans the pasture, or the highway, or the
grove; it hovers about the playing fountain, or the spray
from the hand-pump; it is familiar, yet as elusive as a
spirit.

Is there not much in nature and in life that is symbolized by the rainbow? Nature is not all solids and fluids and gases; the unreal, the fantastic, the illusory play a large part in our lives.

Sept. 1

The more we live upon the breath of the newspapers, the more will the mental and spiritual condition out of which come real literature and art be barred to us. The more we live in the hard, close, cutting, calculating business spirit, the further are we from the spirit of literature. The more we surrender ourselves to the fever and haste and competition of the industrial spirit, the more are the doors of the heaven of the great poems and works of art closed to us. The more we live and move and have our being in the scientific spirit, the spirit of exact knowledge, the fewer monumental works of literature we leave behind us.

Oct. 21

The eye of a fly must, after all, be a very delicate instrument. Is his power of vision multiplied by all those hundreds of eyes? Try to bring your hand down upon one. See how he watches and waits for you to strike, raising his wings a little, to be ready on the instant. Not often is your hand quicker than he is. How surely he sees when your hand starts on its downward deadly stroke, and springs for his life! How much mind has he?

Dec. 8

Write in my Study on Bergson's view of the intellect, and on the chill of science. Health very good. Writing fatigues me less than ever before; been at it now nearly five months.

Dec. 11

Indian summer weather continues. A strange stillness has fallen upon the weather. It seems asleep and dreaming of October. No wind, no cloud, and but little frost. A thick white haze muffles all the landscape and lies banked around the horizon.

Dec. 12

The newspaper is good for relaxation. You can read it with your eyes alone. It is a mental laxative. If you are congested with literature and philosophy, read the newspaper and you shall not know there is such a thing, or ever has been, in the world. You will soon be empty of all thoughts of them. It taxes the mind about as much as whittling does the body. To talk of the educational value of the newspaper is like talking about the educational value of horse-trading, or of the stock exchange.

Dec. 13

Hud dug out a snake the other day — a garter snake — about two feet under ground. The snake was bunched up in a kind of knot, and stiff and stupid. I brought him to my Study and the warmth soon made him very lively. I kept him three days and then let him go. He steered for the wood-pile. I hope he finds a safe retreat.

Dec. 22

To John Bigelow's funeral with Mr. Howells. See several famous, and some infamous, men there.

Dec. 27

Have just been reading St. Paul. How eloquent! what good literature! These Epistles would never have come down to us had they not been good literature. They are full of the wisdom of the soul — full of the things that save us in this world. Paul was really the Father of Christianity.

Chattanooga, Tennessee, Feb. 10, 1912

Began snowing in the night; looks like winter on the Hudson. Snows all day, ten inches. A lunch at the Country Club. Many fine people. Winter without, but warmth and cheer and hospitality within. I hear myself eulogized in true political-orator fashion. On the 12th we go over the Chickamauga battlefield. See two broods of quail on the ground where the soldiers bled and died.

Athens, Georgia, March 13

Write in forenoon; walk and catch crabs with De Loach in P.M. Last night the cackle of the marsh-hens was to me a pleasing sound. Now and then we see marsh hawks beating about over the marsh, or dropping into it. Yesterday morning a great blue heron went heavily over it. The marsh looks like a vast tawny rug.

March 24

Am reading Fiske's 'Cosmic Philosophy.' Too much an echo of Spencer. 'The dissipation of motion,' and 'the integration of matter' — these wooden terms play as prominent a part here as in Spencer's pages, while Fiske has not that perfect mechanical rhythm of sentences, and the art of nesting his ideas, the one within the other, like a set of boxes, that Spencer has. Spencer has worked his system out with the regularity of the multiplication table; his ideas follow each other like twice two make four, twice four make eight. Such logical coherence and consistency would be hard to equal. Such precision — and such barrenness to the spirit!

April 11

To the Horace Mann School — a fourth birthday blow-out — very pretty and moving. The first time children ever danced before me with roses that they laid at my feet — enough to move the heart of a stone — all the work of Jean Dwight Franklin. Her poem of four lines in the 'Atlantic,' a gem. ['Away with Clocks and Sundials!']

April 16

News of the terrible disaster at sea — Titanic goes down. Probably 1400 lives lost. Her first voyage. The largest ship ever afloat. Horrible to think of!

April 21

Oh, what a lovely morning! with bird voices in the air, and I am haunted by the vision of that great ship, with her 1000 bodies, two miles deep in the sea!

A hundred or more purple finches in song for two days in the trees about us — a sort of low, half-suppressed rehearsal of their songs. Never heard them do anything like it before — like the goldfinches' spring jubilee and match-making picnics.

May 9 [Roxbury]

Curtis seems better than when I came. Yesterday afternoon I read to him from his beloved 'Signs of the Times.' Poor, feeble stuff to me — a kind of echo of what the 'Signs' used to be forty years ago, under Elder Beebe — but a comfort to him.

May 20

Work in garden at Slabsides. The shovel and wheelbarrow dispel my blues. In morning work on my geological papers for new book ['Time and Change'].

May 26

Come home [from Slabsides] at four and find telegram from Hattie that Jane died yesterday morning — the last of my four sisters. A tender, affectionate, and hard-working woman; not much intellect, but good sense, and good wholesome instincts. She piloted me to school in our childhood. How the shadows around me deepen!

May 28

Out to South Gilboa. Jane's children all there, tearful and forlorn. The old, old story — the children in the house of the dead parent. Jane looked very natural. Oh, the calm of that eternal sleep of death! She had died in peace; dropped away suddenly. She would have been seventy-seven on the tenth of June. Poor child! she had a pretty hard life — hard work and self-denial all her life. How little she knew of what the world holds, or of what men have thought and done.

June 15

Start for the lakes in Hamilton County with the Talbots. A good run of fifty miles to Speculator, on Pleasant Lake. Meet 'Uncle' David Sturgis, an old trapper and guide, and now a hotel-keeper, eighty years old. Very shy and gentle and sweet — a real product of the backwoods; knows much about wild life. Experienced religion last year and joined Methodist church. Like him much.

June 16

Cloudy, foggy, with some rain. We sit before the open fire and hear much talk. One has to be very artful to draw 'Uncle David' out — must approach him in a roundabout way, stalk him, in fact. He interrupts his recital of his wood experiences with frequent laughter, or half-suppressed laughter, more to himself than to his listeners. Tells no big yarns, understates rather than overstates; never heard a panther in the Adirondacks, but once caught one in a trap baited for marten; thinks there have not been any in these mountains for many years. Ravens used to be plenty, rarely see or hear one now. 'Why?' 'Because the wolves and the panthers are gone. The ravens feed on the leavings of the "kill" of these animals. Now they get little to eat in the woods.' A good reason.

June 24

Just at dawn this morning, as I lay on my cot on the porch [at Woodchuck Lodge] Frank Caswell came along, and, seeing me there, spoke to me. 'Are you awake?' 'Yes.' 'Well, Curtis [1] passed away last night.'

[1] His brother.

I was prepared for it, but I could not parry the blow. I shall never forget the effect the news had on me, there in the gray June morning.

July 4

Put a bird, or an insect, in a new and strange position, as on the inside of a closed window, and what a mere machine, for a time at least, it becomes! it is a victim of heliotropism. It reacts constantly to the light, and keeps up its efforts to get out till exhausted, or dead. A butterfly, one of the fritillaries, is now fluttering against the window in front of my desk. It is, for the time, a machine kept going by the attraction of the light. But a big 'blow-fly' on the window that I try to catch is wiser and, when pressed, darts away from the window and eludes me in the free space of the room. When he takes to the window again, and I make a dive for him, his wits again save him. This usually happens with big flies. Are they wiser than birds and butterflies? They seem to be, under such conditions. It is hard to corner one on a window.

July 21

Randolph S. Bourne came Saturday. Glad to see him here — a fine mind in a poor body. Has a future, I think; has already written several essays for the 'Atlantic.'

July 27

An Italian sculptor, C. S. Pietro, began to make a clay bust of me on Monday, doing well.

Sept. 17

[At Woodchuck Lodge.] These peaceful broad open valleys, and the long mountain lines seem greatly to enhance the splendor of such a bright day. In a country of low horizons, the day would be less striking. These valleys hold it and set it off. I think of Emerson's line, 'Tenderly the haughty day fills its blue urn with fire.' These valleys are vast blue urns, and they hold such a generous portion of the sunlight.

In the afternoon I walk to 'Scotland' over our old trail and get a few blackberries. Find a mouse's nest in a niche under an overhanging ledge, where one looks for a phœbe's nest — thought it was one at first — covered with moss, just like a phœbe's. The body of the nest of thistle-down, thick and compact, with a small hole to a cavity in the center. A prettier nest I never saw — three feet from the ground, but not occupied. The moss was from rocks where water trickles in wet seasons — long, yellowish-green. The bottom of the nest covered with moss also, so it could hardly have been for protection. A unique find.

Sept. 20

Some sunflowers at Hobart arrested my attention — such an almost human attitude of dejection! Their broad leaves pressed down wrapped them in a kind of cloak drawn close about them; their heads were bowed till they wholly faced the ground. I could but pause and look at them. 'Why are you so bowed and weighed down, you lovers of the sun — shutting all the world from your gaze but the little circle of ground at your feet? Your attitude oppresses me. There is the sun and sky overhead. Do look up and let the wind under your cloak.' If the sunflower could have answered, what would it have said? Probably this: 'I have had my day. I have followed the sun in his course across the sky all summer. I have had my fill of him. Now my seeds are ripened, and they are my only care. I must turn them down, away from the rains and the fowls of the air. The back of my head makes a good roof over them. I have done my work. I have had my day, and here I wait for the knife of the harvester.'

Nov. 6

Election goes for the Democrats; might have been worse — might have gone Republican. I wanted to vote for Wilson, but voted for T. R. on the score of friendship — a thing he would not have done — a thing no man should do.

Feb. 3, 1913

Wake up in Washington this morning; raining and sleeting; rains all day. Go to Capitol. Meet Underwood, who says he will support our [McLane] bird bill.

Feb. 4

Go to Bergson's lecture at Columbia. Not one word of his French can I understand but *donc*, but I do not tire of looking at him. Small, thin man of the Emersonian type, an idealist, a prophet of the soul. Superb head. The rather austere Emersonian smile; manner animated; heavy eyebrows, small, deep-set, but expressive eyes; thin hands — look cold; strong chin and nose. A wonderful mind.

Feb. 19

` To Columbia [University]. At the tea given in his honor, meet Bergson face to face. He knows about me. I told him of my great pleasure in meeting him — that Emerson was the inspiration of my youth, and he the inspiration of my old age. With a deprecating gesture he seemed to disclaim such doubtful honor, and then began to talk of the unexpected idealism he found here, in Emerson, in James, and others. Then he was whirled away to face some other admirer. One of the most symmetrical and beautiful heads I ever saw. A small man; not an imposing figure; not an aggressive and dominating personality; but a wonderful mind, and a gentle heart.

Met Eucken also. A white, bushy top, like myself. Not a striking head or figure. He, too, knows my work, and is very cordial in his German-English. His work has not yet made an impression upon me.

March 4

Go to MacDowell Club at night with C. B., to a reception to Alfred Noyes. Large, strong, healthy young Britisher; looks like a University man — not like a poet. He lectures on the future of poetry, but does not convince us that poetry has any future. Then recites some of his own poems. Does it well, but he is not a great poet; nothing in his poems that goes to the heart or to the soul; one page of Wordsworth or Arnold is worth it all.

March 10

To Poughkeepsie in afternoon. Greatly alarmed over the condition of Ursula — double pneumonia; fear the worst. Just begin to realize all she has been to me, and all she has done for me.

March 18

Mrs. B. doing well. Clear, lovely day.

April 8

At Slabsides, writing on Vitalism. Ran the car yesterday afternoon to Port Ewen, and then came home and ran it into the locust tree just inside our gates. Never look back while driving your car! I looked back as I came through the gate, to see if I was going to hit [it], and the little beast sprang for that tree like a squirrel. Broke or bent her forward spring so we can't crank her.

May 1

No more perfect day ever came down out of heaven. Warm, still, clear. Orchards piled with apple-bloom. The wood thrush this morning. A thin veil of foliage over the trees. Drive Wife in the car to Clintondale, a beautiful drive.

May 3

Have just taken a run of a few miles in the car. The blind, desperate thing still scares me. How ready it is to take to the ditch, or a tree, or a fence! I fear I have not the mechanical type of mind ever to feel at my ease with it, or to feel perfect master of it.

June 5–8

In Detroit with Mr. Ford and Mr. Buck. Have a fine time. Mr. Ford pleased with me and I with him. His interest in birds is keen, and his knowledge considerable. A lovable man. So is Glen Buck. Mr. Ford's plant a wilderness of men and machinery covering over forty acres. The Ford cars grow before your eyes, and every day a thousand of them issue from the rear.

June 28 [Roxbury]

In the afternoon drive Julian and the girls down to the station. Return in good shape with the girls; but, in driving the car in the old barn, get rattled and let it run wild; it bursts through the side of the barn like an explosion; there is a great splintering and rattling of boards and timbers, and the car stops with its forward axle hanging over a drop of fifteen feet. As the wheels went out, the car dropped on its fly-wheel, and that saved me; the wheel caught on less than a foot from the edge; had it not, it would have landed at the foot of the steep hill, and I should have landed on the other side of Jordan! A lucky escape! The top of the radiator is badly crumpled, otherwise the car is unhurt.

I am terribly humiliated, and, later, scared at my narrow escape. The thing I had feared for weeks happened. Thus does fear deliver us into the hands of the thing we fear!

Sept. 1

With the Ford party drive out to Concord. Pick up Sanborn and we lunch at hotel. Sanborn of the Emersonian type — tall, gaunt, deliberate, sharp-featured, stooping; with Emerson's manners and ways. A rather dry, lean nature, but an interesting man. Hates Roosevelt. We drive about town, to Walden Pond, to the Emerson house, etc. Spend some time in Emerson's house. Just as he left it. Very impressive to me; his dining-room, his study, his library, his bedroom, all look like Emerson — the home of a scholar and thinker.

Sept. 2

In Boston to-day. To Country Club for lunch; then to Arlington, to see Trowbridge and Nixon Waterman — two charming, lovable men. Trowbridge well, ruddy and spry; Waterman very humorous and bright.

Nov. 4 [Roxbury]

Draw writings with John C. [Burroughs] and receive the deed that makes the old place mine, thanks to the generosity of Mr. Ford.

It is just as impossible to prove or disprove the freedom of the will, as to lift yourself over the fence by your boot-straps. If I feel, or think, my will is free, that is enough for all purposes of my life. If I do not feel or see the necessity that rules me, it is as if it did not exist.

1914–1921

[IN the remaining seven years left to him, despite his own declining health and many bereavements and the almost overwhelming oppression induced by the World War, Burroughs continued to write. Many stirring War letters to the New York dailies came from his pen, the responses to them from all over the country showing that, by means of that pen wielded amid the peace of the hills, he was valiantly supporting the cause of the Allies. Moreover, six books of enduring worth are the fruits of this period of storm and stress — 'The Breath of Life,' 'Under the Apple-Trees,' 'Field and Study,' 'Accepting the Universe,' 'Under the Maples,' and 'The Last Harvest.' The two last-named were published posthumously in 1921 and 1922, respectively.

Chief among the friends he lost by death in those darkened years were William Vanamee, John Muir, Hamilton W. Mabie, W. D. Howells, and Theodore Roosevelt. Nearer losses still were those of his wife in 1917, and his brother Eden in 1919, this last leaving him the sole survivor of his family.

The gloom of these years was, however, brightened by many events of happy import. Early in 1914, at Fort Myers, Florida, he found in Mr. Thomas Edison and Mr. Henry Ford the best of playfellows, and in subsequent years joined the Edison-Firestone-Ford auto-camping parties in their jaunts in the Adirondacks, the Green and White Mountains, and the Great Smoky Mountains.

After May, 1914, when the present editor established

her home in the little cottage — the Nest — at Riverby,
Mr. and Mrs. Burroughs became members of her household, continuing to live there, except when at Woodchuck Lodge in midsummer or when wintering elsewhere, till the close of their lives.

The American Academy of Arts and Letters, in 1916,
awarded a gold medal to John Burroughs for excellence
in Belles-Lettres, but the honor coming to him, an octogenarian, and when his fellow academicians were dropping thick and fast around him, and his wife was rapidly
declining, could give him but little pleasure. His best gift
on his eightieth birthday was that great message of President Wilson's which came out on April 3, 1917, a message, he said, written across the sky for all the world
to heed. When peace was declared, he rejoiced that it
had been vouchsafed him to see the most fervent and devout hope of his life realized.

An event of years to him was the friendship formed in
the summer of 1919 with the young poet John Russell
McCarthy, whose work had moved him profoundly. Mr.
McCarthy visited him twice at Woodchuck Lodge, and,
during Burroughs's third winter in California was, for a
time, a member of the Burroughs party.

The last few months were marked by a steady decline
in health, but even then, at La Jolla, by the sea, and later
at the Bluebird Cabin in Pasadena Glen, he busied himself with rereading the Correspondence between Emerson
and Carlyle, with rereading Bergson, with arranging the
matter for his two unpublished books, writing in his
Journal, studying the trap-door spiders on the beach, and
the barking seal in the waves, and seeing many friends.

Almost the last literary work he did was to dictate a brief paper to be read at the Memorial meeting held at the American Academy of Arts and Letters for William D. Howells. By a fitting coincidence the last sentence he ever penned, when editing some of the essays which were published in 'The Last Harvest,' was about Emerson. The last bit of consecutive writing he did, at about the same time, and to be found in the same book, is called 'Facing the Mystery.'

In February his condition necessitated a month's stay in a hospital in Pasadena; this was followed by another week at the Bluebird Cabin in the Glen, and then the homeward journey. He realized the seriousness of the undertaking but was eager to set out. The end came on the train, in the early morning of March 29, twelve hours before reaching home. Characteristic of one of the deepest attachments of his life, the last word on the lips of John Burroughs was the word 'home' — a few minutes before the Silence — 'How far are we from home?']

Feb. 25, 1914

Here at Fort Myers with the Edisons and the Fords. Midsummer weather, a real tropical scene; reminds me of Jamaica and Honolulu. I can eat these oranges and grape-fruit. A cocoanut tree loaded with fruit out of my window. Pretty nearly an earthly paradise here, lacks only the mountains to lift one up toward heaven.

March 10

Been here since 22d of February. Bright days most of the time. Write mornings; fish, drive, walk in afternoon.

Edison and Ford good playfellows. Edison sleeps ten or twelve hours in the twenty-four; says he can store up enough sleep to last him two years. A great mind — a great philosopher — loves jokes and good stories. Mr. Ford a lovable man, a great machinist, but not the philosopher that Edison is; a shy, modest man, shrinks from any publicity and from those who would make a fuss over him. No vanity or conceit at all; he is not puffed up; thinketh no evil; has a good will for all. A real nature and bird lover, and lover of his kind.

March 28 [*Experiment, Georgia*]

I drive De Loach's car every afternoon, and am getting master of it. It makes me tremble only a little now when I back it out and drive it in. De Loach and I sit in the study at night and read and discuss scientific matters. He often gives me good hints, but quite unconsciously. My mind these days is like a trout looking for flies.

May 2

[Purple finches] are feeding on the seeds of the sycamore balls — a hard feat for them, owing to the long string (stem) by which the ball is held.

A downy woodpecker drumming, morning after morning, on the stub of a dry limb of the big maple up by the side of the road. One morning I saw the female come to the tree and busy herself searching around a large limb some distance from the drummer. He was evidently instantly aware of her presence. He drummed rapidly twice, then, after a moment's pause, dropped down a few feet and clung, silent and motionless, to the stub. The

female worked nearer and nearer; but the male made no
sign. Finally she alighted upon the branch upon which he
was perched, and busied herself on the opposite [side] of
it. Still he made no sign. After a few moments, he flew
swiftly away and disappeared in some trees near by. After
about a minute the female disappeared in the same direction. She seemed more ardent than he did. Maybe he
was not drumming for her — had perhaps drummed up
an unwelcome female, and would have none of her.

May 8

Mr. Vanamee died last night, an old friend of forty
years; a man of much talent and many admirable traits.
Books his dissipation; his library in Middletown was a
resort of mine for many years. Peace to his ashes!

July 13

The blueness of the waters of the Great Lakes is remarkable; so unlike river water, or the colorless water of
our mountain lakes. The vast expanse of the blue sky
above them seems to have colored them; the heavenly
blue is contagious and affects the water. There is a hint
of the sea in the Great Lakes. In the smallest of them
that I have seen (St. Clair) there is a strange, far-off,
elemental look. Superior is the father of it. You feel that
that water has been somewhere, and has had unusual
experiences.

July 18 [*Roxbury*]

8 A.M. Here I am again at my Barndoor Outlook. The
old familiar scenes and sounds. I hear two scarlet tan-

agers singing up in the woods, their strong, rather harsh notes rising above the continuous warble of the red-eyed vireo and the occasional *per-chick-a-pee* of the goldfinch.

Aug. 25

Write a little, but not with much zest. The terrible War in Europe depresses me. That war-drunk Kaiser my special detestation. He will bring ruin upon his country, and great injury to the whole world. But if the militarism of which he is the embodiment is crushed and cast out by the War, there will be great gain.

Sept. 6

I wake up in the night and groan in spirit over the carnage in Europe. If that military bully, the Kaiser, was only compelled to go to in the fore-front of the fight! But what can save him, as long as England and France are supreme on the seas, I cannot see.

Sept. 20

Reading 'Pan-Germanism' and much impressed by it. I did not dream of such scheming, such jealousies, such rivalries and animosities among the nations of my own day. Civilization seems to have done nothing toward eradicating greed and selfishness among the races. For nations to live together as brothers and neighbors seems out of the question.

Work a few hours each day with the men, prying rocks and stones. It does me good. I am all the time bruising the head of German militarism.

Oct. 8

How much labor the old ice-sheet has caused mankind — covering the soil and packing into it rocks and stones over all parts of a large section of the globe! For many weeks I have had men and teams battling with these obstructions in a field on the old farm. In many places the soil is packed with rocks; there are medial moraines nearly all over the field. Many of the rocks and larger stones that we move are rounded and rubbed and grooved on the bottom, as if they had been sliding down hill. The ice-sheet nearly or quite doubled the labor of the first settlers in this part of the country, and added much to the labors of their descendants. Without it New England and New York land would have been as easy to clean up and make tillable as land in Georgia or Tennessee.

Oct. 10

Anything we can write or say without emotion is not poetry, whatever else it may be.

Dec. 3

The one overwhelming and all-absorbing event of this fall, the European War, finds hardly an echo in this record. It is too tremendous. It occupies more than half my thoughts. I can read little else than the newspapers. I even read the yellow journals, lest some scrap of news escape me. But the news I most want — the utter defeat of the Kaiser's armies — I do not yet find. The struggle in Poland now seems to be the crucial battle.

Dec. 23

At Yama Farms Inn, Napanoch, N.Y. Work in the

Hut, revising the chapters of 'The Breath of Life.' A letter from a German professor at Wurzburg protesting
against my Tribune letter. Not a strong reply.

Dec. 25

News comes of John Muir's death — an event I have
been expecting and dreading for more than a year. A
unique character — greater as a talker than writer; loved
personal combat, and shone in it. He hated writing, and
composed with difficulty, though his books have charm of
style; but his talk came easily and showed him at his best.
I shall greatly miss him, though I saw him so rarely.

Feb. 23, 1915

A great thing is to know what you want to know, so
that your reading and studies may not be aimless and
profitless. In my youth I knew that I wanted to know
the birds, to know geology, and astronomy, and all natural knowledge.

March 15

Go to Stone Mountain [Georgia]. A fascinating climb,
an hour or more on top. Probably the biggest single
granite knob or lump in the world.

April 11

Lounsbury died suddenly two days ago. A lovable
man, I liked him best of all the Academicians. My last
word and talk with him last November. He told me then
that his heart was his weak point. He would not hurry to
catch a street car, as I was inclined to do. He made a

most effective criticism of a statement of Arnold's in one
of his later essays. Hopkinson Smith died also, at same
age, seventy-seven. . . . Smith orated when he talked.
Both should have lived to see the end of the War.

April 25

One hundred and ten Vassar girls yesterday at Slabsides, and a dozen High School girls from Poughkeepsie,
also President McCracken and his wife. I like the young
man much. Rare April days. Jenny Wren here this
morning.

May 6

To Carnegie Hall, to the Civic Forum function in honor
of Edison. An interesting ceremony. Much speech-mak-
ing, but Edison will not say a word. The gold medal
presented him is large and fine. Edison hates all the talk
and palaver — the whole thing a bore to him.

May 8

To Sing Sing. Visit Osborne and the prison. Go
through the prison and then see the 1800 march in to
dinner — the rag-tag and bob-tail of humanity — very
depressing to look at their crude, unfinished faces. Not
one in ten with any foundation for character-building.
An atmosphere of content seems to pervade the place.
Osborne a great success — treats the prisoners as human
beings, and gives every man a show. Incredible that for
ages the State should have aimed to punish and torment
its prisoners, instead of trying to make better men of
them! Osborne has abolished nearly all guards and spies,
and tries to let the men govern themselves.

Mr. Ford and I both had to make little speeches in the big dining-hall, after the men were through dinner. How they did clap Mr. Ford! He said he had never made a speech in his life. He was much embarrassed; he only spoke a dozen words. Among other things I said it was their bad luck that they were there, and probably my good luck that I was not there — which made them laugh. If they had all been as well-born as I was, and brought up to industrious habits on the farm, etc., etc.——

July 22 [Roxbury]

Great indolent clouds floating about the sky, not sure what course they should take. The smell of blooming clover on the air. Telephone peas ready yesterday. Few birds in song. Bilberries just ripening. Farmers backward with their haying. The country very sweet. Strawberries yet linger in the orchard. Hear the migrating calls of the bobolinks in Caswell's meadows. Strength returning, but heart still unsteady after meals and often at night. [After a serious attack of autointoxication.]

Aug. 1

Saw a gray fox early this morning pass up the wall between us and Caswell's, followed by a mob of cawing crows. The crow is the typical alarmist.

Aug. 13

Pietro comes to model me again.

Sept. 3

Day of the More Pageant.[1] Perfect day, fine affair, a

[1] A pageant in Roxbury depicting its pioneer history, in which a tribute to J. B. was given in the Nature Interlude.

great picture. The Nature scene the best of all. I am deeply moved. Johnson says it is a great honor to me. Before the Pageant we lunch with the Finley Shepards in the big tent. A gala day indeed.

Dec. 4

In New York. See Mr. and Mrs. Ford till 2 P.M. Go to the steamer [Peace Ship] with them. Mr. Ford's heart is bigger than his head. A great crowd at the steamer. Ford is sanguine and happy. He might as well try to hasten spring as to try to hasten peace now. I told him as much.

March 15, 1916

The idolators are just as truly religious as the Christians, or any other sect. What they worship and pray to is an idea which their idol represents to them. The Christian God is an idea which is symbolized more or less by the man Jesus Christ. Christ is represented by the Cross. This is the Christian's idol. The heathen with his idol is just as near the truth. All peoples and tribes make their own gods, and make them, largely, in their own images. All religions are a kind of idolatry, and I respect them all alike.

March 31

I sit here boiling sap, sparrow songs all about me. Robins calling and running over the bare ground. Phœbe looking about under the porch. A highhole calls below me, near the river. Bluebirds calling and warbling everywhere — the plaintive note of the female, and the happy, eager note of the male. Three starlings go by — a new form against the blue — none of our birds make just the same figure. Sweeping down the hill, with half-closed wings, they suggest arrow-heads.

How the old days, when I helped boil sap in the home sugar-bush and looked off over the fields through the lucid air come back to me! I was happy then. I am happy now — except when thoughts of my poor suffering wife cross my mind.

April 1

From our old sap-bush I used to look across the valley, two or three miles in an air-line, to the farm of Seymour Older on the broad slopes of the Batavia mountain. His sugar-camp was in the mantle of woods that covers all its upper portions. At night we used to see his campfire. Many times when we were boiling sap in the early part of the night, have I looked across to his bush, and seen his speck of light shining out through the miles of darkness. Seymour boiled sap there during many March and April days. His farm was the only one that stood tilted up on the mountain-side, giving us a full view. In spring we could see his plow at work, turning over the sod; in summer we could see his hay-making and hay-gathering, and his grain-harvesting. I was never in his house, nor ever saw his wife or children, but I shall never forget him. He was a tall, slender, small-eyed man, a good farmer, a good citizen and neighbor, and a man of some education. When I was a clerk in the Treasury Department in Washington, in 1866 and '67, I was called from my desk one day in the office by the head of the room, Mr. Kennedy, and I looked up and saw there before me Seymour Older. I had not seen him since my boyhood. Had I beheld my great-grandfather, I could not have been more astonished. I certainly was glad to see him. How kindly the past looked out of his small blue eyes! I never saw him later in life.

April 19 `

Looks as if we might break with Germany on the submarine issue. Hope we will, and that War will follow. It might be our good luck to share in the honor and glory of helping the Allies crush this pirate of the seas and desperado of the land.

Two eggs in the robin's nest in my summer-house.

April 27

In the afternoon walk down by Gordon's and Seeley's ponds. In Seeley's pond saw a muskrat come ashore and gather up a mouthful of dry leaves, take it to the water again, swim down the pond, and then dive for his hole, which led to his nest in the bank above the water-line. By what sleight of hand he expected to keep those leaves dry, I could not imagine. Probably he knew they would dry out in his nest.

I noticed that the muskrat, in swimming, appears to scull himself along with his tail — at least his tail has a twisting, undulating motion. It does not passively drag behind.

Roxbury, May 10

A strange white opacity in the air, like a little milk mixed with a pail of water. [Two hours later.] Still the curious white mist in the air; the wind has no effect upon

it. After breakfast I walk up the side-hill above the house
to the lingering snowbanks. How dirty they were! —
leaving a deposit of soil on the stones and ground where
they had melted, a border of dripping ground a few feet
wide all around their lower margins. Prairie horned
larks were feeding about them, close up to their margins,
evidently picking up the seeds of grasses and weeds that
the wind had brought over the hill from the other side.
They were very busy. On the top of the hill, where I
could look over into the West Settlement, the wind blew
so hard that I could not stand it long. I crouched behind
the stone wall awhile. Then made my way across the hill
to the upper snowbank and, standing up, slid swiftly
down one of them for thirty or forty feet. Then, by the
head of the spring, out of which a big volume of water
was running, I cut my initials in the bark of the old
beech tree that stands there. The initials that were there
in my youth are all obliterated.

This spring was a vital part of the home. How many
times has Father said to me, 'John, you must go up to
the head of the spring and clean the leaves off the
strainer.' The little elm sapling that then stood in the
corner of the wall is now a large, superb tree, three feet
through. Three times did I see the 'pump log' that
brought the water to the house renewed in my youth —
once with poplar, once with hemlock, and once with pine.
Some old fellow from Mooresville [now Grand Gorge]
used to come with his long auger and bore them. It was
to me an interesting proceeding. It was quite a trick to
bore a log fifteen feet long, and keep near the center of
the log. The poplar logs proved a failure — soon decayed,

as did the hemlock; pine lasted well. Now, for many years, an iron pipe conveys the water, but does not keep it so cool and fresh in summer.

How lovely the country looked! The intense green of the grass, the fresh brown of the woods, the blue of the sky. Wind still violent in the afternoon. Every lone tree in the fields like a cataract, and the woods resounding like the multitudinous seas.

May 14

The goldfinches of a large area must have assembled here by appointment, or mutual understanding, community of mind, or how? They fill a dozen treetops at a time along the road. They feed on the half-matured elm seeds, rifling the winged disc of its germ very skillfully. Bands of them make a little excursion into the vineyards and garden for the green seeds of the chickweed. This morning a large number of them came down around my Study and attacked the closed dandelion heads, and dug out their green seeds. They are evidently hard-put for food. They made no provision in advance of the gathering of the clans. But they evidently get fun out of it all, and laugh and sing the day through. . . . I cannot make out whether it is the males alone that make that subdued musical chatter. It has an air of privacy and screened seclusion — just the bursting buds of song. I visualize it as matching the half-unfolded elm and maple leaves. Probably the passers-by along the road under the trees do not notice it at all. It is a mist or fine spray of song, coming from no particular point, but from everywhere in and about the trees. . . . How contented and confiding

the tones are, expressing only joy and affection! Few
birds have such pretty ways as the goldfinch.

May 17

Mrs. Burroughs gains very, very slowly, if at all. Fear
she will never be any better.

May 19

How much live natural history goes to waste every day
upon every farm, even in our dooryards and gardens.
There are at the moment (that I have found), twelve or
fourteen robins' nests in my lot of eighteen acres, a
wren's nest, two bluebirds' nests, one song sparrow's
nest, two wood thrushes' nests, one phœbe's, and the
chippies and vireos and orioles and warblers have not
yet begun to build. On a large farm, how many more
nests there must be! Think of the interesting natural-
history incidents that occur in a whole township in a
single day, or in the county, or in the State, and during
the whole season! Not one in ten thousand is ever witnessed or recorded. How few I myself witness, or make
note of, of those on my own few acres! If I spent all my
time in the open air, on the alert, how many more I would
see! The drama of wild life about us is played quickly,
the actors are on and off the stage before we fairly know
it, and the play shifts to another field.

May 23

Life is its own excuse for being. It seeks myriad forms
of expression, but rests with none. There is no finality
in the universe. On and on, around and around, with no

stoppage. The streams flow to the river, the rivers to the sea. Is that their end? No, through the air they flow back to the land, and begin the circuit again, forever and ever.

The creek that flows through your fields or past your house — what an individuality it has! none other just like it, though the waters of all are just the same. The meadow brook, the pasture brook, the forest brook, the mountain brook — how they all differ, what a distinct impression each of them makes, and yet all of one identical element! The conditions, the environment, are what makes the difference. They have each a different body, so to speak. Rocks give one character, sand and gravel another, silt and loam another.

The music of the brook is evoked by the obstacles in its way. If there is no friction, there is no sound. Does the brook make the valley, or the valley make the brook? In a world of clashing seismic forces, valleys result, and then water comes and enlarges them. The rains carve the clay bank into ridges and valleys. Physical laws rule it. The serpentine course of a stream through a plain is inevitable.

June 3

News of the great sea-fight. Much disturbed by it. If England fails upon the sea, as she has upon the land, the Kaiser will have her, sure as the Devil!

June 9

[At the Fords', Dearborn, Michigan.] In the afternoon I lay the corner-stone of the bird-fountain in which I

have cut my name. The fountain, the walks to it, and
the terraces above it, all made of stone from Woodchuck
Lodge — stone that I helped my brothers pick up for a
wall in my youth.

July 18 [*Roxbury*]

The place looks as good as ever. Sleep on the porch.
At 4 A.M. a sparrow sang, *Very peaceful, very peaceful!*
And so it was. No disturbing sights or sounds — only
the disquieting thoughts of the War, which one cannot
escape from. A world of grass. Never saw such meadows
and pastures before. The air is sweet with the perfume
of meadow and pasture. The foliage of the wood and
field trees as rank as if it had had some special fertiliza-
tion — as if the blood spilled in Europe had soaked
through and fertilized the roots of all vegetation.

July 20

Great shining, perfumed summer day. A luxury to
live.

Aug. 2

When the paper comes, I want to run away to some
secluded spot and read it undisturbed, as I would a love-
letter. First I skim the headlines hurriedly to get the
import of the big print; then read the details of the more
important events; then the less important — impatient
of all spread-out accounts of our own local and home
news. Only the news from the War is of vital and world-
wide, and age-wide importance. Our Mexican troubles
I brush aside as I do the fly that tickles my scalp. The

stake of the world, and of civilization, is in the European
conflict. If the Huns triumph, woe be unto us! A robber
nation will again overrule the world.

After dinner I go over the news again and glean where
I reaped before. Or I get hold of another daily and read
its version; the change in type and heading freshens the
news up. By lamplight I often glance over the news
again. In magazines and weekly periodicals I look only
for War news, or War discussions.

Aug. 5

I never cease to wonder at the incessant cawing of the
crows; at all hours of the day, from all points of the
compass, their voices reach me. Are they so truly social?
are they always calling to one another for company,
signalling back and forth to keep in touch? or what is the
reason? What purpose does this endless caw-cawing
serve? They caw from the treetops, from the ground,
while on the wing, while alone, while in company; in the
spring, in the summer, in the fall. [The crow] is more silent in winter, apparently because life is more serious then.
In beating his way home to his rookery at sunset, against
a cold winter wind, he has nothing to say. Hence I infer
that his ceaseless cawing is only the expression of his
festive and social nature. He has a good time; he loves
his fellows; he knows his enemies; and life is sweet.

The 4th was one of those summer days when the slow-
moving clouds pile their snowy peaks high in the blue
depths of the sky — the Alps and Andes of cloudland.
As I sat over by the woods, feasting my eyes upon them,

a red-headed woodpecker climbed up high in the air and overtook some bug or other insect (I could faintly see it) and picked it out of the air easily, and returned to a dead branch in the woods. The same hour I saw cedar-birds doing the same thing, lower down. They moved slowly and, here and there, seized some winged insect. This is a common practice of cedar-birds in late summer. They do the thing rather awkwardly and deliberately, as we do slowly a feat which a professional does with a quick stroke. With the professional fly-catcher it is a flash and a snap, and the bug is gone.

Aug. 29

Came Edison and his party to take me with them on a motor-trip. They camp in my orchard — an unwonted sight — a camper's extemporized village under my old apple trees — four tents and large dining-tent, and, at night, electric lights; and the man Edison, the center around which it all revolved. Wednesday afternoon we start for Albany. Next day off to the Adirondacks by way of Saratoga and Lake George.

Oct. 4

Walking up the road this morning at seven, I saw where the birds had been wallowing in the dry earth. There were the prints of their wing-quills, and the prints of their slender feet. How curious, I thought, that these dainty creatures of the air should want an earth-bath — should feel the need of sifting the soil through their plumage, of charging every feather, for a moment, with the earth dust! Does it strengthen them and renew them? How suggestive it is! To come to earth again, after your life in the air, to hug it close for a few moments, to interpenetrate yourself with it, how sanitary and renewing for birds and men! Nearly all the animals love to get back to the earth. Behold the delight of the horse in rolling on the ground. The bull loves to tear up the soil with his horns, and then paw the earth over his back. The dog, the pig, the cat, love the contact of the soil. So do children.

Is it only the scratchers among birds that earth their wings? I do not know that birds of prey, or crows, or woodpeckers do so, or water-birds. The latter seem to find the water and mud sufficient.

I suppose the intellectual man gets from a walk in the country, in some degree, the equivalent of the bird's earth-bath. What he gets is very intangible, but it refreshes and heals him. Is it partly physical, from the exercise in the open, and partly mental and spiritual, from the play of his senses upon the objects around him? Whitman says, 'I recruit myself as I go,' as we all do.

Oct. 6

Great Britain is, of course, arrogant. Arrogance is a part of the British constitution. Her conduct upon the sea has always been high-handed. Natural enough: she is an island empire, and her existence, as such, depends upon her supremacy upon the sea. Let her have it. Why should the elephant be jealous of the whale? Let the continental empires go their way. Germany wants both the sea and the land, to the exclusion of England.

Oct. 8

I find that the editing of my MSS. tires me more than the writing of them. There is something exhilarating in the original writing, but editing is drudgery.

Oct. 10

Lady Russell, author of 'Elizabeth and her German Garden,' with her beautiful daughter, called. The Whiteheads brought them. It was a rare treat. Lady Russell is a very beautiful woman, small in stature, with very regular features; with the fresh, youthful English complexion. I divined something about her that was unusual before she got out of the car, and before I heard her name. It was her manner. She had manner — not put-on manners — something bred in the blood, a low, gentle, easy tone and bearing. Manners are an Old World, aristocratic product. They do not flourish in a democracy like ours. I myself have none. I am natural, unaffected, but my naturalness has never been touched with this something extra — this perfume of manners. The same is true of her daughter — tall, darker, and very beautiful; she, too, has manner.

We had tea before the open fire, and Lady Russell ate one of my strawberry apples, and told me of reading my books in Berlin. She is a woman of genius. Her books are charming — nature and art and society happily mingled.

Oct. 13

Roosevelt loads his gun too heavy. The recoil hurts him more than the shot does his enemy. He is bound to make a big noise, but the kick of the gun is so much power taken from the force of the bullet. People react vigorously against him, as they always do to this surplus verbal energy. It is poor politics, to say the least. He has made me take Wilson's side. His is a case where the half is more than the whole. I do not believe that the people of this country can be bullied and browbeaten into supporting any man. I believe they will resent the course of an ex-President who, on all occasions, pours out upon the President a flood of what savors of vindictive personal abuse.

Roosevelt would be a really great man if he could be shorn of that lock of his hair in which that strong dash of the bully resides. He looks up to Lincoln — why can he not copy a little of his humility and modesty? His fierce attacks upon the President are humiliating to the whole country. Is our chief public man, then, entitled to no respect? Is the country the victim of a fraud and a humbug?

Nov. 7

In the afternoon I walk up to Esopus to vote for Wilson, but do not expect he will be elected. This may be my last Presidential vote, and I vote on principle — only a revenue tariff; and for the man the pro-Germans don't want. Wilson is a much stronger man than Hughes. Put their pictures side by side and see the difference — good humor and a fine sensibility in one, and strength of will and of character in the other. But the masses never want the best.

Nov. 9

The magazine writer has a new problem: how to address himself to the moving-picture brain — the brain that does not want to read or think, but only to use its eager shallow eyes, eyes that prefer the shadow and ghosts of things to the things themselves, that [would] rather see the ghosts of people flitting around on the stage, than to see real flesh and blood. How an audible dialogue would tire them! it might compel them to use their minds a little — horrible thought!

For my own part, I am sure I cannot interest this moving-picture brain, and do not want to. It is the shallowest brain that has yet appeared in the world. What is to be the upshot of this craze over this mere wash of reality which the 'movies' (horrible word!) offer our young people?

Nov. 12

Mrs. B. does not know how serious her case is. . . . Oh! how emaciated she is! She wants to talk with the doctors about her case. I tell her a part of what they say; that it is very serious, and that the chances are against her; but I tell her to will to get well. She says she will do all she can.

Nov. 17

To Academy [1] Meeting. The Gold Medal is conferred upon me for excellence in Belles-Lettres — mainly my essays, I think. A great surprise, but, near eighty, it means little to me.

Dec. 3

Must rest from my writing for a few days. Have written nine essays since May, three on birds, one for 'Youth's

[1] American Academy of Arts and Letters.

Companion,' one for the 'Art World,' called 'The Good Devils,' two on Nature Lore, and one called 'The Natural Providence,' and one called 'The Price of Development,' or 'Biology and War,' or 'Development and War' — which?

Dec. 30

The sound of an axe in the winter woods — how I love to hear it! It suggests heroic warmth.

Jan. 6, 1917

My friend Hamilton Mabie was buried on the 3d. I should have gone to the funeral. I miss him from the world. I saw him on the 17th of November at the Academy meeting. He wrote me that he was happy in the prospect of being as well as ever again. Alas! alas! He was a lovable and helpful man; not one of the original men, but a very serviceable man in a literary age. I doubt if his books will last; but his friends will not forget him. He did not touch Nature directly, but through books; he sustained first-hand relations with very few things, which is true of most of us. He shone in some of his editorials in the Outlook; and how he did shine as toast-master at a club, or a public dinner! Never saw his equal. And now the eternal darkness and stillness surrounds him!

Jan. 14

Writing on Emerson's Journals. The hideous War, with talk of peace, still fills all the horizon.

Feb. 22

[On board the yacht Sialia, *en route* for Havana.] All day on a blue, placid sea, calm as the Hudson River, though one feels the slow pulse of the sea under all. Ten knots an hour. I walk and sit and read upon the deck. Not a flaw in anything, except at table, where my appetite is too good, and the food too rich and abundant. But I am on my guard.

A little warbler, the red-poll, I think, comes aboard and hangs about the yacht for a long time, apparently very hungry. A troop of gulls hover over our wake and stern all day. What grace, what ease, what mastery of flight! Oh, if we could do things in words with the same grace that gulls fly! — that were literature.

Feb. 23

In the midst of a steel-blue shield all day, sailing, sailing, and never getting off the magic shield. It journeys with us.

Feb. 24

Yesterday a pretty sight — two porpoises racing with our boat, only a few feet away. We could look down upon their backs as they ran like hounds, side by side, easily keeping up with us (twelve miles an hour), and, so far as I could see, not moving a fin. The subtle and powerful muscular propelling effort of the whole body could not be seen. I fancied their ears lain back like a racing dog's. They followed us an hour or more, now on one side of the ship, and then on the other, evidently in high glee that they could keep up with us. What jolly, sportive creatures they are — the school-boys of the sea!

Feb. 26

Every night between eight and nine, our wireless man

picks the news out of the air with his wire net. Think of it! over our heads, here in the dark air, darts and shoots all the important news of the day, and no one the wiser except as it is revealed by his instrument. A network of pulsing lines overhead. News of the great War, of world calamities, of doings in distant countries, which our senses are too dull to apprehend — all about us these news vibrations come and go, and cross and re-cross one another, and we know it not! What magic! what spirits are here! The operator sits there in his little room on the upper deck, with the receiver in his ears, and writes as the messages from the heavens are conveyed to him. Such things reveal to us how much more fine and marvellous nature is — the coarse common nature about us — than we had dreamed. If we could reach its real interior, and interpret it, would there be any room for spirit? would not matter and spirit be seen to be one?

March 2 [Havana]

We are off on a fifty-mile ride inland to see some large sugar plantations. A superb road; for twenty or more miles the road is arched by huge Spanish laurel trees; their branches interlock overhead, making regular green Gothic arches. A prominent feature of the landscape, the scattered royal palms, their plumes streaming back or waving in the wind like the head-gear of Indian chiefs. No country homes or farms, in our sense; thatched, windowless huts, here and there, with open doors; the dwellings of the better class in villages toeing on the street. No glass in even the best houses; windows with iron gratings and blinds; houses low, only one story, and always with a colonnade front and ornamental. No pretty creeks or streams; plenty of broken limestone everywhere in the fields, often a serious obstruction to cultivation.

In the afternoon we visited the large plantation of Señor Pelayo at Rosario, a truly imperial plantation of 13,000 acres of the best sugar lands — level and stretching away on either hand as far as the eye can see. The mills are on a scale to match — very clean and orderly and pleasing to look upon. The output is 1200 bags a day for about three months. The house of the owner is one of the best I have seen, and his Spanish hospitality perfect. His quiet dignity and courtesy were very pleasing. The garden behind the house is a tropical thicket of several acres, a dense green retreat of all kinds of tropical and semitropical trees and vines, the cinnamon tree among them. It is an ideal spot where one wanted to linger and dream.

March 7

In the afternoon, as I sit alone on the upper deck, reading an editorial in New York 'Evening Post' on Mr. Howells's eightieth birthday, a telegram comes from C. B. saying my wife died peacefully yesterday — a blow I have been daily looking for, and which I thought I was prepared for. Here, in this peaceful harbor, on this calm summer day, with the big ships going and coming about me, came this sad news. A long chapter in my life, nearly sixty years, ended. I am too much crushed to write about it now.

March 8

The Ford party off into the country fifty miles. I have no heart to go with them, but crave a little solitude on the

near-by hills. At 11 A.M. the launch puts me ashore and
I walk up on the ridge overlooking the sea. Even Nature
in her harsher aspects in the tropics soothes and heals.
I stand and loiter long on the breezy ridge and look north
upon the great blue crescent of the sea. I have but one
thought, and am glad to be alone with it on the hills.

March 9

How I go over and over my last days with her. One
cannot foretell the pain that the death of near and dear
ones is bound to bring. When the fear becomes the reality, how naked we stand! I had anticipated these days,
over and over, and felt secure. Forewarned I was, but I
could not be forearmed. In my old age this bereavement
falls upon me, and I am less able to meet it than I should
have been years ago. Then life had more future, now it is
so nearly all in the past tense. Without C. B. and Julian
and his children, what would I do!

Finished reading the 'Life of Emerson' with long, sad
thoughts. How much, since we have been in the Harbor,
have I lived with Emerson and Carlyle through this life of
him, and through his 'English Traits'! How these two
men do come home to me!

Cabot omits two incidents in Emerson's life known to
me — his presence at the Holmes seventieth-birthday
breakfast, at Hotel Brunswick in Boston, in December,
1879, when I saw him and spoke with him (and with
Holmes and Whittier). He took no part, except to eat his
breakfast with the rest of us, but he looked as serene and
godlike as ever. The other incident is Emerson's visit to

Baltimore and Washington in December (I think), 1871, when he lectured. Walt Whitman and I went over to Baltimore and met him, and heard the lecture. It was then that Emerson said: 'I have your "Wake-Robin" on my table. Capital title, capital title!' but said nothing about the contents.

I heard him also in Washington — on Manners, I think. I met him, or waylaid him, at the B. and O. station, and carried his satchel into the train, and got a little talk from him. It was then that he said, on my naming Whitman, that he wished Whitman's friends would quarrel a little more with him about his poetry. He said also that Agassiz was his teacher rather than Darwin. He went back to Baltimore for another lecture, and I sent my 'Notes' on W. W., and a letter, but got no reply.

March 10

As I walk the deck I look off yearningly toward the green and brown hills where I walked with my sorrow on the 8th. I left something of myself on those hills. I lived in that solitude one hour of intensified life. No other point in the horizon so attracts me now. Thoughts of my poor lost one consecrate those hills. Oh, if she could only know how my heart went out to her that day!

April 3

[At the Nest.] My eightieth birthday. A deluge of letters and books and flowers. President Wilson's great message my best gift to-day — a great message to the whole world. I read it with profound emotion. I believe it will play a great part in the future political history of mankind.

May 9

Just finished 'Walden' for the second time. Many delicious pages in it — enough to keep it alive; but a vast deal of chaff without any wheat. Such an exaggerator! His trick always to say the contrary, the unexpected thing. He writes his fractions large — enormous denominators, enormous numerators. Reduce them to their simplest terms and it takes the conceit out of them. He abounds in forced and false analogies. A great deal of ingenuity spent in trying to wed things that will not be wedded. Oil and water will not mix, churn them as you will. Little or no wise counsel in the book — throws no light on any of life's serious problems. It is, as he suggests, the crowing of the cock in the morning, a pure piece of brag; and, if the cock had not had the home barnyard larder to resort to, he would have crowed a different tune. If Thoreau woke up his neighbors, to what purpose did he awake them? Not to be better farmers, or better mechanics, or better tradesmen. He shirked all civil and social responsibilities, and was able to live his life in the woods, off and on, for two years, because others stayed at home and helped make the wheels go round. His refusal to pay his poll-tax, and going to jail till a friend (probably Emerson) payed it, is a sample of how petty and futile his views of the State were. The act was childish and grotesque. Not a great man, like Emerson; not a great soul; but, at times, a very clever, stimulating, and suggestive writer. With reference to his times and country, he was like a knurl on a beech or birch tree — hard and fine-grained, but containing little available timber. His best books are his 'Maine Woods' and 'Cape Cod.' About half of 'Walden' is precious. The 'Week' has little real stuff in it.

May 17

We drive up to the school [at Tongore]. As large a
school as I had, 35 or 40 pupils, but half of them, or more,
foreign born; not the bright, clear, rosy cheeks I looked
upon. The little schoolma'am was very gracious; she
knew of me, but did not know that I had preceded her in
that school by more than sixty years. No legend of me in
the place, it seems. I told the staring children that I had
been a teacher there sixty-three years ago, but that I did
not see a face there that I saw then. They looked very
solemn over my attempted joke.

June 8

I sit on the porch and see the maple trees slowly clothe
themselves with verdure, and I say, 'What an agitated
and troublesome world the leaves must think they are
born into!' Never a moment of rest; ruffled and swayed
and tossed by the wind at all hours; furiously torn and
lashed at others; the hosts of tender leaves driven together like the waves upon the beach, making shipwreck
of the whole treetop seem imminent — hail, tempest,
tornado, wreaking their vengeance upon them; and yet,
in most cases, suffering no visible injury. The wind dies
down and they fall into their places, and spread their
green palms to the air and sun, and are as ready to clap
them in gladness as ever they were. The flexible, yielding
character of the leaves, and of the branches that hold
them, saves them. Their clashing is like the clashing of
a girl's ringlets, or of a willow's pendant boughs. When
the autumn comes, and the leaves are ripe for their fall,
rarely is one seen to be seriously torn or deformed by the
periods of storm and stress it has passed through.

Roxbury, July 7

That caressing, reassuring wing-gesture of the blue-bird seems peculiar to it. How pretty it is, accompanied by that soft, affectionate warble addressed to its mate. So many birds have little ways and maneuvers of their own. The flicker bows and bows to his mate, and calls to her in a coaxing, reassuring tone peculiarly his own; while the courtship of robins and sparrows seems attended with a certain violence, as if they sought to carry the female by storm. Of the bobolink the same is true. 'Touch me and I am yours,' the female seems to say, and away she goes, with her black and white suitor in pursuit. I have never seen any wooing of the cuckoos, nor of the meadowlarks, nor of the vireos.

July 26

When little puffs of air strike the meadows now, they carry away clouds of white smoke — the pollen of the blooming timothy.

July 28

I hear the indigo bunting, singing, singing, in a remote field all the morning. He is perched on the top of some tree, a bit of [sapphire] amid the green, and he sings as if all the world were listening. What is he singing to? His brooding little brown mate in a low bush may hear him. Does it cheer and comfort her? We are humans when we ask this question. She broods on just the same when he stops singing.

Aug. 2

Every morning in my walk I call upon the junco on her nest in the little mossy bank, at the threshold of the

beechwoods. I see her light beak and her black shining
eyes there in the small cavity, partly screened by various
wild green growths. That spot seems a little different
from any other. That bit of wild feathered life appeals to
the imagination. I linger about it. I put up some poles
and brush to ward off the grazing cows. I sit a long time
on a rock near by, partly to enjoy the cool breeze, and
partly to be near the junco. I see the male occasionally
lingering near. How interesting that he should seem to
understand what keeps his mate there! This is doubtless
their second brood. I fear some fox or skunk or coon or
squirrel will find her out. In the early winter or spring
maybe she and her brood and mate will come to me on the
Hudson.

Aug. 4

Eden comes on the train at 10.30. It is his seventy-
seventh birthday. Health seems to be returning to him in
his old age. Thirty years or more ago his hold upon life
seemed very slight and precarious. The doctors told him
he was near his end. It did not disturb him at all. 'I shall
not die till my time comes,' was always his reply. He is
now talkative and jolly. I greatly enjoy his visit. We walk
over Home in the afternoon. The Old Home, I know, looks
good to him. Every height and mountain-peak around
the horizon recalls his fox-hunting. It is one of his staple
subjects of talk. Before his famous hound, Old Wilder,
died, he shot 240-odd foxes. This was his greatest hound.
I remember him well — a dog of fine breed, with a very
musical bay.

Aug. 13

These are the August days, bright, warm, tranquil; cool at night, warm by day. The tide of the season has reached its height, the corn is topping out, the oats are turning, the hay-makers are near the end of their harvest, the bird-songs are failing, the swallows are lined up on the telegraph-wires getting ready to depart, the hills are browning a little, the woodchucks are fat and lazy, the hen-hawks soar and scream, the buckwheat is in bloom, the cedar-bird is brooding, and the goldfinch also, the crows caw in the distant woods and pastures, and on cool still mornings there is a hint of fall in the air. At night the August meteors cut the black vault with their swift, straight lines, and the milky way stretches its broad band across the heavens.

Aug. 15

A small red weasel up on the hill, by the roadside, intent on crossing the pasture-lot bars, but springs back as he sees me, his boldness and activity in such contrast to that of the chipmunk. He thrusts his head and neck out and eyes me intently. He appears first at this opening in the wall, and then at that, and surveys me at different angles. He carries on a hurried investigation of this strange animal, and then as hurriedly turns on his tracks and disappears. The other day a chipmunk at the same bar-way sat motionless several minutes, and eyed me, and then turned and went back.

Killed a woodchuck this forenoon with his mouth filled with dry grass and stubble to carry to his hole. My bullet was like a stroke of lightning; he dropped and never moved.

The young cedar-birds in the orchard are about ready to leave the nest. When I approach, they stand and stretch their necks up in the same scared way their parents do about the nest, with their beaks pointing upward and feathers depressed.

Aug. 17

President Wilson's words are nearly always equal to the occasion. How rare the men, and Presidents, of whom this can be said!

Aug. 25

Climb to the top of Old Clump in the forenoon — Clara, Eleanor, Harriet, and I. Not over-fatigued by the trip. Three or four years since I was there. Do the climb easier than I could have done it a year ago. Heart much steadier than last year. No birds, no wild life of any kind, save woodchucks in the sheep pasture on our return.

Sept. 15

When I casually open 'Leaves of Grass,' after the book has been long closed to me, it is like coming suddenly upon the ocean, after years of absence from it. I have been reading the verses in the magazines, or in the volume of some recent poet, and opening Whitman is like coming from an enamelled bathroom to the ocean beach. Such large, free ways, such elemental force and simplicity, such freedom from the subtle and the over-refined, such fundamental statements, and absence of elaboration, such magnitude, and, at times, such absolute justness of phrasing! Emerson in his Journals may well speak of its 'Alleghany lift and sweep.' It is like the forest primeval, like the great plains, like the mountain-peaks, yet steeped in humanity and brotherly love. It is refined as the sky is refined, as the Great Lakes are refined, as the rain and the dews are refined. It is not culture, or poetry, or art, as we commonly use the terms — it is something greater, and better.

Sept. 26

A bird's nest is always a surprise and delight, especially when placed upon the ground, the waste and litter of the great outdoors taking such pretty shape, and enclosing such pearls.

Oct. 24

Very lonely. Oh, the falling leaves! They move me. Her house is like a tomb. Felt her loss afresh when I went over to the kitchen door and found the leaves clustered there as if waiting for something. They were waiting for her broom. For over forty years it had not failed them, and now they lay there, dulled and discouraged. Oh, the unswept stones and entry-way — what a tale they tell!

I never could have believed I should miss her so much. Yet I do not want her back — but if I could only know she was well and happy somewhere in the land of the living!

Over forty years we two sat here and saw our days go by; saw the leaves come and go and the seasons change. Now they come and go for her no more — the dust in her house, the leaves at her door, are undisturbed. Why do I mourn for her? why this loneliness? I suppose it is for

my vanished days, for my life buried with her. She was
a part of my youth, of my manhood, of all I did and
thought, and, though a discord in my life, I mourn her
just the same.

Nov. 24

So eager for War news that I go to the post office before breakfast. British victories in France mighty good
reading.

A new path now — from my Study to the Nest. My
path to the house faded out. I kept it open for near forty
years. Alas, alas, no more! As I pass up the drive in the
morning, I often see a reflection of my own form in the
kitchen window and it fairly startles me. So often has she
come to that window and called to me!

Dec. 6

The great thing about Wilson is that he grows. Few
men in political life grow under the pressure of new conditions and new demands. Wilson has grown as the occasion demanded. He is now the foremost man in the
Allied nations; his word leads all others. All his utter-
ances have high literary value, without posing at all as
literature. They are too serious and earnest for that. To
call them literature is almost to detract from them. Yet
Lincoln's Gettysburg address is literature, so is Paul's
Letter to the Corinthians.

Dec. 11

Ice fast in the river. Eat, sleep, and work well, but am
thin. The horrible War — who can store up fat in such
times?

Walk to Slabsides in afternoon. Start up a partridge from under my shed. The sight and sound of her hardy wings did me good. No other tracks on the snow, save an occasional mouse and red squirrel. Surface of the snow everywhere fretted and etched by wind-blown leaves and twigs.

Dec. 31

Down to 20° below. A struggle to keep warm with furnace heat and open wood fire. The poor birds almost succumb to the cold. My little song sparrow hangs on and accepts my offer of cream of wheat. Intense cold and suffering all over the country; shortage of coal adds to the calamity. Another letter to Tribune, sent on 29th.

Jan. 1, 1918

The New Year finds me in pretty good health, writing in morning, and sawing and splitting wood nearly an hour in afternoon. More easily tired than one year ago, but my interest in the War, in Nature, in books, as keen as ever. Weigh about 132. Sight and hearing good, memory a little uncertain. Appetite good as ever. Sleep fairly good. The old Adam slowly hauling in his horns.

Have written at least half a volume the past year, though have published but little. Four or five letters on the War and the Germans in December bring many responses.

Papers written since last April: 'The Spring Bird Procession' (Atlantic), 'A Mid-summer Idyl,' 'The Singing Birds,' 'Atoms and Orbs' (all in the hands of Harpers), 'Is Nature Cruel?' (in hands of Century), 'What I get from Science' (unfinished), a paper in New York 'Times' Supplement on 'Might and Right,' and at least five or six other short papers, on phases of nature.

What of good and bad does the new year hold for me? I am glad I do not know. If it only brings the end of the War, — on the terms of the Allies, — that will be good enough.

Jan. 6

Writing, past week, on Thoreau, and a short article on the might-makes-right fallacy; also a letter on the economics of war after the War.

March 1 [Tryon, N.C.]

I long to be back at Riverby, out of the accursed South. Feel that my own land and clime will bring me back to normal. I can see nothing beautiful in the Southern landscape. The everlasting blood-red soil, and the dark pine woods, the disheveled fields, the houses upon legs, ready to run away, the mud-bespattered horses and vehicles and pedestrians, the absence of grass, etc., etc., — all offend my eye. All day we hear the boom of the guns five miles away, on the artillery range, where our boys from Spartanburg are learning the art of War.

A long line of honking wild geese have just passed over, a good sight and sound. They will reach the Hudson ahead of me.

March 8 [Tryon, N.C.]

A call from Dr. Emerson a few nights ago. Like him much. Strangely like his father in the upper part of his face, but not his father's strong chin and mouth. A good, easy talker. A great event to me! The son of Emerson! Only a little gray. Moves and walks briskly; about seventy-two.

March 19

There is good sawed timber in Brownell's essay ('Standards'), but I do not see a green leaf anywhere.

July 17 [*Ocean Bluff, Mass.*]

We drive to Plymouth, twenty miles. A fine old town, solid and clean. We see Plymouth Rock — a small affair. The monument on the hill rather impressive. All this part of Mass. looks homelike and thrifty and well-ordered. Good State roads and fine gardens and meadows — the New England look and order everywhere. Much more satisfying than similar things in N.Y. State.

Oct. 9

No writing this week. War news too exciting. Wilson is as great in diplomacy as Foch is in war. My hardest trial now is to wait from one newspaper to the next.

Oct. 15

Exciting days — momentous War news. The Hun is breaking. Kaiserdom is doomed. The German empire is in the throes of revolution. The day of reckoning has come. The cyclone of the World War, which the military power of Germany unloosed, and which it expected to ride and control, has got out of their hands, and they are now

its victims. Germany will be impoverished in men and
money for generations. The bills she must pay are stag-
gering. President Wilson equal to the occasion — a man
of the ages. The law of moral and intellectual gravitation
seems to center the Allies' cause in him. All sponta-
neously look to him to speak the right word, and he speaks
it. Few words, but they are written upon the sky, where
all may see and read them.

Oct. 17

The trial each day is to wait the arrival of the postman.
How the hours drag! How we watch for him down the
road! Often we have to wait till one o'clock to know the
War news, but every day brings the end of the Hun
nearer.

Oct. 31

Roosevelt criticizes Wilson severely. Yet here is the
fact over all: We have won the War. Germany is beaten
to her knees, and is begging for mercy. That is what we
set out to do, or help to do, and it is done. Two men in
the world have contributed to that end more than any
others — Foch and Wilson — one in the field, the other
in the Councils of the Nations. Wilson's lofty ideal of
justice and international fair-play has been our guiding
star; he stated our cause in terms of world democracy, and
his words have been an inspiration; in the field Foch has
been his equal, and we (the Allies) have won the War.

Nov. 11

Woke up this morning at five to hear a faint, confused
din of bells and whistles in the direction of Poughkeepsie,

heralding, I fancied, the end of the War. Got up and
dressed and sat by the open fire till daylight. The mail
at 6.15 told the story. The Hun had capitulated. Glory
to God! — not to the Hun's God, but to the Christian
God of the Allies!

Go to Poughkeepsie in the afternoon. Bedlam turned
loose. Such a racket! Everybody bent on making a dis-
cordant noise. Soon tire of it.

Nov. 12

Every hour I have to nudge myself and say, 'Wake up,
wake up! Don't you know the War is ended?' It seems
incredible that my life should go on just as before. I saw
wood, doze before my open fire, read the paper, walk a
little, ponder over Moulton's 'Introduction to Astronomy,'
dream of the old days, receive callers, or sit vacant in my
chair. And yet the most fervent and devout desire and
hope of my life has suddenly come true! It is a relief like
that the early man must have felt when he saw an eclipse
of the sun passing off. The world is at last freed from the
grip of this monster, and his claws are drawn. Not in this,
or in any other generation, can he make another spring,
if he ever can.

Dec. 3

At noon. A flock of evening grosbeaks in the maple in
front of my window, the first and only ones I ever saw
here, in the forty or more years I have sat here. Eight or
ten of them picking at the buds. A pretty sight. The
impulse to leave seemed to seize them all at the same
instant. When one felt it, they all felt it and turned their

heads in the same direction. Rare visitants! Will any one else see them? Have they ever been here before? Then I heard the loud hum of an aeroplane, and, looking out, saw one high and dim over Hyde Park, going south; probably the same one I saw yesterday going north over this place. I am convinced that in five years or less, we shall be making journeys in them, and that they will be as safe as the steam-cars or autos.

Dec. 19

[At Yama Farms.] A short walk in the morning. A small oak tree at the foot of the rocks full of clinging dry leaves, one leaf near the top in constant motion, swinging to and fro, while the other leaves are still, or show a slight tremulous motion at times. But the one leaf was visibly greatly agitated. It reminded me of those high-strung, sensitive souls in all large communities who are moved or thrilled by thoughts or influences that the great mass is quite insensible to, or only faintly conscious of — the poets, prophets, seers whose places are high on the tree of life.

Dec. 24

What heathenish, unchivalrous, or non-chivalrous, creatures the birds are! Two nuthatches, a male and female, are feeding, nearly every hour each day, on the piece of suet on the maple tree in front of my window, but there is not the least comity or fraternizing between them. The male on all occasions treats the female rudely and spitefully. He will not allow her to feed at all while he is around. She often timidly approaches, but he instantly

makes a dive at her. He is a little barbarian. When the
downy woodpecker comes there the nuthatch has to eat
at second table. Downy will tolerate no other guest.

Jan. 7, 1919

Heard of Roosevelt's death last night and have had a
lump in my throat ever since. I love him more than I
thought I did. The past two years his openly hostile attitude toward President Wilson has been very irritating.
(It ill becomes an ex-President to deal in denunciations
toward the President — criticism, yes, but not abuse.)
But how quickly death makes us forget all that! We
remember only his great qualities, and his great service to
the country; and I remember his great kindness to me
personally. The old man's tears come easily, and I can
hardly speak his name without tears in my voice.

I have known him since his ranch days in Montana, and
to know him as I have was to love him. I went with him
through the Yellowstone Park in the spring of 1903. My
paper in the 'Atlantic Monthly' on 'Real and Sham Natural History' had pleased him so — there was so much
fight and hard hitting in it — that he asked me to go with
him and see the game in the Park. I have written about
it in my 'Camping and Tramping with Roosevelt.'

He was a live wire, if there ever was one, in human
form. His sense of right and duty was as inflexible as
adamant. Politicians found him a hard customer. His
reproof and refusal came quick and sharp. His manner
was authoritative and stern. He was as bold as a lion, and,
at times, as playful as a lamb. His political enemies at
Albany, early in his career, laid traps for him, in hopes of

tarnishing his reputation; but he was too keen for them. He was scrupulous in morals, and unflinching in what he felt to be his duty.

The world seems more bleak and cold since he is no longer in it. He helped to warm it, and to keep the currents going. Too fond of the lime-light and the center of the stage, from his excess of the sense of leadership. He was a born leader and disciplinarian. Add a little of Lincoln's humility and self-forgetfulness, and we should have had one of the greatest men of history. What a center of energy he was in our affairs! He elevated the standards of business and political morals for the whole country, and intensified the patriotism of every one of us. His Americanism charged the very marrow of his bones.

Jan. 21

Mr. Childs and I drive to Roosevelt's grave in a small cemetery on a knoll partly surrounded by woods, with glimpses of the bay to the north; a beautiful, secluded spot; the grave a mound of wreaths and flowers. Spend a half-hour there, not all the time with dry eyes. How vividly he came back to me, and the days we had spent together! Taft had been there, the guard said, and had wept profusely.

The most potent force for pure Americanism, in the best sense, in our history, was Roosevelt.

Jan. 29

Rereading Huxley. A keen, penetrating mind, the Knight in shining armor of the Darwinian theory. The way Huxley can 'sass back'; the way his irony can bite and blister; the way he can dispel fog and illusion, is a wonder. No other writer of his time, or fore-time, on scientific subjects, was so immanent in his work, so clearly and vividly before his reader. Clear as crystal is his page, and with a distinction like cut-glass. He is brilliant, he is logical, he is imaginative, he is sane and sure, he is rhetorical, he is solid, he is a moral teacher, and he is a trained scientist.

March 28, 3 P.M.

The worst day of the whole winter, blizzardy conditions all day, increasing cold, the air full of driving snow; the snow that fell last night, swept from the surface of the ground and packed behind the knolls and ridges and other windbreaks. The birds about the door and buildings, as if wanting to be taken in. The sky blotted out by a thick veil of snow and vapor; the sounds of the passing trains strangled by the gale; and we, who do not have to be out, sitting by our open fire in 'a tumultuous privacy of storm.' In the old days on the farm we kept the cows up all day on such days, letting them out only just long enough to drink. How we hovered over the stove! what a stamping and sweeping on the doorstone when we came to the house! How the woods roared — like the surf on the shore! How the gusts of wind in snowy winding-sheets stalked across the hills! How bare some places were swept, and how the snow was piled up in others! Long rays of the storm streamed under the door and reached far out in the room; every vulnerable place in the roof was searched out by the wind, and the snow sifted in. A big woodpile and a bounteous larder were appreciated then. The earlier settlers had the wood but did not always have the full larder. The smokers on such days have a resource in their pipes; those handy with tools tinker in their shops; now and then one reads a book — no, I never saw a farmer read anything more than his weekly paper.

March 29

The frolic of the snow ghosts still continues. Juncos and robins starving, I fear. This morning a male junco sat on the honeysuckle vines, here at the Nest, with his head tucked under his wing, fast asleep. It was just a ball of feathers with no sign of a head. I approached it carefully and closed my hand upon it. It struggled and gave a cry, but was soon quiet. We warmed it, and put it in a paper box with ample air-holes, but it soon died — starvation and cold, I suppose.

April 3

My eighty-second birthday. School-children in the morning. Friends and neighbors call. Mr. Roy from Montreal here. Newspaper reporters from ' Sun,' ' World,' and ' Evening Post.' Many telegrams and letters. A rather strenuous day. Woodcock at night in flight-song.

April 9

Read a half-hour in Masters's 'Spoon River Anthology.' Good stuff in it, but no great poetry; no beauty, no great thoughts; but humor, pathos, sympathy. These younger, free-verse poets have been influenced by Whitman, but are not to be named the same day with him —

no power, no grandeur, nothing elemental or cosmic. The trick of it all tires one after a while. I learn nothing new, I love nothing more, I am brought no nearer Nature, or the Infinite. No music or rhythm, as in Whitman. It is good 'shredded prose,' and not good verse.

July 1

These six or seven letters from strangers, called out by my remark in the June 'Atlantic' about Thoreau's standing in the abutment of a rainbow, annoy me a little. Our memories play us such tricks. Tell me what you saw to-day, or yesterday, or last week, not what you saw as a boy. And tell me whether or not you were thinking about this very point. One of the most common things in the world is inaccurate observation; and one of the next most common is a hasty conclusion.

July 4

A hot, hot day. At noon comes John Russell McCarthy, the new poet from Pennsylvania, whom we have invited to spend a few days with us. I was so taken with his poems [1] that I wanted to see him. I am in the big hammock, out in the orchard, when C. B. brings him out to me. A young man of the blond order, twenty-nine years old. I like him instantly. Very modest and unobtrusive; quite ready, on all occasions, to take a back seat. A sweet smile and impressive blue eyes.

July 7

McCarthy leaves us on morning train. I love the youth. Wish we could have kept him longer. His wise,

[1] 'Out-of-Doors' and 'Gods and Devils.'

sweet smile haunts me. He was companionable without being talkative; just his presence was enough. He was his own poem 'June' in the flesh. Hair cropped close, and a fine-shaped head. Has read very extensively, but knew little of Wordsworth. He has a great future, I think. His acquaintance is the event of years to me. His poems have quality, like some rare new fruit.

July 9

Why the thought of death does not trouble us, or over- whelm us, more than it does, is a mystery. If we were under judicial sentence to be shot or electrocuted at no distant day, would not the thought of it harass us day and night? But we go about with Nature's death-sentence upon us, even in old age, when we know the day is near, as cheerful and contented as ever we did. Normal old people do not seem to be disturbed. Our fathers have struggled so long with the thought of death that the race of man has become immune, or callous. Our inmost self has come to accept it. Or is it because, never having ex- perienced it, we cannot take in the thought? We are blank and indifferent, when we should be agitated and un- happy. We visit the graves of our friends, and visualize them lying there in the utter silence and darkness, and know that we shall soon follow them, and yet we go home and are soon absorbed in a book or a paper, or are asleep in our chair! Blessed are we in not being able to realize the thought of death!

July 18

Two hours at Eden's. . . . The place speaks so clearly of him that I feel as if I had really seen him. The turf on his

grave beside Hiram's is green. I could hear his voice:
'John, time will fetch us.'

Aug. 10

[In camp, Green Mountains, auto-camping trip.]
Ten A.M. Edison not up yet — the man of little sleep! He
inveighs against cane-sugar, yet puts two heaping tea-
spoonfuls in each cup of coffee, and he takes three or four
cups a day! He smokes three or four cigars each day. He
eats more than I do, yet calls me a gourmand. He eats
pie by the yard, if he can get it, and he bolts his food.
O Consistency, thy name is *not* Edison! Yet we all defer
instinctively to him. He is a big-brained man, genial
and good-natured. Never saw him grumpy or in ill-
humor yet; has a big fund of all kinds of stories. His
head is full of all kinds of facts, figures, and formulæ. . . .
A wonderful man, and a striking figure. It takes a great
man to do a big work in any field — invention, research,
art, literature, science. Mr. Ford is a great man also. His
face is striking and original; his brow, nose, and chin
show great force of character. A little car, but a big
man back of it.

Aug. 11

Not any drift boulders in Green and White Mountains,
because the old ice-sheet plucked them from these mountains and dropped them over the landscape to the south;
here they lie like a herd of slumbering elephants with their
calves, sleeping the sleep of geologic ages. The view of
the White Mountains very impressive. We came through
the Crawford Notch, down and down and down, over a

superb road, through woods, with these great rocky
peaks shouldering the sky on each side. Simply stu-
pendous!

Aug. 12

Granite New Hampshire produced one great man — a
giant man in many ways — Daniel Webster. He is the
granite contribution to humanity.

Aug. 27

Coming from New England, or from Connecticut, into
New York is stepping down to a lower level of everything
that relates to home and village life. We have left the
country of the grand old elms, the village green, the attractive village church, the conspicuous public libraries,
and the solid, homelike, unpretentious dwelling-houses,
and have entered a region of bald, naked dwellings, or
highly ornate, showy villages. The country opens and
unrolls, and the farms are better, but life is far less attractive; more wealth, but the art of living at a low ebb.
Newness, baldness, rawness take the place of sobriety,
simplicity, stability.

If the sun has an orbit, its curve is as yet undetected.
But no doubt it has an orbit. Here we are, traveling at
the rate of a thousand million of miles in a year, and yet
never getting away from home! The earth is as much at
home in one place in the universe as in another. There is
no locality in empty space.

Nov. 23

[At Yama Farms.] Make my first acquaintance with
Horace — a man after my own heart. My tastes were his

tastes. Care little for his poetry, but get much out of his letters. He had the gift of self-portrayal. He and I would have flourished well together at Slabsides, or at Wood-chuck Lodge — a real countryman, capable of self-entertainment; a sweet, simple, candid soul.

Christmas at La Jolla, California. The Pacific furnished the music, the sky furnishes the glory, and Miss Scripps furnishes the dinner.

The wave blossoms when it breaks.

Jan., 1920

The swells that beat upon the ocean are not the result of a local agitation of the water; the pulse of the earth is in them; the pull of the sun and the moon is in them. They are more cosmic than terrestrial. The Earth wears her seas like a loose garment which the sun and moon constantly pluck at, and shift from side to side. Only the uncharted ɔceans feel the tidal impulse — the heavenly influences. The great inland bodies of water are unresponsive; they are too small for the meshes of the solar and lunar net. . . . What a puzzle the tides must have been to early man! What proof they afford of the cosmic forces that play upon us and hold us in their net! . . . The pull of the sun and moon is upon you and me also, but we are unconscious of it. We are bodies too light to affect the beam of the huge scale.

Jan. 10

A Mr. Clark has just called — an engineer on some northern railway, deeply interested in birds, and in psychology. His appreciation of my books knows no bounds. He says, as others often say, that I have little conception of what my books have done for people. I hardly know why I am so indifferent to such testimony. It goes in one ear and out the other. The reason probably is that I did not write my books to please the public. I wrote them to please myself. If I had made any sacrifices, or undergone any hardships or self-denial, to please others, I should be pleased if I found that I had succeeded. But there is no merit in my success; I could not help it; it was all for my own pleasure.

Jan. 17

On Monday we drove over to the Imperial Valley, 120 miles, most of the way through and over great warty granite mountains. Toward the last they were like huge piles of gigantic potatoes, in size from pumpkins to that of elephants, and larger. Rocky avalanches were hanging over you and waiting below you. Death and destruction seemed imminent on all sides. Very little vegetation, and none at the last. The naked earth, the colored boulders lay blistering in the sun. They had weathered smooth, and were clinging at the angle of repose — a succession of piles of granite *pommes de terre*, two or three hundred feet high. It was all like a nightmare. Never saw mountain scenery further removed from the green, smooth, restful hills that I know so well. They tired me like a fever — a leprosy of stone, or the granite smitten with small-pox. At last we struck a cement road and rolled swiftly, thirty miles, into El Centro.

April 2

Hurrying up with the copy of my new volume, 'The Faith of a Naturalist,' [1] these days.

April 3

My eighty-third birthday. Spend it at Yama Farms. Thirty or more of my friends come to celebrate with me. A perfect day, clear, mild, and lovely. In the evening a great ovation. I am nearly snowed under with poems and speeches. I get on my legs and 'sass back' as best I can. Henceforth I know the hill will become steeper and steeper, and my breath shorter and shorter. I must gird up my loins to make the climb.

April 28

Dr. Johnson said of Dr. Berch that he was as brisk as a bee in conversation, but no sooner did he take a pen in hand than it became torpid to him and benumbed all his faculties. I once heard Emerson say a similar thing about Alcott.

I heard Frederick Douglass say that the best way to keep a man out of the mud was to black his shoes.

One of the drawbacks of old age is that one outlives his generation and feels alone in the world. The new generations have interests of their own, and are no more in sympathy with you than you are with them. The octogenarian has no alternative but to live in the past. He lives with the dead, and they pull him down.

[1] Later named *Accepting the Universe.*

May 18

The death of Howells, a few days ago, gave me a shock.
I had known him long. He was my senior by only one
month. It had been two years or more since I had seen
him. Last December I read his charming paper 'Eighty
Years and After,' and enjoyed it greatly. It is a master-
piece. No other American man of letters, past or present,
could have done that. In fact, there has been no other
American who has achieved the all-round literary crafts-
manship that Mr. Howells achieved. His equal in his own
line we have never seen. His felicity on all occasions was
a wonder. His works do not belong to the literature of
power, but to the literature of charm, grace, felicity. His
style is as flexible and as limpid as a mountain rill. Only
among the French do we find such qualities in such perfection. Some of his writings ('The Day of their Wed-
ding,' for instance) are too photographic. We miss the lure
of the imagination, such as Hawthorne gave to all his
pictures of real things. Only one of Howells's volumes
have I found too thin for me to finish — his 'London
Films'; it was too filmy for me. I had read Taine's 'London Notes' and felt the force of a different type of mind.
But Howells's 'Eighty Years and After' will live as a
classic. Oh, the happiness of his style! One of his late
poems — the latest of his I have seen — on growing old,
'On a Bright Winter Day,' is a gem.

June 20 [*Roxbury*]

A wonderful morning, clear, calm, and warm. The
valley full of fog, which does not take flight, but ebbs
and flows and melts till, at eight, not a vestige of it

remains. At seven, not a leaf was stirring, only the plumed grasses waving a little. I walk up the road. See a hummingbird bathing in the big drops on the foliage of a small ash tree. Never knew before how the hummer bathed. Saw a highhole, a red-headed woodpecker, a kingbird, and a scarlet tanager in the same tree, a basswood. The flight of the highhole is with four or five wing-beats, then, skipping one, and going some feet with wings closed. The red-head flies in much the same manner.

Discovered that the webs of the little spiders in the road, fairy napkins, saturated with minute drops of moisture, exhibit prismatic tints. In it we see one abutment of a tiny rainbow. Step a pace or two to the other side, and you see the other abutment. You never see the completed bow, because the web is too small. These fragments are as unapproachable as the bow in the clouds. If you think you can step on one of them, try it. The colors go when you make the attempt. I also discovered that when a suspended dewdrop becomes a jewel of rainbow tints, you can see only one to the right or left of you. It also is a fragment of a rainbow. It seems to me there ought to be a point where you could see an entire bow in the wet grass, but I could not find it — drops too few, and not all presenting the same angle to the sun.

June 24

I believe the goldfinch can describe a longer arc in the air with closed wings than any other bird.

July 5

The noiseless butterfly. Even the tiniest gnat hums a little. In fact, all winged things that I know make a

sound in flying except butterflies and moths. They whisk
about your face without a sound.

July 8

The song of the hermit thrush this morning in the
beechwoods. I had almost forgotten how divine a strain
it is.

July 14

Visit the graves of my dead in the Old Yellow Church
burying-ground, and in the Presbyterian burying-ground
in the village. I stood long and long at Father's and
Mother's graves, and seemed very near them. And at the
grave of dear Channy B. [Deyo]. . . . I lingerered about
them all, and said good-bye to them all, and said I would
come again if I lived.

July 22

Had a skunk in a trap I had set for a woodchuck, and
in trying to liberate him got some of his essence. Had to
change my clothes and shoes. What marksmen they are!
I held his tail down with a stick, but he managed to un-
cork his bottle all the same.

July 27

Not a cloud in the sky this morning, but one needs an
overcoat and gloves. Something must have happened to
the sun these days. Into what cold, interstellar spaces
has he dragged his little family of worlds?

Aug. 12

When the chipmunks have worn out the stone walls by
traveling upon them — ground them to powder; when

the swallows, and the other birds, have worn out the telegraph-wires along the road, by perching upon them; when the woodchucks have reduced to powder the rocks upon which they bask in the summer sun — why, I shall not be here!

Oct. 3

The most impressive moment of the day, here in the mountains, is at sunrise. From my cot on the sleeping-porch I see the first flash of his coming. Before that moment, I see his rays glint here and there through the forest trees that give a mane to the mountain-crest. The dawn comes very gently. I am usually watching for it. As I gaze, I gradually become conscious of a faint luminousness in the eastern sky. This slowly increases and changes to a deep saffron. And then, in eight or ten minutes, that fades into a light bluish tinge — the gold turns to silver. After some minutes the sky, just at the point where the sun is to appear, begins to glow again, as if the silver were getting warm. A minute or two more, and the brow of the great god is above the horizon line. His mere brow, as I try to fix my eyes upon it, fairly smites me blind. The brow is magnified by the eye into the whole face. One realizes, in these few seconds, how rapidly and steadily the old earth turns on its axis. You witness the miracle of the transition of the dawn into day. The day is born in a twinkling. It suggests one of those moving pictures where the element of time is cut out and we see the flower open. Is it Browning who uses the word 'boiling' to describe the moment? 'Day boils at last!' Gilder, I think, speaks of it as a scimitar flashing on the brim of the world.

I watch for it each morning as if I were seeing it for the first. It is the critical moment of the day. You actually see the earth turning. Later in the day one does not note in the same way the sun climbing the heavens. The setting sun does not impress one because it is usually enveloped in vapors. His day's work is done, and he goes to his rest veiled and subdued. He is new in the morning, and old at his going down. [See 'Under the Maples,' pp. 97–98.]

Oct. 7

If Harding is elected in November, I shall be ashamed that I am an American. I am so intolerant of that gang of reactionaries in the Senate, led by Borah and Lodge, that, more than ever, I would like to see the Senate abolished. Let the House make the laws. What great thing ever came out of the Senate? There have been great men there, but not for a generation or more. They are mostly mere politicians.

Nov. 3

For the first time in my life, I am ashamed that I am an American. If I were in Europe now, I could not hold up my head and confess I was a citizen of the United States of America. I must be crazy: I had supposed a League of Nations was a good thing. I knew, in advance, that it would be impossible to hold the people of this country up to a sense of high moral obligation, yet the concrete reality has cut me deeper than I thought it could. I am shocked. It seems as if the great mass of the people had overwhelmingly saddled all the trouble of the

last eight years, the World War, and everything, upon
poor President Wilson — the high prices, the crimes, the
disorder, the taxes. It is probably always so — the administration is always to blame for everything disastrous
that happens, almost for the bad weather. Thank
Heaven, I was not carried away by the landslide! I am
proud to belong to the saving remnant — the minority
who still have some sense of moral duty. We cannot shirk
nor repudiate this debt we owe the world. The welfare of
one nation should mean the welfare of all. We all con-
stitute one family. What injures one, injures all. Nations
can no longer exist and grow rich by preying upon one
another. That is barbarism. If this Republican landslide
means that we don't care a damn for Europe — that we
must keep aloof from all its affairs — we deceive ourselves. One extreme follows another in politics, as in the
weather. If this incoming administration is attended by
hard times, a landslide will carry it off in the same way.

Dec. 6

The sparks from soft woods like hemlock and chestnut
are, for the most part, harmless. They do little else than
blacken your rug. But get the snappings from hickory or
oak, then beware! there is fire in their hearts. Hickory
occasionally fairly explodes and sends live coals across
the room, and may burn your house up. So you need not
fear the sputter and threats of superficial and irritable
men — they are only skin deep; but beware the anger of
the grim, silent men of few words. They are like dogs that
bite, but do not bark.

Dec. 10

After one has become an octogenarian, the freaks and tricks of memory are very curious. Proper names are so easily recalled sometimes, and so difficult at others. Ideas, too — how they slip out of the mind, like eels, often when we are making an effort to hold them! There is no trouble about the language one commonly uses in writing or speaking, but proper names — what a game of hide-and-seek we play with them! I find it very difficult now to commit to memory a bit of poetry or prose. Probably, during the past six months, I have spent several whole days trying to memorize a poem of Edward Fitzgerald's, but with poor success. Some passages in Whitman — some of those tremendous lines about the orbs — have given me the same trouble.

Dec. 12

The greatest cradle on earth — the cradle of the Pacific — is rocking in front of my window, some days a little more gently than others, but the foot or hand that nudges it is never idle. What a vast cradle it is! What myriad forms of life it holds, both beautiful and hideous beyond words!

Dec. 29

The brilliant sunshine continues. I begin to look for a day with the lid on. Oh, for the shut-in feeling of a storm! — the privacy of storm! I think I could get closer to myself on such a day. At any rate, it would be more like home.

La Jolla, California, Jan., 1921

I was greeted this morning in a very hearty way by the village barber. He had read my books and liked them, and was sure we might be real comrades. He promised to tell me what he knew about skunks — seemed to know I was interested in the subject.

All great men are men of sorrows; the weight of the world rests upon them. Look at Johnson, Wordsworth, Carlyle, Darwin, Whitman — all with feelings too deep for tears. No, not all great men — Emerson was a great man, and he had not this look of sorrow. His look is more like a divine smile. Emerson had more of the divine in his face, and in his life, than any man of his time.

Jan. 17

Have been reading again the Correspondence of Emerson and Carlyle, and living for a week or more with these two great spirits, and sharing their troubles and triumphs. What an experience it has been! I feel lonesome. Like Emerson's letters the best. One tires of Carlyle's groaning and appealing to Heaven. He did no work cheerfully or uncomplainingly. He should have been thankful that he had work to do. What an outcry! and yet all the time invoking the Silence! The Old World sorrow and pessimism in one, and the New World optimism and courage in the other!

I sit here through these sunny days and look out, till I am weary, upon this great Sahara of the Pacific, where brine takes the place of sand. You would die of thirst there the same as in the sand. The waves would bury you in the one case, as surely as the sand-storm in the other.

Feb. 4

Came to Pasadena Glen on the 3d — a little bunga-
low called the Bluebird, snug and comfortable. . . . [Re-
cords improvement in symptoms, after recent illness.]
Life seems worth living again. Drove to Sierra Madre
post office to-day. Now, at seven P.M., I hear the patter of
rain.

THE END

INDEX

Abbott, Lyman, deeply religious, 165.

Accepting the Universe, xvii, 276, 330 *n.*

Adam and Eve, beautiful myth, 99.

Adamana, Arizona, 254.

Addison, Joseph, 88.

Adirondacks, B.'s first camping in, 31; gem of lakes in, 219, 268, 276, 294.

Adirondacks, The, xv, 32, 33.

Aeroplane, B.'s prediction about, 319.

Æschylus, 51.

Africa, South, and Boer War, 215–16.

Agassiz, Louis, 305.

Alaska, Harriman Expedition to, 137, 212, 213, 216.

Alcott, Bronson, 330.

Alexander, S.

'All Souls,' pseudonym of B., xv.

Allen, Rev. A., neighbor of B., 241.

Allen, Francis H., vi.

Allen, James Lane, 257.

America, dominated by industrial spirit, 149–50; sentiment of beauty scarce in, 150; fermenting and democratic, 170; a crude people voiced in Emerson's *Literary Ethics,* 217; fails to stand by the League of Nations, 335–36.

American Academy of Arts and Letters, 277, 278, 299, 300.

Amiel, B. quoted on, vii, viii.

Ampersand, 219.

Analogy, B. ever a seeker of, 14.

Andover Review, quoted, 147–48.

Anecdote, German damming the Danube, 18; thieving farmer, 73; weeding corn, 83–84.

Angle-worms, 218–19.

Antæus, 58.

Apple, 6, 125–26.

April, in Washington, 58–59; a day in, 70, 79, 86, 94, 110, 132, 148, 149, 192, 211, 217–18; nectar, 157; tokens in, 167; poem, notes for, 182–83.

Arbutus, 36, 182.

Aristotle, 25.

Arizona, petrified forests in, 254–55.

Arnold, Matthew, 63; described, 103–04, 105; *Arnold's View of Emerson and Carlyle,* 104; his lecture on Emerson, 105; B. writes on, 119, 122; quoted, 122, 170; not for most serious moods, 128; death of, 148–49; comments on, 148–49, 189, 214–15, 273; Lounsbury on, 284.

Art, blending of natural and divine, 6; artist must paint opposites, 22–23; must give glimpses of the unattainable, 24; Ruskin on balance in art, 25; the nude in, 190; inner voice of, stirs soul, 194.

Art World, 300.

'Artemus Ward,' 195.

Ash, falling stems of, 162.

Ashland, N.Y., xv, 1.

Ashley, Mrs. M. C., 254, 255.

Asia, Central, Lamp Rock in, 161.

Astronomy: moon, 7, 10, 12; and eclipse of, 146–47; stars, 13; Big Dipper, 10, 16; laws of spheres, 11; Pleiades, 22; discoveries in seem inspirations, 41; opens up new fields, 56; furthest fixed star, 85; stages of an orb's life, 120; earth, evolution of, 121; Venus and Jupiter play see-saw, 178; aurora, 181; meteor, 219–20, 310; meteoric dust, 231–32; sun's orbit un-